Daily Blessing Devotional

365 Life-transforming, Spirit-filled Devotions

Daily Blessing Devotional

365 Life-transforming, Spirit-filled Devotions

by Oral Roberts Evangelistic Association

Harrison House
Tulsa, Oklahoma

Author emphasis in Scripture quotations in italic.

07 06 05 04 10 9 8 7 6 5 4 3 2 1

Daily Blessing Devotional:
365 Life-transforming, Spirit-filled Devotions
ISBN 1-57794-709-6

Published by Harrison House, Inc.
P. O. Box 35035
Tulsa, Oklahoma 74153

Happy New Year

by Richard Roberts

First of Two Parts

On this New Year's Day, I would like you to read a Scripture that God has laid on my heart to share with you. "Remember ye not the former things, neither consider the things of old. Behold, I will do a new thing; now it shall spring forth; shall ye not know it? I will even make a way in the wilderness, and rivers in the desert" (Isa. 43:18,19).

Notice those words, "Remember ye not the former things." Are there things that happened last year that you'd just as soon forget? I can think of a few bad things that happened last year that I don't want to remember again. God is saying, "Don't remember them. Forget about those things that happened in the past."

Isn't that what Paul said in Philippians when he said, "I count not myself to have apprehended: but this one thing I do, forgetting those things which are behind, and reaching forth unto those things which are before, I press toward the mark for the prize of the high calling of God in Christ Jesus"? (Phil. 3:13,14).

I believe with all of my heart that God is going to do some mighty things this year. I base that on everything I read in the Word of God. I base that on my own spirit and what I'm feeling from the Lord. I base that on my Holy Ghost prayer language with God.

A young man—a minister and singer—was on our nightly program recently. He shared with me something that he heard my father say some years ago: "Faith is your way to reach into the future." When I heard him say that, I realized that our faith helps us reach out to what God has for us.

Then he added, "Faith is God's way of helping you reach out into the future." It dawned on me what I can do by the use of my faith. I can take the faith that God has put in my heart (for Romans 12:3 says God has given to every person the measure of faith), and with that faith, I can reach into my future and get into a position to receive miracles.

The Measure of Faith

by Richard Roberts

Second of Two Parts

I can reach into my future with my faith and get myself into a position for miracles. Second Kings 4:1-7 tells of the woman who was in debt and her sons were about to be sold into slavery. The prophet Elisha instructed her how to use her pot of oil, and God got her into a position to receive her miracle.

In John 6:9-11, when Jesus multiplied the loaves and fishes, He first had all the people sit down. And then they saw the miracle as the loaves and fishes were distributed. God always does something to get you in a position to receive a miracle. God always commands you to use your faith.

When Jesus was about to preach to the multitude on the shores of the Sea of Galilee, He borrowed Peter's boat. Then He said to Peter, "Thrust me out a little bit from the shore" (Luke 5:3).

Jesus was always getting people to do something before they received their miracle, and He hasn't changed. He is the same yesterday, today, and forever. He was telling Peter, "Launch out into the deep with your faith, for it's your faith that you use to touch the future."

Quit dwelling on the past. In Isaiah 43:18-19 God says, "Remember ye not the former things, neither consider the things of old. [Put them in the past. Bury the ghost.] Behold I will do a new thing; now it shall spring forth." He is ready, willing, and able to do it. But we've got to believe. We've got to put the past in the past and reach out for what God has now.

Miracles are coming toward you or past you every day. "Faith is the substance of things hoped for, the evidence of things not seen" (Heb. 11:1). It's the substance of things you hold on to, the things that you believe for. It's the essence of what you hold on to, to launch into the future of things you haven't seen. It's what you use to reach into the future.

Always a God of hope and the God of the future, He is saying, "I will make a way for you." He is saying, "I am your Way."

Forgive First, Then Pray

by Lindsay Roberts

"For assuredly, I say to you, whoever says to this mountain, 'Be removed and be cast into the sea,' and does not doubt in his heart, but believes that those things he says will be done, he will have whatever he says. Therefore I say to you, whatever things you ask when you pray, believe that you receive them, and you will have them."

Mark 11:23,24 NKJV

We like to speak to our mountains, our problems, and tell them what to do, but there's a "rest of the story" to that Scripture. There's something we must do first if we want that Word to come to pass.

The next verse starts with "And." And what does "and" mean? It means the rest of the verse has to be done in order to complete the circle.

"*And* whenever you stand praying, if you have anything against anyone, forgive him, that your Father in heaven may also forgive you your trespasses. But if you do not forgive, neither will your Father in heaven forgive your trespasses" (v. 25).

When we pray, we have a job to do if we want our prayers to be answered. That job is to forgive. If we do not forgive, neither can our Father forgive us. Therefore, He can't fulfill the first part of that Scripture.

Forgiving someone doesn't justify or make right the wrong they did. We don't have to agree with it, but we can't harbor bitterness. We have to say, "Lord, I give them to You." This keeps our hearts free of bitterness so that our prayers can be answered.

Do You Know Your Heavenly Father?

by Oral Roberts

You have two fathers. One of them is your heavenly Father. Do you know *Him?* Many people know only their natural father—their "birth father," in today's language.

The more important father to know is your heavenly Father—the Father who not only gives you spiritual birth, but who created all that you are!

Your natural father gave you an inheritance—a genetic code, a link to the past, a family tradition. Your *heavenly* Father also offers you an inheritance—a spiritual genetic code to make you into His likeness, heaven as your ultimate home, an abundant life on earth, and an everlasting future!

Jesus told us many things about our heavenly Father. Our relationship with God is to be that of a child and his daddy. Jesus described our heavenly Father as our eternal Father—the One who will never abandon or leave us.

Our heavenly Father is all-loving, the One who never gives up on us. He is our omnipresent Father, the One who is always available to us and who has unlimited patience with us. He is our forgiving Father who graciously forgives us when we repent of our sins and gently leads us toward righteousness. He is our wise Father who knows everything about us and how to work everything for our good. He is our generous Father who wants us to have His presence in our lives and who is willing to share all that He has and all that He is. Oh, what a Father we have!

Sometimes our earthly fathers get lonely. We children can remedy that by calling them and having a long talk with them or, as children, by crawling up onto their laps and giving them a hug. Reach out to your daddies today...both of them.

Building God's Dreams

by Kenneth Copeland

Kenneth Copeland Ministries

People always talk about building their "dream home." But did you know that you can begin to build dreams out of God's Word? A good foundation for them is Deuteronomy 28. I can tell you from experience, it is good dream-building material.

God intended for man to be a dreamer. He built into us the capacity to do it. But He didn't intend for us to be limited by natural thoughts and circumstances. He meant for us to dream beyond them.

That's what Abraham did. He locked into God's dream—and it was bigger than anything he could have thought on his own.

It will be that way for you too. God's dream for you is bigger than your dream for yourself. It is exceedingly, abundantly beyond all you can ask or think! (Eph. 3:20.)

Once you get that dream inside you, things will begin to change. No, all your problems won't disappear overnight any more than mine did. But you'll respond to them differently.

When they rise up in front of you and threaten to defeat you, God's dream will stir in your heart.

You'll start saying, "Wait just a minute. I'm the head, not the tail. I'm blessed, not cursed. I don't have to tolerate this situation. I happen to be a child of the King Himself. He sets my table in the presence of my enemies. No weapon formed against me can prosper!" (Deut. 28:13; Psalm 23:5; Isa. 54:17.)

Building your dream home is great! But building God's dreams inside of you, and then seeing those dreams come to pass, is glorious![1]

Strength in Time of Trouble

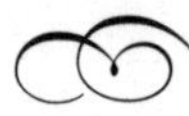

by Evelyn Roberts

First of Two Parts

First Samuel 30 tells the story of David and his army going into battle and destroying the Amalekites. When David and his men came home to Ziklag, they found that the Amalekites had burned the city and taken their wives and children captive. David and his men wept until they had no strength left. Then, because they wanted to blame someone for what had happened to their families, David's men began talking about stoning him.

Have you ever had something bad happen to you and you wanted to blame someone for it? That's what happened with David's men. When we're grieved and hurt, we often do and say things we don't really mean. I know I've hurt people's feelings when I've been feeling hurt myself, and later, after realizing what I'd done, I have apologized for it.

David didn't know what to do. So what do you do when you don't know what to do? You go to the Lord. He is the only One who can help you when bad things happen. Friends will try to help you all they can, but really, nobody but Jesus can help you when something really bad hits you. Verse 6 says David encouraged himself in the Lord his God.

I remember the day Oral and Richard told me that our son, Ronnie, was gone. It broke my heart. I cried my eyes out, and then I got on my knees and prayed. Like David, I didn't know what to do, but I found strength in the Lord. I turned to Him. I've learned that the Lord can always strengthen you and help you when you call upon Him in time of trouble. (Ps. 86:7.)

Know Who Your Enemy Is

by Evelyn Roberts

Second of Two Parts

It's important to know who your enemy is and when to go into battle. David made his plans to attack the Amalekites carefully, striking the enemy at just the right time. (1 Sam. 30:11-20.)

Now, of course, we don't fight our battles with guns, or with spears and bows and arrows as David did. Ours is a different kind of battle. Christianity is a spiritual war. God and the devil are fighting, and we're caught in between. So when problems hit us, it's the devil fighting against us. If we can ever understand that it's the devil who's fighting us and not people, then we won't be so hard on those around us.

David and his men found the enemy, and they fought all night and all the next day. And verse 19 says David recovered all!

What weapons of warfare can you use against the devil?

Your faith. One of your greatest weapons is to know that God loves you and He is going to take care of things.

Prayer. The devil doesn't like it when you talk to God because prayer is an effective weapon against him.

The Word of God. God's Word is full of strength and power.

The Name of Jesus. Before Jesus went back to heaven, He gave us His name to use in prayer. He said, "Whatever you ask the Father in My name He will give you" (John 16:23 NKJV).

The word of your testimony. Another great weapon you can use is your testimony. Revelation 12:17 says we overcome by the blood of Jesus and the word of our testimony.

We know the enemy, we have the weapons, and we now have the power to attack!

Something Better

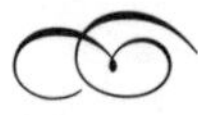

by Richard Roberts

When I was young, I had dreams for my life. I wanted two things: to be a nightclub singer and a professional athlete. What I didn't want was anything to do with God!

But God had other plans for me. Through the prayers of my parents, I stopped running from God's love and turned to Him and received His salvation. And it was then that He began to reveal His plans for my life.

In Proverbs 19:21 NIV God says, "Many are the plans in a man's heart, but it is the Lord's purpose that prevails." God had something better in mind for me. When I gave my life to Him, His plans became more important to me than my own. I wanted to go His way, and I began to seek His direction. In Isaiah 30:21 NIV God tells us, "Whether you turn to the right or to the left, your ears will hear a voice behind you, saying, 'This is the way; walk in it.'"

Today, instead of being a nightclub singer or professional golfer, I am in the healing ministry. I hold three degrees from Oral Roberts University, the very university I ran away from. I am now the president of that university! I have found that God's plans are much better than mine.

God has plans for you too. And His plans for you are far beyond anything you have even thought of or imagined. I've quit asking God to go with me and my plans. I ask Him if I can go with Him because He knows where we're going!

God's Not Mad at You

by Kenneth Copeland

Kenneth Copeland Ministries

I have six simple words for you: God is not mad at you!

The first time I found that out, I hadn't been a Christian very long. I had heard all my life about the terrible things God would do to you. He would make you sick and keep you poor. He would bring you trouble to make you strong. I heard He did bad things to you, but it was all right because He was God.

Then one day I came across Isaiah 54. God is not mad at us! That's earthshaking news—such good news that some people have a hard time believing it. They start thinking of all the sin they've allowed into their lives, all the wrongs they've done.

But God did something about that: He sent Jesus to the cross.

Read Isaiah 52. All of us have seen paintings of the Crucifixion. Yet none of them come close to the horror of what happened to Jesus that day. When He bore the sins of mankind, His body became so marred, He didn't even look human. (v. 14.)

Yet it was this very event that freed us forever from God's wrath. Jesus' death on the cross was enough to pay for your sins and mine. As far as God is concerned, it's all over. We just have to accept it.[1]

Overtake Your Situation

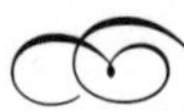

by Lindsay Roberts

When I first married Richard and became part of this ministry, my father-in-law taught me a very simple, but important, lesson. He told me, "Lindsay, you can either react or respond to life's challenges." He was right! His words still ring true for me today.

Whether you react or respond to the events of life can make the difference between defeat and victory, between a life of failure and a life of success. When difficulties arise, if you *react* to the situation, it will overtake you. But if you *respond*, you can overtake the situation!

Problems will always be around. If it's not your health, it could be your finances. If it's not your children, it could be your marriage. If it's not terrorism in this country, it's conflict and war abroad. The issue is not whether or not you will face problems; the issue is *how* you will face them. Each of us has a choice.

Jesus declared, "My peace I give to you. Do not let your heart be troubled, nor let it be fearful" (John 14:27 NASB). The world doesn't give you Jesus' peace; therefore, the world can't take it away. And Deuteronomy 31:6 NKJV reassures you that God *will not leave you nor forsake you.* He is with you to give you His peace no matter what problems arise.

You can *react* to your circumstances with fear, doubt, and worry, or you can respond with prayer and the confession of God's Word. Whatever your situation, respond to it in faith and allow the peace of God that passes all understanding to flood your heart.

God Has a Place for You

by Gloria Copeland
Kenneth Copeland Ministries

God has a plan for each of us, but did you know that He also has a physical place for us? When God created Adam and Eve, He made a place for them in the Garden. When He established the children of Israel as a people, He gave them the Promised Land.

I believe God has a physical place for us, but to receive it we are to diligently seek Him and His way of doing things. When we seek after God, we find His wisdom, we run into His goodness, and we open the door for the kingdom of heaven to be manifested, so we can live life supernaturally.

We don't have to live like the world lives. We have a Father in heaven who is in control, and He wants us to be like Him. That's why He gave Adam dominion over all things. Then God gave him instructions on how to live in the Garden.

Everything was perfect, nothing missing, nothing broken, until Adam and Eve failed to follow the wisdom of God for their lives and disobeyed Him. As a result, they lost their Garden.

God has a place of blessing for you, and I believe that if you'll stay connected to Him and follow His wisdom, your "place" will continually increase. You can't follow the wisdom of God and not increase.[1]

'Launch Out Into the Deep'

by Tommy Barnett

Phoenix First Assembly

First of Three Parts

God has given me a revelation of power from Acts 1:8, which says, "Ye shall receive power, after that the Holy Ghost is come upon you: and ye shall be witnesses unto me both in Jerusalem, and in Judaea, and in Samaria, and unto the uttermost part of the earth."

Every week I go someplace and preach. Sometimes I preach to large audiences of several thousand, and sometimes I may speak to just a dozen. But I pray this prayer every time before I get on the plane:

"Lord, I don't care if there are a thousand or if there are a hundred people present. All I ask You, Lord, is if on this trip You'll give me just one person, if I can change one life, if I can get just one person to touch their believing button, somebody will build a great church, somebody will start a great ministry, somebody will pray for the sick, somebody will help the hurting.

"Lord, I am looking for one man or one woman. I believe when I finish my sermon, a great church is going to be built. I believe that healing ministries are going to spring up. I believe that hospitals which are vacant all over the land are going to be spiritual healing centers. Lord, just give me strength and power and anointing that I might deliver what You would have me to. In Jesus' wonderful name."

Jesus had a magnificent way of speaking words on two levels at the same time. The words He spoke would address the intellect of man, and that man would begin to respond. Even as he responded, it would get down into his heart. It seemed to have a double meaning. The Bible is full of such events. In Luke 5:4 Jesus said to Peter, "Launch out into the deep, and let down your nets for a draught." Peter stopped to obey the command of God, but he stopped as if to say, "I think He has a deeper meaning than fishing for fish." Jesus Words are so impregnated with heaven that they seep down through the intellect, down into the spirit of man.

Room for One More

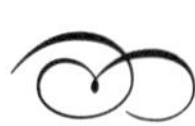

by Tommy Barnett
Phoenix First Assembly

Second of Three Parts

It is so sad to watch people who are talking about the kingdom of God while they are operating in the kingdom of this old world—churches jockeying for power, divisions in churches over petty issues. It has always been that way.

Did you know that the people who resist the move of the Spirit in their generation the most are always the people who have the most ecclesiastical turf to protect? Historically speaking, when anyone slams the door in the face of the Holy Spirit and says, "Not this way, not here, and not now," it's not ever really genuinely over a theological issue. It's actually an argument over who is in charge.

A lady came to me one day and said, "Pastor Barnett, our church is growing big. It's too big. We've got to stop right now for a while and just analyze things and take care of what we've got. We are big enough." I tried to tell the lady that the church is only big enough when everybody in the city has been saved.

A few weeks went by. She came to me one Sunday and said, "My son is coming in from out of town. He's unsaved. I want him to get saved. Preacher, will you preach good? Will you give an altar call?"

I said, "Yes." Then I said, "No, lady, I've changed my mind. The church is big enough." She got my point.

She said, "Well, I think we've got room for one more."

'Love Is Not Love Till You Give It Away'

by Tommy Barnett
Phoenix First Assembly

Third of Three Parts

If you want power, serve your generation. The Bible says that is how Jesus built His kingdom. He served His generation. If happiness to you is "palms up," you'll be happy only on your birthday and at Christmas. But if happiness to you is "palms down," you'll be happy 365 days a year. The happiest people I know today are those who have tasted the joy of serving other people. They never want to be served again.

Whatever you want in life, to get it you've got to give it away. It sounds like a paradox, but if you want joy, then introduce joy to those who have no joy. Joy says, "Look, I'm glad to meet your friend, but the one I really want to meet is you."

If you want happiness, spread happiness wherever you go. If you want love, become a lover, because everybody loves a lover. Somebody ought to write a song about that.

All three of my children are different, and they all interpret love just a little bit differently. Luke is the uncomplicated one. All you have to do is kiss and hug him a couple of times a day, and he's happy. Luke is like me, so I understand him.

Matthew is not that affectionate. He interprets love as talking to me. When I go to Los Angeles, I sleep in one room and he in the other. When we turn off the lights, you would think we were at the Waltons' house. "Dad," he says, and for another two hours I'm trying to go to sleep. But Matthew interprets love as your talking to him.

Then there is Christi. She's not that affectionate. She likes a hug and a kiss, and it doesn't matter if you talk to her much or not. Christi interprets love as your giving her something, buying her something.

Many times I have heard Oral Roberts say, "Love is not love till you give it away."

Money With a Mission

by Dr. Creflo A. Dollar
World Changers Church International

The children of Israel, three and a half million people, had wealth transferred into their hands. (Ex. 12:35,36.) God led them into the wilderness where there were no malls to spend their money. They did not understand the purpose for the money. And when you don't understand the purpose for money, you will build idols instead of sanctuaries.

In Exodus 25:8, we see the purpose for money. God says, "And let them make me a sanctuary; that I may dwell among them." Now what does that mean? Is God talking about just church buildings here? No. Of course, we need those, but He's talking about when somebody can turn on their television and get saved because your money bought the equipment and the television time that enabled them to hear the Word and accept Jesus into their heart. That is a sanctuary, a place where He can dwell.

That is the purpose for money. It's called money with a mission. And if you're not ready for the mission, don't expect the wealth. Prosperity is not real until prosperity is coming from you, going to somebody else.

I'm talking about growing up. You don't grow up in prayer until you start interceding for someone else instead of just for yourself. You don't grow up in faith as long as you use faith just for yourself. You grow up when you start using your faith for somebody else. Nor do you grow up in prosperity if you're getting it just to squander it upon your own desires.

When you use money to be a blessing in somebody else's life, then God says, "Now you are My distribution center. I can give you more because I know what you are going to do with it."

Go Into Praise and Worship

by Richard Roberts

God has been pouring into me these words: "Seek Me first. Quit talking to Me about all these things. I already know about the things. Talk to Me about Me. Praise Me, worship Me, see Me, seek My kingdom, My glory, My righteousness. And then as you do that, all these things will be added to you." (Matt. 6:33.)

So I've changed, and it has totally revolutionized my prayer life. I've quit saying, "Gimme, gimme, gimme. God, do this. God, do that." I've just gone into praise and worship.

Each morning before we make our television programs, I drive the short distance to the studio singing, "Put on the garment of praise for the spirit of heaviness; lift up your voice to God. Pray in the spirit and the understanding. O magnify the Lord."

I arrive at the TV studio praying in tongues, lifting my hands in praise, putting on my spiritual armor—taking my helmet of salvation (protecting my mind); putting on my breastplate of righteousness (protecting my heart in which I believe); girding my loins about with truth (which really is soul winning in its most beautiful form); putting on my gospel shoes to walk over the devil's roughest territory with the sword of the Spirit (which is the Word of God); taking my shield of faith so I'll be able to quench the fiery darts of the wicked one; and the seventh piece, praying in tongues.

As I do these things, I get direction. And although hell may be all around me, I can walk right through it, and I don't have to stop. My wife says I am an oblivious person. Well, I am oblivious to the things that I should be, because I made up my mind that I'm going to seek God first—His kingdom, His glory, His righteousness. And when you do that, the Holy Spirit begins to speak to you. You do things that are unusual, and the world doesn't understand them. Your family may not understand them. But if you will hold fast to what God has told you to do, you'll see Him work.

The Tenacity of a Puppy

by Lindsay Roberts

I once had a little puppy, part Pekingese and part Poodle. He was so persistent! I remember a time when he got hold of an exposed tree root, and I watched him as he pulled on it. I admired his tenacity. I thought, *Bless his heart, he thinks he can move that whole tree!* Before he was finished he had that small root pulled right out of the ground. He even pulled the root loose from the tree!

Watching him reminded me of when my mother used to say, "Lindsay's like a puppy to a root." I'd say, "What does that mean?" I learned it means that like a puppy to a root, when you grab on to something with your faith, you don't let go until you are successful in achieving what you're striving for. Even when adversity comes and you don't see immediate results, you hold on and you don't give up.

James 5:16 describes tenacious prayer. It says, "The effectual, fervent prayer of a righteous man availeth much." An effectual prayer is one that is "continual, heartfelt, and powerful." Fervent means "red-hot, with intensity." A righteous man is "a person who is in right relationship with God, who knows what God's Word says and is living in obedience to it." That kind of prayer avails much. It does the work it's supposed to do.

When you pray according to James 5:16 with a tenacity like my puppy had, you can be confident that God is at work in your life.

The Measure of Faith

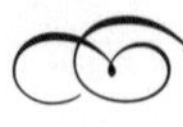

by Oral Roberts

First of Two Parts

The apostle Paul said in Romans 12:3, "God hath dealt to every man the measure of faith." When you come into this world, God slips faith into your heart. God gives you the power to believe Him. As a matter of fact, the strongest force in your being is this measure of faith. It's easier to believe God than it is to believe the devil. It's easier to believe your best friend than it is to believe your worst enemy. It's easier to believe God will heal you than it is for the devil to oppress you. It's easier because God has put faith in your heart. He put in a measure of faith. You have it.

I used to pray, "O God, give me faith." Nobody had ever told me that I had a measure of it. I would read the Bible, but you can read and skip over some of the most important teaching in the Bible. I had read those words, "God hath dealt to every man the measure of faith," and never even thought about it.

One day I discovered Romans 12:3. I have faith. God said to me, "Faith is not something you get; it's something you already have." So I didn't pray anymore to have faith. You don't ask God to give you something He has already given you. You've got it! But you can waste it, and you can throw it away.

Jesus never accused His disciples of not having faith. He just said, "Where is it? What have you done with it? Why aren't you using it? Why have you hidden it in the midst of indefiniteness? Why have you laid it aside in the hour of trouble?"

Jesus and His disciples were on a boat, which was rocking in the storm, and the disciples were terrified. They wakened Him and said, "Master, carest thou not that we perish?" (Mark 4:38). And He arose and spoke peace to the storm, and there was a great calm.

Faith Comes by Hearing

by Oral Roberts

Second of Two Parts

Romans 10:17 tells how your faith operates: "So then faith cometh by hearing, and hearing by the word of God." Notice how verse 13 fits exactly with the word "cometh." "For whosoever shall call upon the name of the Lord shall be saved."

Verses 14 and 15 continue: "How then shall they call on him in whom they have not believed? and how shall they believe in him of whom they have not heard? and how shall they hear without a preacher? And how shall they preach, except they be sent?"

The past several years, millions of people have lost faith in everything—in government, the police, the church, and preachers. People have lost faith in about everything you mention. But as I am sharing with you right now, your faith is coming up out of your heart. That measure of faith is becoming active. It's stirring around inside you. The miracle that you've been waiting for—the miracle for your soul to be saved, the miracle for your body to be healed, the miracle to call in the finances you need, the miracle to set your life free, the miracle to turn it around for you—has come!

Put On the Word of God Every Day

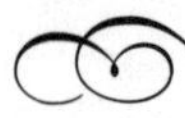

by Richard Roberts

Do you brush your teeth every day? Do you put on your clothes every day? I'm sure you do now, but when you were a baby you didn't. Someone had to help you learn to do those things and develop a habit of doing them.

When I was born, I didn't lie in my crib and look up at my mother and say, "The Lord just impressed me that I need a toothbrush." No, it didn't happen that way at all. I learned how to brush my teeth because my parents forced me to. In the morning and again before I went to bed at night, they would say, "Richard, have you brushed your teeth? Let me see your toothbrush." And they checked me every day until I developed a habit of brushing my teeth. It was the same way with learning to put on clothes.

When I was a baby I was comfortable with no clothes on. But as time went on my parents taught me that I must put on clothes! And today I wouldn't dream of leaving my home and walking onto the set of my daily TV program, or anywhere else, without putting on my clothes.

I also wouldn't dream of leaving my home each day without first "putting on" the Lord Jesus Christ and putting His Word in my heart. I've developed a good habit of having a daily relationship with God and His Word.

By developing a good habit of putting on God's Word every day and then acting on that Word with your faith, you'll be well prepared to face the onslaught of emergencies that the devil throws at you. And not only that, you'll win!

A Threat to the Devil

by Jerry Savelle

Jerry Savelle Ministries International

I had a lady tell me once, "Brother Jerry, I saw you on TV the other day. You were talking about how the devil came against you and how you and Carolyn had to stand and stand until you finally won the battle.

"Shortly after that," she continued, "I was watching Kenneth Copeland on television. He was talking about the adversity he and Gloria had been through and how they'd had to fight the good fight of faith, and they'd won.

"And then I turned on the TV and there was Oral Roberts talking about how the devil had come against him and how he and Evelyn had stood on the Word and fought the good fight of faith and won.

"I don't understand it," she said. "It looks like the devil is after you guys all the time. He doesn't ever bother me."

"Well," I replied, "apparently you're not a threat to the devil."

What makes you a threat to the devil? You are a threat to him when you are deeply committed to the cause of Christ and the standards He gave us for living a Christian life. The devil attacks everybody, but he goes full force after deeply committed Christians. They are, by far, the most serious threat to him because they can stop his operation in their own lives and his efforts in the lives of others.

If you want to be a Christian God can use, make an unwavering commitment to walk with Christ. Ephesians 6:10-11 NIV says, "Be strong in the Lord and in his mighty power." Put on the full armor of God so that you can take your stand against the devil's schemes. Such commitment is Satan's worst nightmare.

Be Aggressive About Your Harvest

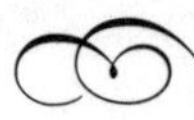

by Taffi L. Dollar
World Changers Church International

It's harvest time, and we must not let our harvest die in the field! I want to encourage you to be aggressive about the things of God. Aggressive means to be bold, ambitious, to desire to be used by God, to live in the will of God, and to carry out His purpose. Aggressive also means to be persistent and not take no for an answer. It means to be go-getting. I believe that as believers we've got to go get from the devil what belongs to us.

I've never seen such wickedness as in these last days. Satan is trying to intimidate Christians. Last year I had family members who were outside God's will. I began to lift the Word up before God. I said, "God, the Word says my household is to be saved." And I have since seen those family members come to God.

It's time to become an aggressive reaper in these last days and not just sit back and let the devil do anything he wants to do in our homes—create havoc, break up our marriages, and infiltrate our children with all kinds of evil things. We've got to put the Word inside them. Every seed produces a harvest, but it's up to us to lay hold of it and begin to seize what is ours.

Matthew 11:12 AMP says, "From the days of John the Baptist until the present time the kingdom of heaven has endured violent assault, and violent men seize it by force [as a precious prize]—a share in the heavenly kingdom is sought for with the most ardent zeal and intense exertion." We're in a race, and just as a runner runs to win the prize, I believe we must exert the same amount of intensity, the same amount of fervency, to lay hold of the prize that's been set before us.

Coming to the End of Oneself

by Eastman and Angel Curtis
Destiny Church

All my life I heard the Scripture, "Train up a child in the way he should go: and when he is old, he will not depart from it" (Prov. 22:6). I've even heard people say about their child, "He's running from God now, but he's going to come back."

But *The Amplified Bible* says, "Train up a child in the way he should go [and in keeping with his individual gift or bent], and when he is old he will not depart from it."

For example, our son is musically talented, and when we see that natural gift in him, we are to encourage him in music as part of his destiny and guide him in that direction. We're to encourage the giftings we see in our children.

But what if you say, "My child is smoking and drinking right now, and I never raised him (or her) that way"?

I think we need to see them through the eyes of faith, seeing those things which are not as though they are. We need to see them as whole, going to church, loving God, and fulfilling their destiny in the call of God.

Also, pray the mercies of God over them as they're going through that wilderness time. Pray, "God, bring them to the end of themselves," because that's what the prodigal son had to do.

While God is bringing them to the end of themselves, we parents—moms especially—want to jump in, write the check, and save them. But only Jesus Christ can be their Savior. It is to Him they need to turn. And that's where we as parents have to get on our knees and say, "God, You teach me how to give this child up to You." For God brings us parents to the end of ourselves too. He wants us all—parents and children—to depend only on Him.

Follow God's Counsel

by Lindsay Roberts

King Jehoshaphat reigned successfully over Judah for twenty-five years. The Bible says "He walked in the ways of his father Asa and did not stray from them; he did what was right in the eyes of the Lord" (2 Chron. 20:32 NIV). But as time went on, Jehoshaphat lost his focus and started wavering in his devotion to God. He listened to ungodly people. He did not remove the altars of foreign gods from the land, and he joined in an alliance with wicked King Ahaziah to build a fleet of trading ships.

The money in building ships probably looked good to Jehoshaphat, and he began to seek the advice of the ungodly king, who was very prosperous. When Jehoshaphat listened to the voice of God, he had prospered. In one battle he acquired more treasures than he could carry off in three days! (v. 25.) God never told him to get involved in ship building. Maybe Jehoshaphat thought the two men would just be in partnership together and he wouldn't serve Ahaziah's gods. But everything Jehoshaphat did after that failed. The ships were wrecked and totally destroyed. The next thing we read about Jehoshaphat is that he died. How sad!

Earlier Jehoshaphat himself had said, "Believe in the Lord your God, so shall ye be established; believe in his prophets, so shall ye prosper" (v. 20). None of us can afford to depart from the Word of God and follow counsel from the wrong people. When Jehoshaphat followed God, he was established. When we believe God and follow His counsel, He can establish and prosper us in every area of our lives.

He Is Relevant

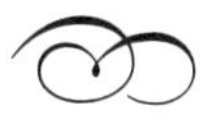

by Richard Roberts

There is a great question being asked across our nation today, and it is this: Is God relevant, or am I the center of the universe?

Some humanist theories devoid of God will tell you that we human beings are the center of life and that God has no relevance. I'm here to proclaim to you today that God is relevant! Furthermore, without Him we can do nothing of our own power that counts for eternity.

God is relevant to the lost soul. No man can save himself from sin, cleanse his own heart, or fill himself with the Holy Spirit. Salvation is a free gift of God, given to us when we repent. There is nothing we can do in our humanity to earn it, achieve it, win it, or buy it. (Eph. 2:8,9.)

God is relevant to the lost city. The Bible says, "Except the Lord build the house, they labour in vain that build it: except the Lord keep the city, the watchman waketh but in vain" (Ps. 127:1). No city council, no city police force, no city fathers can save a lost city. Only the power of God flowing through that city can truly cleanse it of crime, poverty, and destruction.

God is relevant to the lost nation. The Bible says, "Blessed is the nation whose God is the Lord; and the people whom he hath chosen for his own inheritance" (Ps. 33:12). No federal agency, no task force, no branch of the military, no law of the land can save a nation that turns its back on God. According to the Bible, only the Lord can truly build up a nation from the inside out and turn it from destruction to prosperity.

It's not really a matter of whether God is relevant, but whether we choose to make ourselves relevant to Him and choose to receive His forgiveness, His Holy Spirit, His prosperity, His wisdom, and His miracles! John the Baptist had it right when he said, "A man can receive nothing [good from God], except it be given him from heaven" (John 3:27). Let's put ourselves into position today to receive from God as we make Him relevant to our lives and the Lord of our lives.

Walking in Divine Overflow

by Cathy Duplantis
Jesse Duplantis Ministries

Most people know the story of the twelve spies Moses sent out to scout the Promised Land and how all but two—Jacob and Caleb—returned with a negative report.

In Numbers 14:9 NKJV Moses told the people, "Do not rebel against the Lord, nor fear the people of the land, for they are our bread; their protection has departed from them, and the Lord is with us." I've learned from that verse that to live in God's divine overflow we need to:

One, rebel not against the Lord. Isaiah 1:19 NKJV says, "If you are willing and obedient, you shall eat the good of the land." If God speaks to your spirit, don't shrink back. Stand firm and obey Him.

Two, get rid of fear. Second Timothy 1:7 NKJV says, "God has not given us a spirit of fear." Fear comes to all of us, but don't share it. Recognize that fear is not of God and take authority over it, in Jesus' name.

Three, know the limitations of your enemy. Numbers 14:9 NKJV says, "Do not...fear the people of the land, for they are our bread." While there were giants in the land, Joshua and Caleb recognized that what the people in that land had accumulated was intended for God's people. It was bread for them.

Four, know the power of your God. Mark 10:27 says, "With God all things are possible, and when you believe, nothing shall be impossible unto you" (Matt. 17:20). It's important to recognize that God is all-powerful, He loves you, and He wants to do awesome things for you. Knowing this can enable you to walk out of lack into God's divine overflow.

Daily Communication

by Lindsay Roberts

One night I was so exhausted that I climbed into bed at about 9 o'clock. I'm a night owl. My regular bedtime is in the wee hours of the morning, so going to bed that early was highly unusual. But I was so tired that I fell asleep before anyone else.

My mother called the next morning and said, "I couldn't go to sleep last night...you didn't call me like you normally do." Mom was right. I call her every evening to talk to her and pray with her, and I hadn't done it that night. The absence of our regular communication gave both of us a strange feeling.

Even though I'm a grown woman, my mother and I like having daily contact with each other. In the same manner, I believe our heavenly Father wants us to communicate with Him on a regular basis. No matter what our age, we are His children, and He loves us. He wants us to take time to talk with Him, and He misses us when we don't keep in touch with Him.

Maybe you feel as if you don't know how to communicate with God. A good way to open up a line of communication with Him is to praise Him. Turn in your Bible to the Psalms. Use Psalm 103:1: "Bless the Lord, O my soul: and all that is within me, bless his holy name." Start with that verse and build on it. When you begin to fellowship with the Father regularly, you establish a relationship with Him like you've never had before, and you begin to look forward to your daily communication together.

The Will of God

by Richard Roberts

Wherever you go in life, you'll find Satan there. If you get into obedience and do what God has spoken to you to do, the devil knows that you're going to make a difference. We must understand that even though we're on the way to fulfilling God's calling on our lives, our adversary, the devil, who, as a roaring lion, walks about seeking whom he may devour, will try to do everything in his power to steal, kill, and destroy. (1 Peter 5:8; John 10:10.) Satan is defeated, but he is not destroyed yet.

Genesis 37:50 tells the story of Joseph, a young man who dreamed dreams, and his brothers hated him for it. They threw him into a pit and smeared the blood of an animal upon his coat, then took it back to his father and said, "Your youngest son is dead."

Joseph found his way from that pit to a slave caravan heading to Egypt, where he was later imprisoned for his faith. Certainly through all those years and all the things that Joseph went through, he must have wondered if he was in the will of God. But along the way, God was directing his steps and working all things together and in His timing. And when it came God's time, everything came together.

Proverbs 19:2 says that it is not good to be hasty and miss the mark. Moses got ahead of God's call on his life. One day he saw an Egyptian strike a Hebrew, and Moses took the situation into his own hands. Before he knew what he had done, in trying to break up a simple fight, he had killed an Egyptian and had to run for his life. Then on the backside of a hot, blistering desert, he met God through a burning bush. A voice from heaven spoke to him out of the bush, which was not consumed by the flames. God said to Moses, "Take off your shoes; you're standing on holy ground. I've seen the afflictions and heard the cries of My people, and I have selected you to tell Pharaoh, the king of Egypt, to let My people go. The last time you went in your strength, but this time you will go in mine." (Exodus 1-3.)

Radical Faith

by Marilyn Hickey
Marilyn Hickey Ministries

Part One of Two Parts

In this day we can't be namby-pamby about what we believe. We need radical faith. We need to aggressively press in and expect extraordinary things from God like one woman I heard about who lives in Mombassa, Kenya. Her husband was unfaithful to her, and he was a con man who could easily have gone to prison. A minister was preaching in Mombassa, and this woman drove him back and forth to the meetings. It was very hot, and the minister would sweat while he was preaching. The woman said, "I'll take your shirt home, wash and iron it, and bring it back clean tomorrow." She did that each day, and he was grateful for her thoughtfulness.

What the minister didn't know was that she took the sweaty shirt home each night and wrung the sweat out over the bed where her husband slept, saying, "Father, I am believing that the sweat of a godly man will bring deliverance to my husband."

Now that's radical faith! Within three weeks her husband became so conscious of his sins that he couldn't stand it. He got saved, and now he is serving as a deacon in the church and prospering!

One definition of *radical* is "a considerable departure from the usual or traditional." What that woman did may seem far out, but God honored her faith. In Matthew 9:29, Jesus said, "According to your faith be it unto you." I believe God honors radical faith. When we dare to believe Him for the impossible, that's when miracles can happen!

Tracts Instead of Shoes

by Marilyn Hickey
Marilyn Hickey Ministries

Part Two of Two Parts

Radical faith gets radical results! Once I met a man in Guatemala who demonstrated radical faith, and he ended up more prosperous than he ever dreamed he could be. Manuel was a poor Indian whose life completely changed when he got saved. He couldn't read or write because he'd gone to school only a few years, and he had never owned a pair of shoes in his entire life.

After Manuel received Jesus, he got a job. When his first paycheck came, he thought, *Should I buy a pair of shoes?* But then he thought of his tribe, none of whom were saved or had heard about Jesus. So instead of buying himself his first pair of shoes, he spent his whole paycheck on tracts to distribute to his people, and many of them became Christians.

Now that's radical faith! Because of Manuel's radical faith to sow and reach out to his tribe instead of spending his paycheck on himself, God gave him the idea for an invention that helps save gasoline, and it has made him wealthy! Proverbs 8:12 says, "I wisdom dwell with prudence, and find out knowledge of witty inventions." Today Manuel is a multimillionaire, and now he's passionate about reaching out to all the other Indian tribes in Guatemala.

Manuel exercised radical faith by reaching out to his tribe, and he got radical results. I believe that when you get radical in your faith for others, you can get radical results in your own life also!

God Loves Us Anyhow

by Oral Roberts

Some people offer their forgiveness based on their feeling that the other person isn't so bad after all...he deserves a break...he has some redeeming virtues to make up for what he has done wrong...perhaps there was a justification for his behavior...or he was a victim of circumstances.

The Bible, however, shows us that forgiveness is much deeper. God does not take us into His fellowship by whitewashing us or in any way minimizing the seriousness of our sins. Nor does He forgive us because we somehow make up for our wrongdoing. It is simply that He loves, accepts, and forgives us anyhow.

Romans 5:7-8 NASB says, "Though perhaps for the good man someone would dare even to die. But God demonstrates His own love toward us, in that while we were yet sinners, Christ died for us." The relationship of love that God offers us is an unearned relationship like that offered by a good parent to his or her child. As a parent, we may not like what our child does. We may disapprove, we may criticize, we may even punish, but we keep the relationship with the child *anyhow.*

The willingness of God not to let what we do, say, feel, or think break His relationship with us is a model to help us forgive and keep on loving one another, with no strings attached.

Don't Buy the Lie!

by Gloria Copeland
Kenneth Copeland Ministries

Satan can't force you to do anything. He doesn't have the power. All he can do is make a presentation and try to sell you the lies he's peddling. He can't make you buy them. He can only present them. You have a choice whether to take him up on his sorry deal or rebuke him and command him to leave you.

So when he makes you a presentation, learn not to toy with it. Don't take the bait. Instead, learn to immediately turn away from his doubts and start thinking and speaking the Word of God instead. Ask yourself, *What does the Word say that guarantees me the very thing the devil just tried to make me doubt?*

Get in the Word of God and find out the real truth. That's where your authority is—in the truth. Satan will lie to you, cheat you, trick you, deceive you, and bait you into bondage, if you'll let him. But God will always tell you the truth. And that truth will make you free.

So don't buy Satan's lies. Once you know the truth of your authority in Christ Jesus, you won't spend your days crying about how bad things are. You'll spend your days telling those mountains to be cast into the sea.

Instead of acting like a whiner, you'll be more than a conqueror in Christ. You'll kick the devil out of your affairs with the words of your mouth. And as you stand in triumph with your needs met, your body healed, and your heart rejoicing, you can laugh right in the face of that snake as he slinks away complaining about his defeat.[1]

You Can Live in Victory!

by Jerry Savelle

Jerry Savelle Ministries International

When I was younger, I ran from God and from His call on my life because I associated God with a message of defeat. All of my life I'd heard people say things like, "Woe is me." They let me know that if I did anything wrong, God would "get me." I decided all that gloom and defeat just wasn't for me.

But then I heard the Bible's message of victory! I found out that Jesus destroyed the works of the devil, and because of my covenant with Him, failure and defeat weren't in my future. When I learned that, I grabbed ahold of it with everything that was in me, and I answered God's call to the ministry.

I preached my very first sermon in a little church on a Wednesday night. I was so excited about the message of victory that I figured everyone in the place wanted to hear it. So I preached Jesus' words from John 16:33: "In the world ye shall have tribulation: but be of good cheer; I have overcome the world." As I was preaching, suddenly a man stood up and challenged me. He shouted, "Jesus said that in the world we would have tribulation!" And the people said, "Amen."

I answered, "Yes, sir, that's what it says. But if you're going to quote Jesus, please finish the quote." He said, "I don't know the end of the quote. All I know is that in the world we're going to have tribulation."

Too many of us are like that man, looking only at the trials. But Jesus wants us to identify with the "overcoming," not the tribulation. It's true that as long as we're in this world, we'll have trials. But Jesus has deprived them of their power to harm us! As we believe and trust in His Word, we can live in victory!

We Grow in the Valley

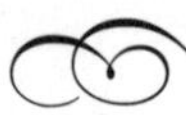

by Evelyn Roberts

I would like to tell you that the Roberts family never has any struggles. But if I tell the truth, I can't say that. My husband, Oral, tells me, "Evelyn, you know you grow in struggles."

I say, "Yes, but I'd like not to grow so fast."

We were in a meeting one night with some of our graduate students at Oral Roberts University and my husband was talking about being so low sometimes that he has to reach up to touch bottom. He asked, "Why do we get that low? Why do we stay in the valley so much?"

One young man replied, "It's because the soil is better in the valley, and that is where the grass grows."

I thought that was a very good answer. We can't stay on the mountaintop in our Christian experience all the time. We must spend time in the valley. But it doesn't have to be a bad time there if we will remember it is in the valley that we grow.

We are never alone when we walk through the valley. The Lord is always there.

What You're Full of, You Will Manifest

by Lindsay Roberts

Some time ago I experienced a physical illness, and I wanted an instant miracle. I went to healing services, and I had several people praying for me. Then God told me, "You're going to walk this one out. And as you walk it out, you'll get closer to Me." It was the hardest walk I've ever made.

When you pray, believe that you will receive. Walking it out is not the easiest road you'll ever walk in your life, but it will be one of the most productive roads you ever walk in your life. The bottom line is, Did you get what it was you were praying for, or did something happen that made you give up and quit?

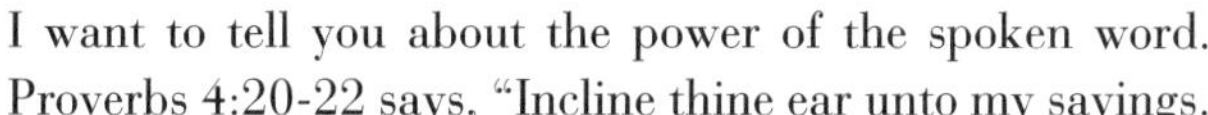

I want to tell you about the power of the spoken word. Proverbs 4:20-22 says, "Incline thine ear unto my sayings. Let them not depart from thine eyes; keep them in the midst of thine heart. For they are life unto those that find them, and health to all their flesh."

We've got to get into the Word of God and understand what Psalm 19:14 says: "Let the words of my mouth, and the meditation of my heart, be acceptable in thy sight, O Lord, my strength, and my redeemer."

Romans 4:17 in *The Amplified Bible* says, "As it is written, I have made you the father of many nations. He was appointed our father—in the sight of God Whom he believed, Who gives life to the dead and speaks to the nonexistent things that [He has foretold and promised] as if they [already] existed."

One day I was mouthing off to God, and He said to me, "I am not obligated to watch over *your* words to perform them. I'm obligated to watch over *Mine*." He said, "When you line up your words with My words, I'll perform them."

I want to share with you about the words of your mouth and the meditations of your heart. If you are using a camera and you take a picture, whatever you focus on will develop. What are you focusing on? What you focus on will develop, and what you are full of, you will manifest. Today you may be full of pride, anger, hurt, or bitterness. And the cold, hard fact is that what you're full of, you'll manifest.

God's Purpose Is for Good

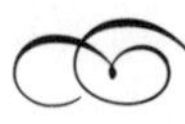

by Richard Roberts

When Jesus spoke to Paul in a blinding light on the Damascus Road, He said to him, "But rise, and stand upon thy feet; for I have appeared unto thee for this purpose, to make thee a minister and a witness both of these things which thou hast seen, and of those things in the which I will appear unto thee;

"Delivering thee from the people, and from the Gentiles, unto whom now I send thee, To open their eyes, and to turn them from darkness to light, and from the power of Satan unto God, that they may receive forgiveness of sins, and inheritance among them which are sanctified by faith that is in me" (Acts 26:16-18).

The Lord's purpose for Paul was very precise. It was also for his total good. I want you to notice three things about the Lord's word of purpose to Paul.

First, the Lord calls Paul to be "a minister and a witness." That is the call of the Lord on each of our lives. We may not be called to preach sermons or be a pastor, but we are all called to minister to others — to show the love of God to them and to help in God's ministry through our giving, our loving, our time, and our abilities. We are all called to be witnesses—to tell freely what we know about the Lord Jesus Christ. Jesus Himself said, "Ye shall be witnesses unto me" (Acts 1:8).

Second, the Lord doesn't tell Paul all the specifics about what he is to say and do in his life. The Lord says to Paul—and to us, "Take ye no thought how or what thing ye shall answer, or what ye shall say: for the Holy Ghost shall teach you in the same hour what ye ought to say" (Luke 12:11,12).

Third, the Lord says that Paul will be used by God to help others—to open their eyes and to turn them from darkness to light, and from the power of Satan, unto God, "that they may receive forgiveness of sins, and an inheritance [from the Lord]" (Acts 26:18). When God reveals His purpose to you for your life, you can count on it being not only for your good but also for the good of those around you.

Trust God today to work out His good purpose in you!

Our Impossibilities Become His Possibilities

by Evelyn Roberts

First of Two Parts

I was thinking about the miracle of Isaac's birth in Genesis 21 and trying to relate it in terms of people who have struggles today. Sarah was not only barren but she was also past childbearing age even if she hadn't been barren.

There are many people whose lives are barren in other ways also. They are destitute. Their lives are not producing, and they've come to impossible situations just as Sarah did. They don't know what to do.

That is when God takes over if we believe in His covenant. When we come to the end of our strength and have done all we know to do, then we must let God take over and do what only He can do. Our impossibilities become His possibilities.

God had promised Abraham and Sarah a son. It was hard to believe they could have a son at their age. By nature's standards it was impossible. But when they doubted, God sent an angel who said to them, "Is any thing too hard for the Lord?" (Gen. 13:14).

Sarah knew God had promised a son, but when it didn't happen right away, she just couldn't wait. She wanted her miracle immediately! So she took things into her own hands and got Ishmael before she got Isaac. Faith is the ingredient she needed to use, and that applies to us too.

How well I know. I have struggles, too. And at times I feel so barren. My life doesn't seem to be bearing any fruit. I pray for something, and it takes so long for the answer to come that I get impatient.

I know I can't get ahead of God. He has perfect timing, a due season. After all, it's His project. I'm only an instrument He uses. Sarah was just an instrument too, but she forgot it was God's project. She couldn't wait for God's timing!

His Covenant Is Better for Us Today, With Better Promises

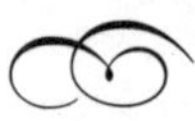

by Evelyn Roberts

Second of Two Parts

Since Sarah could not wait for God's timing, she told Abraham to have a child by her servant girl, Hagar. She got ahead of God. But what terrible trouble she got into by doing that!

I went to my *Amplified* version of the Bible and reread the story. I was really concerned about Hagar, the slave girl whom Sarah gave to Abraham to bear him a son. Hagar had no choice. She had to obey her mistress, Sarah.

As I read the story again, I could see a young mother with her little son being cast out of Abraham's house. She had been used like a piece of merchandise, and because of Sarah's jealousy, she had been sent away into the desert. I really hurt for her!

But right before my eyes was a different story than I remembered reading before. The words seemed to leap out at me! Genesis 21:14 says Abraham sent Hagar away with a loaf of bread and a bottle of water. When the bread and water were finished, she and her son were in the desert, far from home. There was no sign of food or water anywhere. Hagar knew they would die. They were already weak from hunger and thirst. She took her son and laid him under a shrub, then went off a little way from him because she couldn't stand to watch him die. As she was praying to God to supply their needs, her son began to cry. And the Bible says her eyes were opened, and she looked and saw before her a well. Their needs were met!

Jesus promised us a "well of living water" (John 4:14) and even more, for He said we would have rivers of living water—speaking of His Holy Spirit—God's promise to us through the new covenant. Jesus brought the new covenant to us to fulfill the one God gave to Abraham. And His covenant is better for us today, and with better promises. (Heb. 8:6.)

Angels of the Lord

by Terry Law
World Compassion/
Terry Law
Ministries

First of Two Parts

Satan can appear as an angel of light and he does it all the time. Turn on television to the psychic hot lines and they're showing you how to "channel up" your angel.

No, it's not of God, but it does happen. There are real angels that appear as angels of light. The Bible is very clear that there are good angels and bad angels. Probably two-thirds of the angels are good; one-third of the angels fell when Satan fell.

Angels have a special ministry when saints are moving from this world into the next world. Jesus told the story in Luke 16:19-31 of the rich man and Lazarus, who lay at his gate full of sores. When Lazarus died, he was carried by the angels into Abraham's bosom.

I was ministering in Swansea, Wales, and at the end of the service a woman came forward with her husband. She said, "I would like to tell you an angel story. Two years ago I was walking on the curb from a house on a hill. It was in February, and the driveway was icy. I was wearing high heels, and both feet slipped out from under me simultaneously, and I smashed the back of my head against the cement.

"I died. My spirit came out of my body, and I was ten feet up in the air, looking down at my body. My disembodied spirit could see all of that. I saw my husband get out of the car and come running up the driveway. He picked me up and started calling my name. He kept saying, 'In Jesus' name, come back.'

"There were two nine-foot angels on either side of me. And the sense of peace, happiness, and bliss I had from those angels was so overwhelming that when my husband kept calling me, I didn't want to go back. But he wouldn't let go.

"Finally one of the angels turned to me and said, 'Your husband is not going to let you go. You'd better go back.' My spirit came back into my body through my mouth. I opened my eyes, and I gave him a good scolding for calling me back!"

You Can Know Jesus

by Terry Law
World Compassion/
Terry Law
Ministries

Second of Two Parts

For those who are ready to meet God, I believe the first thing we're going to see when we open our eyes in eternity will be the angels of the Lord coming to escort us and take us home to the Father's house. I believe that is what the Bible says.

I was ministering in Montana one summer and had been teaching on Revelation 6:8, which says, "And I looked, and behold a pale horse: and his name that sat on him was Death." And the *Revised Standard Version* says, "And hades [or hell] followed him; and they were given power."

There is no question that hell is a real place or that heaven is a real place. There is no question that death is a state of being. But as I researched the subject of angels, I discovered that the church has always believed in an angel of death. I think there is an angel called Death who rules over death.

This made some sense because Jesus said to the disciples in John 8:51, "I say unto you, If a man keep my saying, he shall never see death." This indicates that when someone dies in Christ, the first thing they will see are angels of the Lord. When someone dies outside of Christ, the first thing they will see is an angel of death.

Sitting in a wheelchair in my meeting in Montana was a Vietnam veteran whose right leg had been blown off by a grenade in the war. He said, "Terry, I was a Methodist boy, raised in Sunday school, and I knew about Jesus, but I was living for the devil. When I was lying on the ground and my lifeblood was pumping out of my leg, I saw the death angel coming for me. I screamed out, 'Jesus, save me!' and I saw that death angel turn and leave when I said those words. Lying on the battlefield with my leg gone, I gave my life to Christ."

You may be like that young man on the battlefield and want to know Jesus. Ask Him to save you, and He will!

God Will Make a New Thing for You

by Lindsay Roberts

On one of our *Something Good Tonight—The Hour of Healing* programs, a person called in and said, "Please pray for marriages."

I believe that God not only heals bodies but also finances and marriages. The Bible tells us to touch and agree. It doesn't say "talk and agree." In Matthew 18:19, Jesus said, "Again I say unto you, That if two of you shall agree on earth as touching any thing that they shall ask, it shall be done for them of my Father which is in heaven." People are reaching out to 1-900 numbers or other different things. They are reaching out because they are hurting. There has to be a void, a lack or emptiness, somewhere to cause you to reach out. You have heard the telephone commercial, "Reach out and touch someone." I believe that God has the supernatural ability to fill those voids, including the ones in marriages.

If you know someone who is requesting prayer for their marriage, share this prayer with them:

Father, in the name of Jesus, I pray for marriages. I believe that marriages are created by You. And if You created the office of marriage, then You can create holy, godly marriages. I ask that You heal marriages in the same way that You heal bodies. You heal spirits, save souls, and bring healing and restoration to finances, so I know that You can bring a healing restoration to marriages.

You may feel your marriage is dead and buried, but that's a good place to have a resurrection. One thing about a death and a burial—following that death and burial is resurrection! In the name of Jesus, I believe for your marriage to be restored and resurrected *to new abundant life.* Let the old things pass away and let the dead bury the dead. Ask God to bring healing and restoration. Don't bring up the old and don't bring up the past, but let God make a new thing for you!

Just Dig the Hole!

by Oral Roberts

Most miracles don't just happen. We usually have to take the first step of faith to set the miracle into motion. In 1968 Oral Roberts University was growing so fast that we outgrew our original dining hall. But we had no money to build a new one. Then I had a strong leading that I recognized as being from God. He said, "Dig the hole." The faculty, student body, and the board of regents gathered around that huge hole, and we all joined hands and prayed. We said, "God, we've dug the hole. Now we're asking You to fill it up."

For seven long months that gaping hole remained just a hole. Sometimes I felt it was mocking us. But one day God began to move, and people started sending in seeds of faith for the new dining hall. Together, we built that building! Thousands of meals are served there each day to ORU students. It's a beautiful, practical building, but it began as a hole in the ground. It started as an act of our faith.

James 2:18 NKJV says, "I will show you my faith by my works." Perhaps God is leading you to do something that seems too huge to accomplish. Don't be afraid to take that first small step of faith. God can take that act and turn it into a miracle. Just dig the hole!

Keep Checking In

by Richard Roberts

When you face battles in life, God doesn't expect you to fight them in your own strength without His help. Proverbs 3:5 says, "Trust in the Lord with all thine heart; and lean not unto thine own understanding." If you try to figure things out and fight your battles with your own understanding, you can get into trouble. A key to success in spiritual warfare is to stay in touch with God and rely on Him in every situation.

Your position is like that of a military unit that goes into battle. Even when the enemy is attacking from all sides—sniper fire raining down and mortars blasting all around—someone in the unit is on a two-way radio checking with headquarters to find out what strategy to use to win the battle. And they follow it!

To win in spiritual battles, it's essential for us to stay in touch with our Commander, the Lord Jesus Christ, to receive our instructions. And we don't say, "Fine, Lord; I got that. I'll take it from here. I'll check back with You when the battle is over." To do that is a guarantee of failure. As we keep listening for God's voice every step of the way, relying on Him completely, He can lead us to a mighty victory!

Taming the Tongue

by Patricia Salem

No human can control everything they say without help from the Lord. In James 3:8 we read that the tongue can no man tame; it is an unruly evil, full of deadly poison. But I know from personal experience that God will help you tame your tongue if you ask Him, because He has done it for me.

When I was growing up, my father wasn't a Christian, and he cursed a lot. I picked it up, because when you're a child and you hear that sort of thing spoken every other word, you just think it's the way people talk.

But one day after I was saved and grown up, I was driving in the car with my children, who were small at the time, and I said my precious Lord's name in vain. I felt so terrible that my little children heard me say it that I turned the car around and went back home. I went inside, got on my knees, and said, "Lord, I'd rather not have a tongue in my head than to use Your precious name in vain. I give my tongue to You and ask You to please change me. I am willing." That was in the late 1950s, and from that time to this, I have never used God's name in vain again. Of course, I say His name every day, but it's to say, "I love You, Lord," or "Thank You, Jesus."

James 4:7 says, "Submit yourself therefore to God. Resist the devil, and he will flee from you." When we ask God for His help in taming our tongue, we have to be sincere. I wasn't capable of taming my tongue by myself, but when I submitted it to God and genuinely asked for His help, He changed me. He will do no less for you!

Many Channels of Blessing

by Kate McVeigh

Kate McVeigh Ministries

As a believer, you don't have to limit your income source to your job. God has many ways and avenues of giving you favor and increasing your income. In my life and ministry, on several occasions, I have experienced supernatural favor in finances, even in little areas.

For example, I've received great deals on office equipment, airline tickets, and even a new dress for preaching. Our heavenly Father cares about the small areas of our lives as well.

I realized one day that everywhere I go I experience God's favor. I may be standing in a long line at a store and another line just happens to open up. When shopping, I always seem to find a front-row parking spot and get things on sale. Or a refund check arrives from my insurance company because my rates have gone down unexpectedly.

It's important not to limit God as to how He chooses to bless us. He has many channels and avenues to get provision to us. We must look to Him as our total Source. Your job is just one avenue of blessing. Take the limits off of God and watch His favor work in *every* area of your life.

The Power Inside Us

by Creflo A. Dollar
World Changers Church International

First of Three Parts

Have you ever looked at the leaves blowing in the trees and said, "That's the wind"? The leaves are not really the wind, but they are moving as a result of the wind. We tend to define the wind by its effects rather than its nature.

Similarly, when we see someone get healed, or they are blessed with a new car or new house, we often say, "Look at that blessing." No, it's not really the blessing we see, but the *result* of the blessing. The blessing is defined as the *endowed power* in you that will result in prosperity and goodness.

Proverbs 10:22 says, "The blessing of the Lord, it maketh rich, and he addeth no sorrow with it." It doesn't say the car of the Lord, the house of the Lord, or the money of the Lord makes you rich, but it says the *blessing* of the Lord. The blessing allows you to get results and have success. The blessing is God's enablement inside you, giving you the ability to do what you couldn't do before you received the blessing.

How do we draw upon that power that is already inside us? The answer is found in Luke 3. Jesus went to John the Baptist to be baptized and the Spirit of God came upon Him. Afterwards, Jesus began preaching, doing great works, and performing miracles. He didn't do those things until He had been clothed with the power of the Holy Spirit and He got into the Word. Luke 4:18 says that Jesus opened the Scripture and read, "The Spirit of the Lord is upon me, because he hath anointed me."

God has already given us spiritual blessings. They're deposited inside us. Now it's time to learn how to draw upon them and receive the *results* of the blessing.

You Become What You Meditate On

by Dr. Creflo A. Dollar
World Changers Church International

Second of Three Parts

So many of us want five easy steps on how to get clothed in the power of God, but there are no five easy steps to receive the results of our blessing. What did Jesus do? He meditated on the Word day and night, to the point that He *became* what He meditated on. He so clothed Himself in the Word that when the time came for Him to yield to the Word, He was used to it.

Let's say we're spending time with our friend, Ray Ray, and Ray Ray has a real interesting way of behaving. We're spending so much time with Ray Ray that before we know it, we're imitating Ray Ray's personality, wearing Ray Ray's clothes, and doing some of the same things Ray Ray does. Somebody might even say, "Look—they're acting just like Ray Ray."

Well, if we spend time in prayer with God, and spend time in His Word, and spend time in the presence of God, then the Word—just like Ray Ray—is going to rub off on us. And when people look at us, we're going to start looking like the Word. Then one day people will look at us and say, "My goodness, they resemble Jesus. *They resemble the Word.*"

Many people are spending time in worry, in distress, and in sickness because that's what they've been meditating on. But when believers are born again and begin spending time meditating in the Word, believing that the Word applies to their lives, then they will yield to what they've spent time with—the Word.

Joshua 1:8 tells us to meditate in the Word day and night and do what it says. Then we will make our way prosperous, and we'll have good success. Meditating on God's Word is our blessing connection.

Meditation Will Mark Your Life

by Dr. Creflo A. Dollar
World Changers Church International

Third of Three Parts

Meditation on God's Word is our blessing connection. The more time we spend in the Word, the more we will have confidence in the Word, the more we will yield to healing and not to sickness, the more we will yield to prosperity and not to poverty. But how long should we meditate?

One time I was teaching about meditation, and that question came up. I had a quick vision, and God told me to take off my wedding ring. He said, "Tell the people to meditate long enough until, just like when you take off your ring, you still see the marks of wearing the ring." In other words, we are to meditate in the Word until we see the marks of the Word on our lives.

Now I could take my ring off and pretend I wasn't married, but if you looked at my fourth finger, you would see the marks of my wedding ring there. I believe that if the body of Christ will meditate and wear the Word like we wear a wedding ring—until the Word makes a mark on our lives—we'll see the anointing connection take place. And the power of God will come on our lives.

As you meditate, the Word becomes part of you and gets inside you. (1 Tim. 4:15.) Meditate means to mutter over and over. It could be compared to rocks in a stream. The water rushing over them causes the rocks to tumble over and over, taking off all the rough edges until they sparkle like diamonds. That's what happens when the Word of God gets inside you.

If we're meditating on the Word, we're spending time in the presence of God. Eventually we'll not only resemble Him in appearance, but we'll resemble Him in demonstration. The result will be prosperity and good success.

Focus on the Goal

by Richard Roberts

Once a king was pestered by a young prince who often led his small army in brief skirmishes against the king's troops. It became bothersome to the king, so he told his commanding general to capture the prince.

When the prince was brought before the king, the king said, "I've had enough. I'm going to have your head cut off!" The headsman was ready to swing his axe when the king said, "I'll give you one chance to save yourself. If you can carry a full container of wine from the outskirts to the center of the city without spilling the wine, I'll let you live." The street the prince had to walk was lined with people, one side cheering for him, "You can do it!" the other side yelling, "Spill it! Spill it!"

The prince carried the container to the center of town and didn't spill a drop. The king said, "You did fine. You will live. But tell me, what were you thinking when you heard the crowd yelling at you?" The prince answered, "I didn't think about anything except not spilling the wine."

The prince had remained focused on his goal despite the distractions all around him. And that's how God wants us to live. The world will try to discourage us from reaching our goal in our Christian walk. But we can do it if we follow the apostle Paul's example. He said, "I keep working toward that day when I will finally be all that Christ Jesus saved me for and wants me to be.... I am focusing all my energies on this one thing: Forgetting the past and looking forward to what lies ahead, I strain to reach the end of the race and receive the prize for which God, through Christ Jesus, is calling us up to heaven" (Phil. 3:12-14 NLT).

Prosperity Versus Success

by Jesse Duplantis
Jesse Duplantis Ministries

I find that a lot of people are afraid of money. They want it, but they're afraid of it. The problem is they've mixed up something called success. They think that's prosperity, but it's not. Success has a price while prosperity has a value.

In Joshua 1:8 God told Joshua that he would become prosperous. Note the word *prosperous* because it implies value. It will go from generation to generation.

It's amazing to me how prosperity was totally accepted in the Old Testament and totally rejected in the New Testament. Yet there are more prosperity Scriptures in the New Testament than there are in the Old Testament.

In Genesis 13 God said Abraham was very rich, Isaac—rich, Esau—rich, Job—the richest man in the East. That's pretty good. David—rich, King Solomon—super rich.

But something happened. The devil sold a bill of goods to the New Testament church, and one was poverty. I said, "Lord, explain that to me."

Then it hit me before the Lord could tell me. I said, "I know why." Because nowhere from Genesis to Malachi does it say, "Go into all the world and preach the gospel to every creature" (Mark 16:15 NKJV). But in the New Testament Jesus said, "Go to Jerusalem, and Judea, and Samaria, and the uttermost parts of the world" (Acts 1:8).

We've got to touch the world, and we're not going to do it without money. So don't be afraid of money. It is God's will for you to prosper and then use the money to do as Jesus commanded—take the Gospel to the uttermost parts of the world!

Working on the Inside

by Richard Roberts

Have you ever prayed for something, and nothing seemed to happen? That's the situation we see in Mark 11:14 when Jesus cursed a fig tree. The Bible says His disciples heard it, but they sure didn't see anything happen at first.

Picture this scene: Jesus was on His way to Jericho to preach. He was hungry. He saw a fig tree and walked over to it to see if He could pick a couple of figs for a snack. But He discovered there were none, so He said to the tree, "You'll never bear fruit again!" Now the disciples were watching because usually when Jesus spoke, something happened. Only, in this instance, it looked as if nothing happened. And Jesus and the disciples went on into town.

But the next morning as they passed by, they saw the fig tree dried up from the roots. (v. 20.) Peter cried, "Jesus, look! The fig tree You cursed yesterday has withered and died!" The disciples found that while nothing appeared to happen on the outside of that tree, Jesus' faith had been working on the inside! Immediately He seized the opportunity to teach the disciples a lesson on faith. He said, "Have faith in God" (v. 22). "Whatever things you ask when you pray, believe that you receive them, and you will have them" (v. 24 NKJV).

I believe this is a key to receiving answers to our prayers. Sometimes when we pray and believe, on the outside it looks as if nothing is happening. But as we keep believing, something is happening on the inside. We just can't see it with our human eyes. So don't give up. You may not see the answer yet, but as you continue to believe, your faith is working on the inside!

God's Love

by Lindsay Roberts

Some people think Benjamin Franklin invented electricity, but he didn't. He just used a key and a kite to demonstrate that lightning is an electrical discharge. He tapped into a power source.

Thomas Edison was an amazing inventor who invented the phonograph, light bulbs, and the motion picture camera, but none of them would have worked if he hadn't been able to tap into electricity, the power source his inventions needed.

Just as Franklin and Edison found the source of power they needed for their scientific work, we, too, have a power source that we can tap into when fear begins to overtake us. That power source is God's love.

In Zephaniah 3:17 NLT God says, "With his love, he will calm all your fears," and I John 4:18 NIV says, "Perfect love drives out fear." God's love is powerful. It can drive out fear of bankruptcy, fear of failure, fear of cancer, fear of death, or any other kind of fear that is trying to attach itself to you. Paul said in Romans 8:38 NLT, "I am convinced that nothing can ever separate us from his [God's] love...." Our fears for today, our worries about tomorrow, and even the powers of hell can't keep God's love away. And His love is always available to us!

If you allow the love of God to operate through you, it can drive out fear. And when fear has been driven out, only faith remains. Claim the power of God's love when you're tempted to fear and let His love drive the fear away.

How Free Is Freedom?

by Richard Roberts

First of Four Parts

How free is freedom? There are four things I want to share with you about freedom and how free it is.

Number one: You are never free enough to escape community. If I hurt you, I hurt myself. Why? Because we are inextricably tied together, and we are responsible to one another.

There is no such thing as absolute freedom. The stars don't have it; they are hemmed in by the heavens. The oceans don't have it; they are hemmed in by the shoreline. Man doesn't have it; we're hemmed in by our relationships with one another. Freedom is not the right to do as you please; freedom is the responsibility to do what you ought.

When America was young and someone had a problem with somebody else, it was no big deal. They just took their families and their possessions and moved over the mountain, and they created Smithboro or Jonesville. But the problem is, as America grew, they ran out of space.

We have to learn how to deal with one another. Jesus said we are to love one another as we love ourselves—whites, blacks, Hispanics, Jews, Christians, rich, poor, illiterate, intelligent. We are to love one another.

But what good is freedom if our freedom of speech does not give us an opportunity to tell the truth and to be men and women of honesty? It's time for us as Christians to stop talking about freedom and start talking about responsibility. Start talking about integrity, start talking about truth, and start talking about character. Start talking about holiness, without which, the Bible says, no man will see God. (Heb. 12:14.)

You Have To Choose in Life

by Richard Roberts

Second of Four Parts

Number two: You are never free enough to get away from your choices. Freedom requires that you choose, and then you live with the consequences of your choices. It's a special message to all married couples. Don't be too critical of your mate's faults because it was those very faults that caused you to marry that person. You made the choice.

In life you have to choose. There is no indecision. You have to choose and live with your decisions. In life, you will decide to do something, or you will make an excuse.

I heard the story of a Civil War soldier who had sympathies on both the side of the Union and the side of the Confederacy. So not knowing what to do, he put on a gray coat and blue pants, and somebody shot him in the front and somebody shot him in the back. You have to choose in life!

Some people decide they are going to be angry all their life. Do you know someone who likes the bitter, angry approach? One woman said, "I always feel the worst when I feel the best because I know how bad I'm going to feel when I start feeling bad again."

Do you know someone who has that bitter approach?

Some people revel in their sickness, and they talk about it all the time. And if God healed them, 90 percent of their personality would go right down the drain.

The prodigal son made his choice. The boy said, "The money is mine. Give it to me. I'm leaving." He chose his freedom. He chose to go from prostitute to prostitute. He chose to waste his substance. He chose to wind up in a pigpen.

Should you make a wrong decision, its not your parents' fault, it's not the government's fault, it's not your church's fault. It's your fault because you made a decision. The question is, Are you making God's decisions, or are you making your decisions?

'Don't Justify Your Reasoning'

by Richard Roberts

Third of Four Parts

Number three: Freedom is never free at the expense of your conscience. To some people, a clear conscience is just an excuse for a poor memory. Secular humanists say that conscience is a primitive leftover. But I've got news. I have a Bible definition for conscience. The Word of God says that conscience is the instrument of discernment within your inner soul to determine right from wrong in a spiritual matter. Many persons today are trampling on their conscience. Reason will justify what your conscience condemns.

You may be driving down the highway eighty miles an hour, ninety miles an hour, or a hundred miles an hour, and a highway patrolman pulls you over. He steps to your window and politely asks, "May I see your driver's license?"

"Officer, is there something wrong?" you ask. "Do I have a tail-light out?"

The officer asks, "Do you know how fast your were driving?"

"No, officer, I don't have any idea," you reply. "How fast was I going?" But your heart is saying, *Officer, I was doing ninety miles an hour. I'm sorry. Forgive me. I will never, ever do it again if you will just let me go.* But instead, you say, "Well, how fast was I going?"

Your reasoning mind tries to justify what your conscience will condemn. But you'll never get away from your conscience. Never!

The carnal mind is at enmity with God. (Rom. 8:7.) Don't ever justify your reasoning and ignore your conscience, because it will live with you all of your life.

Don't say, "It's my life. I'll do what I want, " because you will take your freedom and destroy yourself.

The Way Across the Ocean of Life

by Richard Roberts

Fourth of Four Parts

Number four: You can never be free until you are voluntarily mastered by something greater than you. God never set anybody free for the sake of freedom. When Moses delivered the children of Israel out of Egypt, God set them free, but He branded them with the Ten Commandments.

Jesus came to set the captives free, but not for the sake of freedom alone. Instead, He branded them by saying, "Now take up your cross and follow Me." There are conditions with freedom.

Years ago I heard a story about a famous zoo in the late nineteenth century. The United States was always on the lookout for rare and exotic birds. One particular bird hunter was sent on a regular basis to the far corners of the earth to capture some birds to bring back for viewing in the local zoo.

On one trip to Africa, the hunter captured a number of rare and exotic birds. One bird was so magnificent and beautiful that he knew it would be a prized possession for the zoo.

About ten days out of port, the little bird worked its way through the wooden slats on the cage that had been especially built for it. The magnificently beautiful bird flew in circles around the boat as if to say, "I am free! I am free!" The tiny bird then flew off, getting smaller and smaller in the distance, until suddenly it was no longer visible.

After a couple of days, the hunter assumed the bird had drowned, when all of a sudden he saw a little speck in the sky coming closer and closer. The tiny bird landed on the deck of the ship. His colors had seemed to fade, but he had discovered that, that which he thought was a prison was really his haven of rest. That which he thought had bound him was his only way across the ocean.

And we, too, must understand that the only way across the ocean of life is to have a relationship with God. I have discovered that the only way for me to cross the ocean of life is to make a commitment to the Lord.

The Lost Art of Diligence

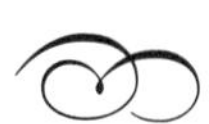

by Lindsay Roberts

We're living in what I call an "instant" society. We want everything now—from instant potatoes to instant information on the Internet. And as our instant society has developed, diligence has become a lost art.

Perhaps you're in a situation where you want an instant solution to a problem. The process of arriving at the solution can be a learning experience that is as rewarding as the answer to the situation. That's where diligence comes in. Instead of giving up—telling yourself that if you can't have the answer now, you don't want to go on—you push through to get to the end result.

It took Moses and the Israelites 40 years to make an 11-day journey. They had to be persistent and steadfast to reach their goal—the Promised Land. And God used those 40 years to teach them an important principle: To be diligent and rely only on Him in everything they did. Some of Moses' last words to the Israelites were that if they diligently obeyed God and His commandments, His blessings would literally overtake them. (Deut. 28:1,2.)

I believe God put the word "diligently" in the Bible so many times because He wants us to perk up our ears and ask why. Throughout the book of Deuteronomy, we're instructed to be diligent: Diligently keep God's commandments (11:22), diligently ask questions (13:14), diligently investigate matters (17:4), diligently observe instructions (24:8), and diligently listen to His voice (28:1). Our part in our relationship with God is to be diligent so He can do His part, which is to be a rewarder of those who diligently seek Him (Heb. 11:6).

'My People Need To Laugh'

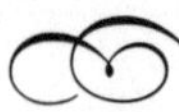

by Jeanne Caldwell
Agape Church

Each year the ladies in our church get away for a couple of days and get relaxed, refreshed, and renewed in spirit, soul, and body. This particular year the Lord had me teach on laughter! He said, "My people need to laugh."

Medical science now acknowledges that the best resistance against disease is laughter. One scientist defines laughter as "stationary jogging," because the muscles and blood pressure react in such a healthy way during laughter. After laughing, the body benefits from its relaxed state.

Recently a clinical psychiatrist who conducts "laugh therapy" said that the physical advantages of laughter are amazing. It affects the heart and digestive system, and enhances the immune system against disease like a preventative medicine.

Laughter releases a chemical called endorphin into the body. Endorphin is a combination of two words: endogenous, which means "something produced within," and morphine, which is "a medication for pain control and relaxation." God, through His love for us, has placed Scriptures in His Word about our having joy. Joy produces the very chemical in our bodies that will help us calm down and stop the pain. It is like morphine that is given externally, but we have it internally! If we would laugh twenty minutes a day, it would release enough endorphin into our bodies to keep us healthy.

Joy is a fruit of your recreated spirit, but it has to be cultivated. (Gal. 5:22.) Philippians 4:4 RSV says, "Rejoice in the Lord always"—not sometimes! Some folks spread gloom and despair everywhere they go. They need to recognize the enemy and resist him, then begin to speak positive words and think positive thoughts. Do something for someone else and get your mind off yourself. Learn to enjoy life and have fun!

A merry heart doeth good like a medicine: but a broken spirit drieth the bones. —Proverbs 17:22

It Is of God!

by Cathie Dorsch

Agape Church/*Kids Like You* Television Ministry

First of Two Parts

When Pastor Happy and Jeannie Caldwell started Agape Church in 1979, they felt very strongly that a children's ministry was needed immediately. Of the people attending, we could count on a third of that number being children. In order to bring in the children of our city, the children's ministry of the church produced *Kids Like You* as an outreach of the church.

I had some children's theater experience in my background and had studied drama in college. After I committed to working with the children's ministry in the church, I was at home with my small baby, and I began to see things on television that grieved me as a young mother. I just couldn't believe what was going on.

I began to pray that God would do something about children's television in America. Finally one day He really stunned me when He said, "*You* do something about it."

It wasn't long afterwards that the idea for *Kids Like You* children's television ministry was birthed in my spirit, and God laid out the first twelve programs for us and showed us how to do them—what topics to cover and the format of the program.

I remember Pastor Happy saying, "I don't think you know how much work you're getting into." But we had a witness in our spirit that it was of God. So we put the show together, produced and pitched it to our NBC affiliate in Little Rock, and began airing it.

The more established we became, the more the station would break from the network programming of NBC Saturday morning prime-time TV, preempting the network in our area in the state of Arkansas, and air *Kids Like You.*

We hear from kids in every corner of the state of Arkansas, telling us that they are receiving Jesus into their hearts as Lord.

We Need To Be There With the Power of God

by Cathie Dorsch

Agape Church/*Kids Like You* Television Ministry

Second of Two Parts

After the children have had fun with the puppets and learned the Bible lessons, we always have a prayer of salvation at the end of the program.

We've gone to a lot of theme parks and asked kids what's on their minds. We've found that there are a lot of Christian kids who are ready to speak up, share their hearts, and share their faith.

We were very concerned about what was on television for our children in Arkansas. Then after our program aired, program directors from around the country started calling us. We didn't really even knock on a lot of the doors. God just opened them for us because the need was so urgent. *Kids Like You* grew from simply airing on that NBC affiliate to airing on almost all of the nation's Christian networks, and some international networks as well. Even other individual network affiliates (of the main secular networks) would air the program.

Children in America will spend about twenty thousand hours in front of a television set before they reach the age of eighteen. That is more time than they will spend in church, reading their Bible, or brushing their teeth, and even more time than they will spend with their parents!

In our nation, this generation is so different from any other one in history. I think we have a responsibility in the body of Christ to be there with the Gospel, training them with the Word of God. We have to reach the kids with something that will appeal to them. So we believe very firmly that we've got to be there with excellence of ministry. The devil's crowd works hard to make their programming look glitzy and attractive. They put a lot of the supernatural and the dark side of Satan's kingdom in children's television. So we need to be there with the power of God, with what is the right spiritual power.

Pray for the generation that is growing up under what we see on television today, and believe that God will touch them.

Excellence Versus Perfectionism

by Lindsay Roberts

When I was a young girl I somehow got the idea that I had to be good at everything, that I had to be perfect. My mom was concerned because I was a perfectionist by the time I was only eight years old! If I got a 99 and not a 100 on a test in school, I would feel stomach distress. My mom wasn't infusing perfectionism into me, and neither was God. He understands how weak we are; He knows we are only dust. (Ps. 103:14 NLT.) But I would never allow myself to let down.

I began to see this same pattern developing in my daughter Jordan when she was eight or nine years old. One day I said to her, "Jordan, go mess up your room." Now most mothers are saying to their children, "Go clean up your room." But I didn't want her to be under a lot of pressure. I wanted her to learn to relax and enjoy herself.

Sometimes children process things differently than we intend for them to. And because Jordan was a straight-A student and I would talk about how she had always been a straight-A student, she began to think, *Mommy won't be pleased with me if I'm not perfect.* Without realizing it, I was putting pressure on her.

There's a difference between having a spirit of excellence and being a perfectionist. Galatians 6:4 NLT says, "Be sure to do what you should, for then you will enjoy the personal satisfaction of having done your work well, and you won't need to compare yourself to anyone else." God does not expect us to be perfect, but to be the best we can be—to have a spirit of excellence without the kind of pressure that destroys. This gives us balance in our lives.

We're To Be Men and Women of Integrity

by Richard Roberts

One of the most important things God has shown me is that we are to be men and women of integrity, that we're to keep our word. Don't you just hate it when someone makes a promise to you and doesn't keep it? I do.

We need to realize that people are watching us all the time. In our daily lives, they could be family members, neighbors, friends, or coworkers. And when one is in ministry, as I am, the media is always watching us. They want to know if we live what we teach, if we do what we say we do, and if we make a promise, do we keep it?

In our private lives, our children watch us the same way. They want to know if Mom and Dad really keep their word. That brings to mind the Scripture in Proverbs 20:7: "The just man walketh in his integrity: his children are blessed after him."

Now I realize there are times when it is impossible to keep a promise, and we need to go to a person and say, "I'm sorry that I'm not able to do what I promised, and this is the reason. But I know I gave you my word, and I'm going to find a way to keep my word and make it up to you at another time." I've had to do that with my own children, and I'm sure you have too.

I've learned that when I give my word to someone, I've got to keep my word or else I lose my integrity. I lose my credibility. I've got to do what I say I'm going to do. Believe me, I ask for God's direction every step of the way, every day of my life, as I want to be known as a person of integrity.

Lean on the Word

by Jerry Savelle

Jerry Savelle Ministries International

Tests and trials have a way of forcing us to choose what we are going to believe. When trouble rises up, we're either going to believe the Word of God or we're going to believe the circumstances.

James 1:2-3 in *The Message* translation says, "You know that under pressure your faith life is forced into the open, and it will show its true colors." It's when you're under pressure that you find out what you really believe. Anybody can talk faith in church or with other Christians. But where it counts most is when you're all by yourself. You can tell where a person is spiritually just by listening to what comes out of their mouth, because under pressure you're either going to talk the Word or you're going to talk the problem.

The devil has a habit of trying to convince us that the Word isn't working, nobody cares, and it's over, or as we say in Texas, "Ship your saddle home." But that's a lie. If we could see into the spirit realm, we'd see angels busily working to get our needs met and causing things to come to pass.

In Galatians 6:9 the apostle Paul said that if we will not allow ourselves to grow weary, we will reap in due season. You never know when your due season is going to come. If you're standing fast on God's Word, you could have a due season today. If not today, it could be tomorrow. God doesn't keep time by hours, minutes, and seconds. He keeps time by "due season." And when you determine to lean on the Word and refuse to give up, God can see to it that your due season is manifested!

God Gave Them Dreams

by Marilyn Hickey
Marilyn Hickey Ministries

The Lord has directed me to speak to you about dreams. God said He has given you dreams to do things for Him. He has given you special dreams to direct your lives.

I went through the Bible looking at dreams and visions because it is the language of the Holy Spirit. I saw that sometimes dreams are given for warnings, as sometimes God will give a dream about something that doesn't have to be. God gives it to break the powers of darkness in the situation. Sometimes dreams are for encouragement. God came to Paul in a dream and said, "Don't be discouraged. There are a lot of people in this city, and they are going to be saved!" So that was an encouragement.

But God's dreams are God's plans. When He gives us a dream, it's the plan He has. It might be encouragement, it might be a warning, it might be direction. But God puts dreams in our hearts. He puts visions in our hearts.

The Bible says, "Where there is no vision, the people perish" (Prov. 29:18). Years ago I had a dream in my heart to go to India and minister there. I can remember praying for India before I was saved. I was invited to go speak in India, and I felt led to go.

After I arrived they told me, "Really, it is not a good idea for them to put you on to speak." In India, they did not believe in women speaking. It was a five-night crusade, and I was to speak the last night. But the last night of the crusade was going to be the biggest night. The man in charge of the crusade said, "You are here to get people saved. They don't believe in women speaking, but God does. So go up there and preach!"

I think we had forty thousand people stand to receive the Lord that night. God had a dream and a plan. I believe, even as a child, God saw way ahead. A lot of things that I thought were desires as a child were actually God's dreams and His plan for my life.

Feelings vs. Faith

by Oral Roberts

Everyone has experienced discouragement. You may have wondered if being a Christian means that you should feel wonderful all the time. But let me tell you that Christians don't live by feelings! The Bible teaches that "the just shall live by faith" (Rom. 1:17). Feelings are fickle—they can change all the time, and they will betray you. Your mood may fluctuate with the weather, your environment, your health, or your circumstances. I cannot say that just because you're a Christian you're going to feel wonderful all the time.

However, Jesus has promised you His joy! John 15:11 says, "These things have I spoken unto you, that my joy might remain in you, and that your joy might be full." His joy is not a fleeting, transitory emotion that the world calls happiness or fun. The joy of the Lord is a deep, enduring assurance that provides you with a contentment that doesn't fade in the midst of trying circumstances or struggles.

That's because true Christian joy is based on faith. Faith stands up to rugged everyday living. No one is immune from troubles, from financial or physical reverses; but you can have confidence that even though troubles come, they can never go beyond the control of God.

Deuteronomy 33:27 says, "The eternal God is thy refuge, and underneath are the everlasting arms: and he shall thrust out the enemy from before thee; and shall say, Destroy them." You can have a sustaining joy in knowing that God is your refuge in any time of trouble, and His everlasting arms are beneath you!

His Word Is the Bread

by Evelyn Roberts

My grandparents were in business when I was just a tiny little girl. My grandfather would say, "Now, Evelyn, you have to save every nickel and dime you have. Don't spend it all."

Little children want to know why they should save. He said, "Because someday you'll get old, and you won't want your children to have to take care of you. So you have to start saving your money now."

My grandfather never believed in insurance. He didn't believe in banks either because he had seen the banks go broke. So he would save his money, and he would invest in different things. I remember him saying, "Oh, Evelyn, just pray with us that our money will hold out until we die. I don't want us to have to live off our children."

We all want to be self-sufficient. Do you know how to be a self-sufficient person? Give. Learn to give to others. It comes back to you and makes you self-sufficient. It's hard for some people to believe, but, really, the more you give, the more you have yourself.

Don't think only in terms of money—although it takes a lot of money to live these days—but there are many, many things in life that money will not buy. When you give of what you have to somebody else, you have more yourself. I think you have more compassion when you give your compassion to somebody else. "[Give] so that you may always and under all circumstances and whatever the need, be self-sufficient—possessing enough to require no aid or support and furnished in abundance for every good work and charitable donation" (2 Cor. 9:8 AMP).

Here's the reason. As it is written in Genesis 11:4, "Let us make us a name, lest we be scattered abroad upon the face of the whole earth." God gives to the poor. His deeds of justice, goodness, kindness, and benevolence will go on and endure forever. We must realize that whatever we have to give, it comes from God. It is God who gives seed. He gives us not only the seed to sow for somebody else but also the bread that we eat.

His Word is also bread. As you grow older, you appreciate the Word of God so much more!

Enduring Hardships

by Richard Roberts

Do you know people who seem never to have a problem? They have plenty of money, are never sick, and everything goes right for them...but they wouldn't know God if they met Him coming down the road? Yet you are struggling.

If you know someone like this, it doesn't take long to start making comparisons. Their situation is on the "green grass" side of the fence, looking good. Your situation is on the other side—battling and fighting everything Satan is throwing at you. You may be at the point of saying, "I don't want to fight anymore. I'm just going to give up."

Don't give up; the fight is worth it! The apostle Paul wrote to Timothy, "Accept, as I do, all the hardship that faithfulness to the gospel entails in the strength that God gives you" (2 Tim. 1:8 PHILLIPS). In another passage Paul told Timothy, "You...must endure hardship as a good soldier" (2 Tim. 2:3 NKJV). In other words, accept the fact that when you serve the Lord, you're going to face some difficulties.

Christians can expect Satan to attack with trials and troubles. But the Bible says, "When all kinds of trials and temptations crowd into your lives...don't resent them as intruders, but welcome them as friends!" (James 1:2,3 PHILLIPS).

"Give me a break!" you may say. "How can I welcome my trials as a friend?" James gives the answer in verse 4. He says that although trials come to test your faith, they produce endurance so that you can stand firm and say, "No matter what, I am going to overcome!"

An Encounter With God!

by Lindsay Roberts

There are times in our lives when only God can change a situation. This was the case with Jacob, who was preparing to meet the brother he had tricked years before. Jacob's name means "deceiver, trickster, con artist," and he had fulfilled it right up to stealing the birthright from his brother. Now Esau was coming with 400 men to meet him, "and Jacob was greatly afraid" (Gen. 32:7 NKJV).

Jacob came up with a plan to divide his people into two groups. He said, "If Esau comes to the one company and attacks it, then the other company which is left will escape" (v. 8). Jacob was still relying on his schemes. But afraid that his plan might fail, he asked God to deliver him. That night Jacob had an encounter with God when a Man wrestled with him until the breaking of day. (v. 24.) During the struggle Jacob gave up his old nature as a schemer, and in return he received the blessing that he sought. (vv. 27-30.)

When you have an encounter with God, He may or may not change other people, but He'll change you. And once God changes you, it gives Him the opportunity to change other people. Between the time of Jacob's distress and his brother's arrival, Jacob met God. And that encounter changed a situation that looked impossible. Instead of seeking revenge, Esau ran to him, and embraced him, and fell on his neck and kissed him: and they wept. (Gen. 33:4.) God can change your impossible situation, too, when you seek Him with all of your heart and yield your will to His good plan for your life!

Facing Desperate Times

by Art Sepúlveda
Word of Life Christian Center

Many people in this world live by an urgency of desperation. It's rooted and founded in things that lead to hopelessness. Urgency can be the measuring stick between conviction and convenience, between the mandate of God and the mediocrity of an individual's life. Living by an urgency can be the key to the vision God would have you fulfill, the standard God would have you set, and the power God would have you impart. You have been given power in Christ through the baptism of the Holy Spirit to literally make a world of difference in the world that you live in.

Don't talk to me about your victim mentality or about your dysfunctional family, because when you become one in Christ, "old things are passed away; behold, all things are become new" (2 Cor. 5:17).

Don't talk to me about your skin color! Don't tell me that you're a Mexican or a black! Don't talk to me about your having curly hair or no hair at all. Don't tell me you didn't get an education. I grew up with all of that and more! Don't use any of these as your excuse because it's not your past that gets you to your future. It's the One called Christ Jesus living on the inside of you who gets you where you've got to go.

You see, today's generation is facing desperate times, but God's unfailing love is ready to answer their urgent cry. Today's generation is looking for answers for a world crisis. They are looking for answers for their personal unrest and unhappiness. Our generation lives in a world that is in turmoil.

It cannot continue as it is. So get ready, because God is about ready to use you. God is speaking to people to get ready to go the extra mile, to get ready to catch the vision, to ready themselves to set the standard and impart His power.

Sufficient Faith

by Jerry Savelle
Jerry Savelle Ministries International

The Bible tells us in Romans 10:17 that faith comes by hearing the Word of God. Notice, that verse doesn't say faith comes by "having heard." It comes by hearing and hearing and hearing, which means we need to feed our spirit constantly with God's Word.

My heart—where faith resides—is much like a checking account. Every time I read God's Word or hear it preached, I'm making a deposit of faith into my heart. At the same time, I'm writing checks on my faith. You could say that I'm always making withdrawals on my faith account, believing God for certain needs or situations. The danger is that we often make more withdrawals than deposits. And when we make more withdrawals on our faith than we've deposited, we come up with insufficient faith, much like we would come up with insufficient funds in our checkbook if we hadn't made enough deposits.

We have to feed our spirits the Word of God on a daily basis because we are confronted with Satan on a daily basis. We can't live on faith that we got from an Oral Roberts crusade in 1952 or from church last Sunday! Why? Because we're writing checks on our faith every day.

First John 5:4 says, "This is the victory that overcomes the world, even our faith." Faith is your conquering power, but you must take advantage of it. Deposit the Word of God into your spirit every day so that no matter what Satan brings against you, you have sufficient faith to conquer him in all situations.

'God, What's Your Plan?'

by Lindsay Roberts

One day Richard said to me, "Lindsay, I've decided that I'm going to stop asking God to bless my plans." I thought, *That's weird.* Then he explained, "From now on I'm going to ask God what His plans are, because His plans are already blessed."

From that time on Richard and I always ask, "God, what's Your plan? What's Your will in this?" When we find out what His will is, we just hook up with it and hang on.

Jeremiah 29:11 NIV says, "'I know the plans I have for you,' declares the Lord, 'plans to prosper you and not to harm you, plans to give you hope and a future.'" We've become so smart in the information superhighway! Because we can just click on the Internet and go around the world, rather than ask God what He wants us to do, we start doing this and that and then say, "Oh, by the way, let's include God in this." No. Let's make God the center of everything we do!

Jesus is not our copilot; He's the pilot! Think about that. He is the author and finisher of our faith. (Heb. 12:2.) He is the Alpha and the Omega, the beginning and the ending. (Rev. 1:8.) He knows and sees everything. (Ps. 139:1-4.) So why don't we let Him be God? Instead of trying to manipulate Him and maneuver Him to fit into our plans, why don't we say, "God, what's Your plan?" then just hook up for the ride, because His plan is already blessed.

I believe that when we get the revelation in our spirits that God is God and we follow His plans, then we can operate in the realm of the miraculous.

Make Your Home a House of Prayer

by Suzanne Hinn

Benny Hinn Ministries

We all know how busy life can be. There are so many things to do. The list is endless. But it's so important for us to make spending time with God in prayer a priority.

God says in Isaiah 56:7 NKJV, "My house shall be called a house of prayer." We tend to think of His house as a church building, but you and I are His house. First Corinthians 6:19 says that we are the temple of the Holy Ghost! God didn't say that His house was to be a house of deliverance or a house of healing. Those things are important, but they are by-products of prayer. Prayer is to be the foundation of everything we do and say.

This is especially true when it comes to our children. They have to know God for themselves. As parents, we can't allow ourselves to become negative and nag them or complain about them. We must press in to God through prayer. That is what will affect our children the most.

There are times when you may think, *I don't have time to pray.* Even though you're busy, take a few minutes to put on a good worship tape and sing along. When you're driving in your car, listen to tapes and pray. Worship the Lord. You may have just a little bit of time, but God looks at your heart more than at how much time you spend in prayer.

I believe that when we make our home a house of prayer, prayer begins to direct our family's steps like a compass, and everything else can fall into place.

'There Is No Substitute for Salvation'

by Richard Roberts

We live in a day of substitutes. Nylon has been substituted for silk, margarine has been substituted for butter, microwave ovens are frequently used as substitutes for regular ovens, and the list goes on and on. But there is no substitute for salvation.

I'd like to list several things that should not be considered as substitutes for salvation. Service is not salvation. (Matt. 23:15.) A person may say, "But I do all those wonderful things." Good works will not get you into heaven.

Turning over a new leaf is not salvation. Man does not get saved by saying, "I'm going to clean up my life and begin anew." That's not salvation. Isaiah 64:6 says, "All our righteousnesses are as filthy rags."

Denying the existence of sin is not salvation either. God does not deny sin; Calvary is God's recognition of sin. Isaiah 53:6 says, "The Lord hath laid on him [Jesus] the iniquity of us all." The first step toward salvation is acknowledging sin, not denying it. That's why we call a prayer for salvation "the sinner's prayer." Through it you acknowledge your sins, repent of them, and allow God to change your life from that day forward.

Also, salvation is not achieved through sacrifice and self-denial. The heathen are masters at this concept. They believe that denying themselves will win God's favor. God is not interested in your giving up soda pop or coffee or a particular food simply to deny yourself. It's not your self-denial He's interested in. He wants a relationship with you. Jesus said, "If any man will come after me, let him deny himself, and take up his cross, and follow me" (Matt. 16:24). That's true salvation, and there is no substitute for it!

Are You Lonesome Tonight?

by Kate McVeigh
Kate McVeigh Ministries

Maybe you remember Elvis Presley's song "Are You Lonesome Tonight?" But did you know that you can be alone without being lonely? I travel all the time and stay in hotels by myself, but I enjoy being alone and spending time with God, and you can too. He is always there for you, and when you draw near to Him, He will draw near to you. (James 4:8 NKJV.)

You are never really alone. The Holy Spirit lives right inside you and is with you wherever you go! In Matthew 28:20 NKJV Jesus says, "I am with you always, even to the end of the age." In Hebrews 13:5 He says, "Never will I leave you; never will I forsake you." Wherever you go, He is with you.

Maybe you are divorced or widowed or have never been married, and you are just lonely. Jesus promised in John 14:18 that He wouldn't leave you comfortless, and in verse 16, He says that He has asked God to give you another Comforter. You can lean on Him when you need comfort.

Going out with a friend of like precious faith can help too. If you don't have a friend like that, ask God to give you one and He will. Being alone doesn't have to mean you are lonesome. God cares. Go to Him for help.

Give-Up Moments

by Dr. I.V. Hilliard
New Light Christian Center Church

When you're walking the walk of faith with God, you meet resistance. And at times you may feel like quitting. When this happens, don't quit! On the other side of your give-up moment could be the miracle you've been waiting for.

When Peter loaned Jesus his boat to use to preach to the crowd that had gathered, Peter had reached a give-up moment. He had fished all night and not caught a single fish. After Jesus preached, He gave Peter a word. He said, Let down your nets for a draught (Luke 5:4). Peter answered, "But, Master, we've toiled all night long and caught nothing!" That was his give-up moment. But then he said, Nevertheless, at thy word I will let down the net (v. 5). And he caught so many fish that it broke his net! On the other side of his give-up moment was the very miracle Peter needed!

We all face give-up moments, but that's when you're got to trust God to keep His Word. Once you find a promise you need in the Word, and God says He's going to do it, you can trust the Word—even when you don't see any results or understand—because it's backed by God. You don't have to figure God out. You just have to trust that He will keep His Word.

We often limit ourselves by forgetting that, as believers, we are spirit beings. That means we have a right to operate in spiritual principles. We can trust God's spiritual laws because they work. When you understand this, you set yourself up for something supernatural to happen for you. So don't give up! On the other side of your give-up moment could be your miracle!

Here They Come!

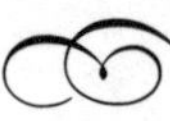

by Oral Roberts

When Jesus died, everyone said, "He is gone." And the news spread throughout Jerusalem—in every back alley, on every front street, on every corner—"He is gone."

His enemies said, "Oh, He's gone. We knew He was a fraud and that there was nothing to Him."

His believers wept and cried, "He is gone. We walked with Him for three years, but now He is gone."

His mother had brought Him into the world. She, who had held Him to her breast and had known He was the Son of God, said, "My baby, my son, is gone."

And all the angels of heaven said, "He is gone."

But His Father in heaven said, "Let Me tell you, today He has just arrived! He is here! He has come!"

Years ago we drove from Oklahoma to the Atlantic coast, and while we were there, we boarded a ship which went ten miles out into the Atlantic Ocean. We stood there with our darling baby Rebecca, our first child, and watched the ships coming into shore and then watched them go out until they were no longer visible.

As each ship sailed out of sight, we said, "Now it's gone." But now, whenever we remember the home-going of our precious daughter, Rebecca, we add, "But on the other side, they're saying, 'Here she comes.' From this side we say, 'There she goes,' but from heaven they are saying, 'Here she comes!'" When our children, Ronnie and Rebecca, arrived in heaven, Jesus said, "They're here!"

The Bible says that when believers die, they are absent from the body but present with the Lord. (2 Cor. 5:8.) Souls slip out of their mortal flesh. While we are saying, "They're gone," the angels in heaven are saying, "Here they come!" And Jesus is saying, "Come on over here." And He puts His arms around them.

Be Willing To Let Go

by Lindsay Roberts

One day in the mail I received an unusual gift from a partner of the ministry. It was a can of Lindsay brand pitted olives. I thought it was a hilarious and thoughtful gift, but it also started me to thinking.

To begin with, olives have a pit for a purpose. The pit is the heart of the olive—the part that connects it to the tree so it can grow. But once an olive is picked, the pit has served its purpose. And in order to make a can full of easy-to-eat olives, the pits have to be removed. Their time of usefulness is over.

We can learn a spiritual lesson from a can of pitted olives. Sometimes we hang on to things from the past and we won't release them when it's time. Maybe they were great for a season, but if that season is over, it's time to let them go.

Maybe you've experienced a radical change in your life. You've lost a job or something else that meant a lot to you. But that job or that way of life may have just been for a season. Its purpose in your life may be over, just like the purpose of a pit is eventually over in the life of an olive. Be willing to release it and move forward with God to the next assignment He has for you.

Jesus said, "No man, having put his hand to the plough, and looking back, is fit for the kingdom of God" (Luke 9:62). Like the pits that had been in the olives I received, we must let go of the past and put some things behind us in order to fulfill God's call on our lives.

God Will Order Your Steps!

by Brenda Timberlake-White
Christian Faith Center

Could you use a miracle today? I think most people would say they could. A miracle is something that you can't do yourself. If you could do it yourself, then you wouldn't need God's help. And most of the time God asks us to do things that we can't do on our own. That's why we need His help. When God challenges us to do anything in life, He challenges us to the degree that it's going to take faith to accomplish it. He wants us to have faith in Him and His Word to believe that He can do it. Whatever God asks me to do, I know that He's going to help me, enable me, motivate me, and equip me to get the job done.

How precious are your miracles to God? Think about it this way. If you lost a diamond ring, you probably wouldn't stop looking for it until you had turned everything in your house upside down and found it. You would do that because the ring is very precious to you. Did you know that the miracles you need from God are very precious to Him—so precious that Psalm 37:23 says He will order your steps? He will even bring people across your path to help you receive your miracles.

Our children come to us with their requests, and they think that Mom and Dad can do whatever needs to be done. It's only natural for them to think that because we've always done everything we can for them. We love our children so much that we exhaust all of our energies and our strength to do whatever they want us to do. How much more does our heavenly Father, who is all-powerful, all-knowing, all-consuming, and who owns everything, love us? He loves us so much that He orders our steps. And when we need something, He touches the heart of the right person to help bring us the miracle we need!

With the Heart Man Believes

by Lindsay Roberts

When Richard became President of Oral Roberts University, he was handed a $42-million debt. He was really frustrated with our financial problems, and he began to talk to God constantly about our needs here at ORU. Then one day God spoke to him and said, "I don't want you to talk to Me about these problems anymore. I already know about these things. Talk to Me about Me. Praise Me. Worship Me. Seek Me first, and all these things will be added to you."

Richard had to totally change his way of thinking. He had to change everything he thought about debt, about life, about God, about what he was going through, and about where he was headed. If you had to talk to God only in scriptural terms, some of us might not have anything to say. Some of us might not know enough scriptural terms to talk to God according to the Word of God. We had to sit down and rethink our entire way of thinking.

In Psalm 19:14 the psalmist prayed, "Let the words of my mouth, and the meditations of my heart, be acceptable in thy sight, O Lord, my strength, and my redeemer." But until the words of our mouths and the meditations of our hearts are acceptable, then He can't be our strength and our redeemer.

A friend of mine once told me that acting in revenge and bitterness, even when the other person is wrong, is like drinking poison and expecting the other person to die. It doesn't work that way. When I heard this, the Lord touched my heart and showed me that my words and my heart were absolutely out of line. I had to line up my heart and my mouth with the Word of God. When you line up your mouth and your heart with God's Word—because with the heart man believes—at that point God will be your strength and your redeemer.

Knowing God

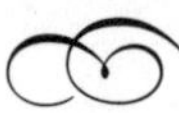

by Gloria Copeland
Kenneth Copeland Ministries

It's time to move into a closeness with God where you live separated unto Him and obey Him in all the areas of your life. When we abide in the Lord and His words abide in us, we have living fellowship with God. And it produces great reward.

Knowing God requires a lifestyle of talking to Him and communing with Him. It's listening to Him and obeying what you hear and what you find in His Word. Learning to live in the place where God can talk to you at any moment is the secret to living an overcoming life.

Knowing God should be our number-one priority, because it is the key that opens every supernatural door. Daily intimacy with Him is the way love works. It strengthens you and undergirds your faith. It produces the anointing that enables you to lay hold of all the wonderful things God has provided through Jesus Christ.

Filling your heart with the Word and the voice of God enables you to abide in Him every single day. And as you feast your heart on His promises and His presence, your future will be one of joy and prosperity, healing and health. Instead of chasing after the blessings of God, you'll find they're chasing you and overtaking you at every turn! Understanding this message has changed my life forever.[1]

Sometimes God Says, "Wait"

by Oral Roberts

Many times a pregnant woman will reach the point where she is weary in body. The baby has grown so large that she finds it hard to sleep at night, awkward to move about, difficult to eat or even to dress herself, and she will say, "Oh, I would just love to have this baby today and get this pregnancy over with!" But the doctors say, "Wait."

"Wait" is sometimes God's answer to us. And just as the doctor tells the pregnant woman to wait in order that her baby might have an opportunity to be born with greater health, so God's answer to us is for our good.

David said in Psalm 40:1-3, "I waited patiently for the Lord; and he inclined unto me, and heard my cry. He brought me up also out of an horrible pit, out of the miry clay, set my feet upon a rock, and established my goings. And he hath put a new song in my mouth, even praise unto our God: many shall see it, and fear, and shall trust in the Lord."

David waited on the Lord because that was what the Lord called him to do. Waiting was God's answer. It was for David's greater good—that he might be firmly established in his inner man and experience a new joy in his spirit.

After the Lord healed me of tuberculosis, with which I was terminally ill as a young man, I became worried from time to time because my body remained so weak. My mother said to me, "Oral, it will take a while for God to restore your strength. Wait on Him." That was good advice. I refused to doubt my healing, and as I waited on God to restore me completely, my strength did return.

God has a purpose in answering your prayer by saying, "Wait." Look for God to do an inner work in you as you wait on Him. You can trust His purpose to be for your good.

Drowning Out the Voice of Fear

by Richard Roberts

Several years ago, Lindsay and I and our children were staying in a hotel in southern California. We were scheduled to minister in a church there the next morning. In the dead of night, we woke up to find the room shaking and rolling all around us. We were right in the middle of a massive earthquake.

The babysitter who was traveling with us was knocked unconscious, and as Lindsay and I scrambled to assist her and protect our children, my life began to flash before my eyes. The devil whispered in my ear, "You're going to die. Lindsay and your children are going to die. You're all going to die in this hotel!"

But suddenly the Holy Spirit spoke to my spirit, and I heard God's still, small voice as clear as a bell: "You have been called to preach in forty nations. You are not going to die in an earthquake today." When those words penetrated my heart and mind, peace began to flood my spirit, and I knew we were going to be okay. The Bible tells us, "God is our refuge and strength, always ready to help in times of trouble. So we will not fear, even if earthquakes come" (Ps. 46:1,2 NLT).

If your life is being shaken, steady yourself with the promises of God. Remember that He is your refuge and strength, no matter what is going on around you. The peace of God can flood your heart as you allow the Holy Spirit's voice to drown out the voices of fear and confusion. Because He is with you, you can handle anything that comes your way.

Bringing Home the Bacon!

by Lindsay Roberts

The word "prosper" means to become strong and flourishing. It means to achieve economic success. A while back, Richard told me a story about how the phrase "bringing home the bacon" came to be, and I'd like to share it with you.

In England, back in the fifteenth century, most people were poor. Only those who had money could afford to buy meat. Of all the meats available, the most expensive was pork. If you could afford to buy pork, you were prosperous. So when someone would buy pork—or bacon—they would invite people over. Then they would take the bacon and hang it over by the door. This way everyone in the neighborhood and the guests that were invited could see it, and the wife could say, "My husband brought home the bacon!"

`It's time for Christians to *bring home the bacon.* It's time for us to put a sign upon the door of our homes which reads *prosperity!* It's time for us to show our neighbors that we're strong, we're flourishing, and we have economic success.

Can you imagine those people in the fifteenth century looking across the street and noticing a slab of bacon hanging by the door of someone's house? "My goodness!" they would say. "That man has brought home the bacon. He's prospering!" What they needed to add to "my goodness" was, "They must be Christians, because the blessings of God are overtaking them. They're blessed in the city and in the field. They're blessed in their baskets and in their storehouses. They're blessed coming in and going out. They're the healed of the Lord, and they're living the abundant life Jesus came to bring them!" (Deut. 28:2,5,6,8,30; Ps. 107:20; John 10:10.) Now that's scriptural!

Flowing in the Spirit

by Bob Yandian
Grace Fellowship

Jesus was a deep teacher. A deep teacher doesn't take simple things and make them complicated; he takes complicated things and makes them simple. We are the ones who often make things complicated. When it comes to flowing in the gifts of the Holy Spirit mentioned in 1 Corinthians 12:7-10, we have made it so difficult that we think only elite Christians can do it.

I've seen some people who, before they start to flow in the gifts of the Spirit, have to go through some kind of transformation—like Clark Kent going into a phone booth and coming out as Superman. They have to bow their heads, close their eyes, and pray before they do anything.

Can you see Jesus doing that? Can you see Jairus going to Him and saying, "Please come heal my daughter," only to have Jesus say, "Give Me two hours in My prayer closet and then I'll be there"? He didn't have to take time to wind up into the Spirit before He could minister to people. Jesus dropped what He was doing and went with the man. Even though the girl had died by the time Jesus arrived, He said to her, "Little girl, arise" (Luke 8:54 NKJV). And the girl was raised from the dead!

Jesus was able to live in the natural, yet He knew how to minister in the Spirit. He knew how to flow in and out of both realms. He could be preaching the Word, but if someone asked Him, "Could You come for dinner tonight?" Jesus could say, "My disciples will be there," and go right back to preaching without missing a beat. Flowing in the Spirit is not mystical. It's not weird. The Holy Spirit relates to us on our level, and when we follow His leading, we can flow back and forth naturally in the things of the Spirit.

Faith Is a Process

by Marilyn Hickey
Marilyn Hickey Ministries

I have learned a lot about faith, and I have a lot more to learn. But I have learned this: Faith is a process. If we don't understand that, we give up too soon. I love to see an instant manifestation of faith, but sometimes a process is involved. Galatians 6:9 says, "Let us not be weary in well doing: for in due season we shall reap, if we faint not."

We see the process of faith in the account of a miracle in Matthew 15:21-28, which tells us how to come into the highest level of faith. While on the earth, Jesus left Israel only once. It was when He went to Canaan where the people were pagans and worshiped idols. Why would He go there? A Syrophoenician woman was there who had faith, and Jesus goes anyplace there is faith. The woman was interceding for her demon-possessed daughter, and Jesus honored her faith. He healed her daughter.

It doesn't matter who you are, where you are, or what your circumstances are. What matters is your faith. Jesus honors your faith. He said there are people with no faith, people with little faith, and people with great faith. These levels of faith show us that faith is a process. Faith has a risk to it. But when you step out in faith, it's not your name that's on the line—it's God's name. And a process is involved.

At times when you pray, you don't get an answer right away. It is as though heaven is brass and nothing is heard. But this is the process of faith. If you are praying the promises of God, the promises of God cannot return void. Your faith is going to go through the fire, but if you will hold on through the fire, you will come forth as gold! (Job 23:10.)

Miracles Can Happen

by Richard Roberts

One day when Jesus was in the city of Cana, a nobleman from Capernaum went to see Him. (John 4:46-54 TLB.) The nobleman's son was at home, deathly ill, and he begged the Lord to come and heal his child. Instead of going with him, Jesus asked, "Won't any of you believe in Me unless I do more and more miracles?" Ignoring the question, the nobleman pleaded with Him, "Sir, please come now before my child dies."

Jesus saw that the man had faith, and He also knew there was no distance in prayer. He said, "Go back home. Your son is healed!" And the man believed Jesus and started home.

When Jesus' word is mixed with faith, it can cause a miracle to happen.

The nobleman knew that his son's life was hanging in the balance. Everything hinged upon whether or not he believed the Lord. He believed the words of Jesus, and he turned around and started home.

Before he got there, some of his servants met him with the news that his son had recovered! He asked them when the boy had started to feel better, and they replied, "Yesterday afternoon at about one o'clock his fever suddenly disappeared!" (v. 52). That was the exact moment when Jesus had told him, "Your son is healed."

Just like that father, when you and I choose to believe the words of Jesus no matter what we see, miracles can happen in our lives!

We Determine Our Standard

by Keith Butler
Word of Faith
International
Christian Center

First of Two Parts

Even before Eve was created, God gave Adam and Eve instructions that they were not to partake of the tree in the midst of the Garden of Eden. Eve found out about that from her husband. That is the way it's supposed to be. God will speak to the head of the household, who will speak life into the rest of the family.

Teenagers are frequently confused. They generally don't know what their roles are. Do you know what your role is? How should you be approaching your single life? What about a married individual? Departure from God's plan for man is the reason why there is so much chaos. Many people have moved away from God's plan, and they have become secular humanistic in their thinking. But if we can get people back to God's plan through the Word of God, they'll see blessings come into their lives.

Here we are in this technological society. Men are working; women are working. Husbands and wives are working. They have families and many spend only five minutes of quality time a week with their children

Every situation is different with every person. One of the reasons we say we have to work is that we have determined what our standard of living is going to be, and we have placed that ahead of our roles.

I think what has happened in many cases is people have determined to have a specific standard of living. They wish to drive certain kinds of cars, and they want their children to go to a certain kind of school. They want certain kinds of clothes. They do what is required to meet that standard, and they pay a price somewhere. The price they pay is with their children and with each other.

God's Plan

by Keith Butler
Word of Faith International Christian Center

Second of Two Parts

God's plan for man clearly is that the husband's responsibility is to go out and bring in the fruit for that family. Certainly women can work. There is no problem with women working. But if she is not doing what is required for her husband and children, they may have wonderful cars and nice houses, but they are going to have kids who get on drugs or have other monstrous problems.

Christian parents are saying, "Why are my children having problems? I took them to church." It is not enough to just take them to church. They must be ministered to at home. If you leave that to someone else to do, they become latch-key children. Many kids today are latch-key children. They have a key to the door and come home to an empty house. We were so blessed as I grew up! We came home from school, and Mother was there to help us become what we are today.

Yes, society is more fast-paced today, but it all comes down to decisions. My wife and I decided to pay the price. She would stay with the children, and I would try to be there as much as I could. We were determined that we didn't want to have what some people think of as PKs—preachers' kids. A lot of times we're told that preachers' kids are the ones who are lost. We made sure that we ministered to our children. We lived at a lower standard economically, but we made that choice!

Today our son is a graduate of a Bible school and is in the ministry. Our daughter is at the University of Michigan and doing very well. We have a son who is saved, filled with the Holy Ghost, loves God, and wants to serve in the ministry.

This is no accident. It happened because we stayed in the right roles, sacrificed our economic standard, and were there to guide our children. Proverbs 19:21 NIV says, "Many are the plans in a man's heart, but it is the Lord's purpose that prevails."

Stop, Drop, and Roll!

by Lindsay Roberts

If you're like me, you're constantly busy, running here and running there throughout the day. But Exodus 14:13 NKJV tells us to "Stand still, and see the salvation of the Lord." I think that often God is trying to get the answers we need to us, but we're so busy running around that we miss His answer that is right in front of our faces!

When you get caught up in your busyness, everyday problems can consume you like a fire consumes a house. And when you are in the middle of that hustle and bustle, you can find yourself running around inside the burning house in a panic trying to find a way out, when the exit is right where it has always been.

So how can we keep our lives from being overcome by busyness? Firefighters tell us that if our clothing catches on fire, we should remember SDR: stop, drop, and roll. The same idea works to keep our lives from being controlled by a busy schedule.

Stop. Stop what you're doing and stand still.

Drop. Drop down on your knees in prayer before God.

Roll. Roll your cares over onto Jesus.

That's a simple formula for coping with being too busy, but it's a biblical plan that can work if you try it.

Sooner Than You Think!

by Sharon Daugherty
Victory Christian Church and School

I believe we are very close to the second coming of Jesus Christ. There are so many signs of the times that are evident that His return is imminent.

A few weeks ago, my husband, Billy Joe, and I returned from Russia, and we saw how God is moving in countries that at one time were closed to the Gospel but now have been opened up for a season. There will be more nations opened up before Christ's return because He said in Matthew 24:14, "And this gospel of the kingdom shall be preached in all the world for a witness unto all nations; and then shall the end come."

God wants a great harvest of souls in these last days. He wants people to know Him. He wants people to come into a relationship with Him. He is such a long-suffering, loving, and compassionate God! Our human minds can't even imagine that He is so compassionate and long-suffering that He has prolonged the end time until He can bring in a great harvest.

I really believe that we're in the day of the harvest of the Lord. The Scripture says that at the same time, the enemy—Satan—is out to try to come against that harvest. We are concentrating on the harvest—on what God is doing and how His glory is being revealed on the earth in the lives of people, whether it's through salvation, through healing, or through deliverance. God's compassion and love for people is all-encompassing.

Be Yourself

by Richard Roberts

Often when I go into a grocery store, people will recognize me and ask for prayer. And when they do, I don't say, "Let's go out in the parking lot." I stop whatever I'm doing and pray for them right there.

One time I was in the frozen food section with ice cream in one hand and frozen vegetables in the other when a woman came up and asked me to pray for her to be healed. When I put down the frozen food and laid my hands on her head, I thought she going to go through the ceiling because of my cold hands. She said, "I didn't know the anointing was so *cold!*" I said, "No ma'am, that was the frozen food."

Why do I tell you that story? Because it's real, just like Jesus was real. Sometimes people see Lindsay and me on television and they want to know, "Are they real?" I believe Jesus wants all of us to be real. We all have our faults and quirks, but God created us to be unique individuals. There's no one else like you on earth.

So if you've been putting yourself down, stop it. Stop thinking you can't be used by God. Be yourself! When God leads you to touch someone with His healing power, don't worry about what to say or do. In Mark 13:11 NIV Jesus told His disciples, "Do not worry beforehand about what to say. Just say whatever is given you at the time, for it is not you speaking, but the Holy Spirit." It's not your power; it's God's—and He wants you to allow Him to work through you. When you're not afraid to be yourself, He can work through you any place in the world, even in the middle of a grocery store!

Who Is This One?

by Richard Roberts

Who is this One who arose on Easter morning?

He is the One who came from heaven to be born in Bethlehem and was laid in a manger. He is the One who was hidden in Egypt, raised in Nazareth, and baptized in the Jordan River.

He is the One who overcame the temptations of the devil in the wilderness. He is the One who turned water into wine, calmed the sea, healed the multitudes, delivered the people, preached the Good News, multiplied a few fish and loaves of bread to feed the masses, and raised the dead.

He is the One who took on our sins and nailed them to a rugged cross. He is the One who bowed His head and died at Calvary. He is the One whose death caused the veil of the temple to be rent in two. He is the One who was buried in a borrowed tomb, because He only planned to use it for three days.

He is the One who on the third day—on Resurrection morning—came bursting forth from His graveclothes and stood outside the borrowed tomb in shining garments, alive forevermore! He is the One who declares to you today, "Because I live, you will live also" (John 14:19 NKJV).

Who is this One? He is the King of kings, the Lord of lords, the only begotten Son of the almighty, everliving God, Jesus Christ, our Savior and Lord!

Extreme Lengths

by Terri Copeland Pearsons
Kenneth Copeland Ministries

Jesus went to extreme lengths to prove God's love to even the most sinful men. Luke 8 tells of a time when He had ministered all day, then got into a boat to go over to the other side. It wasn't an easy trip. They encountered hurricane force winds until Jesus rebuked the storm, putting a stop to it.

When they arrived, a man met them who was so full with evil spirits that he could not be bound—a man who lived in the tombs, thriving off bodies and carcasses, cutting and beating himself. He ran toward Jesus, probably intending to kill Him, but when he ran into the presence of God, those demonic powers fell in subjection. Jesus drove out the demons and set him free.

Think about the extremes Jesus went to. Why did He travel across the lake when He was so tired that He fell asleep shortly after setting sail? Why did He go through the storm? I'm convinced it's because God heard the cry of one desperate man and said to Jesus, "I don't care how bound up by perversion he is or what he looks, smells, or acts like. I love him. Go and set him free."

God hears your cry too, and He has gone to great extremes to purchase your freedom. Be set free today![1]

The 'Little Thing' Test

by Lindsay Roberts

Late one night after hosting *The Hour of Healing*, Richard called me from the studio. Our kids had had a special event at our house, so I had stayed home with them.

"The Lord just spoke the strangest thing to me," Richard said, "I'm to do something, but I don't want to do it by myself. I want you to go with me." I had no idea if he was talking about a late-night trip to the convenience store or jumping off the moon.

"I'm supposed to go up to the office and sign 50 Bibles," he said. Well, that seemed kind of strange. I could understand God speaking to him about going to the ends of the earth to minister, but going to the office to sign Bibles late at night?

We went to Richard's office and signed the Bibles. On the way home, I had to ask, "Richard, why do you think the Lord told you to do that?"

"Oh, it's real simple," Richard replied. "I think it was a test. God knows I'll obey Him and do the big things, but I think He was testing me to see if I'd listen to Him and do the little things."

God needs to know if He can trust us with doing the little things He asks, because if we won't do the little things, how can He trust us to do the big things? God said in Jeremiah 7:23 NIV, "Obey me, and I will be your God and you will be my people. Walk in all the ways I command you, that it may go well with you." Obedience is the key. No matter what God calls you to do, be it large or small, obey Him. Then He can begin to bless you abundantly!

'Now, You Finish It!'

by Richard Roberts

First of Three Parts

This is a true story about Leonardo da Vinci who one day was in his studio with some students. He gathered the paints that were needed, the right canvas, and all the other things he needed to make the shadows and the colors come brilliantly alive. Now he had all the things that he needed, all the instruments of his trade around him.

Leonardo began to draw a picture, outlining various things to bring into various features, and then began to add some color to it. Then, all of a sudden, he stopped abruptly. Turning to one of his pupils, he handed him the brush, saying, "Now, you finish it!"

The student took the brush, and his hands began to tremble as he said, "I can't do that. I'm not even worthy to touch something that the master has touched. I can't do this. I don't have your ability. I don't know how to do it."

Leonardo looked at him and said, "You're right! I just wanted to see if you were sleeping. You don't have the ability to do it by yourself, but I started it, and that ought to call you to do your very best."

God started our lives. He breathed life into us, and He created us in His own image. That should cause us to believe that if He created us and breathed life into us, then the Master started it. But now He has placed the ability to make decisions in our hands. With His presence and guidance we can make wise decisions.

Trust in the Lord with all thine heart; and lean not unto thine own understanding. In all thy ways acknowledge him, and he shall direct thy paths.
—Proverbs 3:5,6

God Starts the Process

by Richard Roberts

Second of Three Parts

What is beautiful about the story of Leonardo da Vinci is that as the student looked at the painting, he could just as easily have put the brush down and said, "Why don't we call it the unfinished work?" Its beauty made him fearful. Instead, he recognized, "The master's here. I can ask him questions. I can ask him, 'Master, would you use this paint or this paint here? I want to put some darkness over here and some light over there. I feel this area is a little bit dark, and I want to bring some light into the midst of it."

"Well, this is what I would do," the master would say.

As we go through the process of life, we have to recognize that God is like Leonardo da Vinci. God starts the process. He trusts us to make decisions. If we will yield ourselves to Him and listen to His advice, we'll be able to paint the mural of our lives with those "brushes" that are the down moments and the high moments of life. We'll be able to find a way to make it the masterpiece that God wants it to be.

John Lennon once wrote a line that was used in the movie "Mr. Holland's Opus." In fact, it was the emphasis of the movie, the key thought of the movie. The line was this: "Life is what happens when you're busy making other plans."

You may be saying, "I want to do something for God someday. My life's going to be so greatly used!" Those are your plans, but you can be sleeping through the process that God wants in your life and has ordained for your life by building your character, by making you reliant on Him, and by telling you who you are.

When you get to the end result and you know that you've gotten the answer to your prayer, then you're able to endure, sustain, be strong, and help others too.

And whosoever believeth on him shall not be ashamed.—Romans 9:33

Part of the Process

by Richard Roberts

Third of Three Parts

My fascination began with the thought of the process. Moses spent forty years in the wilderness, and the Bible doesn't tell us much about those years. But we know that was a part of God's process to get Moses where he needed to be.

Then there was Joseph. There was a period of time between when God placed the dream in his heart and it came to pass. Consider the time in between when Joseph was in the pit and then placed in a prison. Then the time came when Joseph stood before the Pharaoh in the court of Pharaoh. That was all a part of the process to get Joseph to the point where he needed to be. He knew he was a man of destiny. He knew he would deliver the people of God, but there was a process before it happened.

We have believed that it was a short time between the time David killed Goliath with his slingshot and the time he became king. It was not. There was a time in there called "the process" when he was on the run for his life. David didn't know whom he could believe in. He didn't know who would stand with him. But there were those who did stand loyally. David was on the run, wondering if he could have just imagined that he was going to be king.

In fact, Jonathan went to David in one of the caves and encouraged him, saying, "You will be king." Sometimes we need good friends to tell us, "You are who you know you are! Don't let go of the visions and dreams of God."

An enemy is one who tries to divert us and cause us not to see our destiny, to instead make excuses and not allow us to recognize who we are in Christ. But a good friend will remind you of the call of God on your life.

Earnest Prayers

by Pat Harrison
Faith Christian Fellowship International

If you've ever had a legal problem and gone to an attorney to get help, you were searching for a solution to your problem. You meant business. When we go to God for His help, we should be just as earnest in our prayers.

God delights to hear our heartfelt supplications. James 5:16 NLT says, "The earnest prayer of a righteous person has great power and wonderful results." This isn't talking about whiny, complaining, passive prayers, but God-centered, heartfelt petitions that touch God's heart and move Him to action.

How do you pray earnest prayers?

Study to know what God's Word says.

Write down your *earnest* requests.

Write down the promises from God's Word that are in line with your requests and put God in remembrance of His Word.

Then pray: *God, this is my earnest petition, and these are Your promises from Your Word. Give my request Your attention, I pray, and rescue me on the terms of Your promises. I speak forth Your promises, and I expect to receive. In Jesus' name. Amen.*

When our prayers line up with God's Word and we get down to business in our prayer life, He can begin to move on our behalf!

A Balanced Life

by Joyce Meyer
Joyce Meyer Ministries

Car maintenance is necessary. If you don't rotate and balance your tires on a regular basis, they are going to become unbalanced and wear out more quickly. If you don't change your oil regularly, the motor will eventually burn up. It's all a matter of keeping a balance between what's good and bad for your car.

Having a lack of balance in our lives is one of the greatest problems we face, and it's so easy to get out of balance! It might be something as simple as eating too much of a good thing. You might eat it once and then think, *Well, I think I'll have some more of that.* And pretty soon you're letting yourself have some more...and some more...until before long, you've got a big problem. You're eating way too much, and your diet is out of balance.

Being out of balance could be worrying, watching too much television, or spending too much money. We may want to blame the devil for these problems, but really he's on the scene because we got out of balance and opened the door for him to come in. First Peter 5:8 AMP says, "Be well balanced (temperate, sober of mind), be vigilant and cautious at all times; for that enemy of yours, the devil, roams around like a lion roaring [in fierce hunger], seeking someone to seize upon and devour."

A balanced life requires discipline and self-control. The apostle Paul said that anyone who wanted to gain mastery had to restrict himself in all things. (1 Cor. 9:25.) Fortunately we don't have to attempt this on our own. Hebrews 13:6 says, "We say with confidence, 'The Lord is my helper.'" With His help, we can live a life of balance.

Dreaming a New Dream

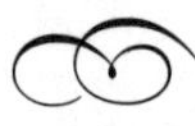

by Oral Roberts

First of Seven Parts

In 1 Corinthians 2:9-10, Paul said, "But as it is written, Eye hath not seen, nor ear heard, neither have entered into the heart of man, the things which God hath prepared for them that love him. But God hath revealed them unto us."

I am speaking of the power of taking the limits off your faith. That works in both the secular and the spiritual world. In 1954, no mile-runner in the history of the world had run the mile in four minutes or less. Thousands of runners had tried to run the mile in four minutes, but seemingly there was an invisible barrier. Just before they reached the finish line, they would be prevented from running that mile in four minutes.

There was a young man in England, a medical doctor, who had been a mile-runner for several years. He had been training and had his heart set on being the first man in history to run a mile in four minutes. Time after time he tried, became discouraged, and backed out. Then he had his vision!

This man, who is a Christian, took the limits off his faith and said, "I'm going to train, and I'm going to condition myself inwardly and outwardly. I'm going to be the first man in the history of the world to run the mile in four minutes."

This was announced several weeks before his try to accomplish that feat. I well remember reading it, and millions of people stood in awe when it was carried live as Roger Bannister ran like the wind that day. When they clocked him, he had run the mile in less than four minutes. He became the most famous runner the world had known!

Since that time, many runners who also had dreamed of running the four-minute mile began to dream a new dream. They began to take the limits off their faith to run the mile in less than four minutes. The power of taking the limits off our faith is immeasurable!

No Limits With Faith So High

by Oral Roberts

Second of Seven Parts

A young man, John Glenn, Jr., badgered NASA and the government to allow him to orbit the earth. He was forty years old, and he had to run the gauntlet in order to be chosen. He was discouraged because of his age, and it was a hazardous thing as America had not yet orbited the earth.

In the Smithsonian Institute in Washington, D. C., I've seen that little 9′ X 7′ capsule into which John Glenn was finally placed on February 20, 1962. Millions of people were holding their breath as the capsule was launched. John Glenn was launched into space and began to circle the earth—not once, but three times. The force of gravity coming against his body was seven times more than the most powerful roller-ride in amusement parks.

Then came the most frightening portion of his orbit in space—returning to earth. When it was time to make the splash-down in the ocean, warning lights suggested the capsule's heat shield had become loose, meaning the capsule could burn and John Glenn would not survive.

He had to have his faith high, with no limits on it! He needed faith with no limits not only to get into that little capsule but also to whirl around the earth three times in less than five hours. He had to believe that his capsule would not burn up, that he would not die, and that he would bring back tremendously valuable material that he had gained by going into space.

As television was covering the return of the capsule, I remember that millions of people were praying as they held their breath. Then we were told that the capsule had safely hit the water! What a sigh of relief!

It was said by many that the most fateful moment in the history of the United States was when John Glenn safely hit the water. He was alive and well and was taken from the capsule armed with invaluable information for his country.

Have the Faith of God!

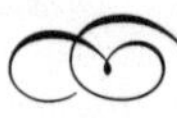

by Oral Roberts

Third of Seven Parts

In the Bible, God taught us how to take the limits off our faith. Jesus said, "Have the faith of God." One translation says, "Have faith in God" (Mark 11:22), but the original says, "Have the faith of God." That has been a difficult thing for me to understand. How can a man have the faith of God? How can I believe as God believes? How can faith work off my believer as it works off God?

In Romans 4:17, the apostle Paul said these words about God: "(As it is written, I have made thee a father of many nations,) before him whom he believed, even God, who quickeneth the dead, and calleth those things which be not as though they were."

The way God uses His faith is to look at the things that don't exist and call them into existence. He calls them before they appear as though they are already here.

Jesus said, "Have the faith of God," which means to take the limits off our faith and look with our spirits to the things that we don't have, that are not part of our being, that will make us what we ought to be or place in our hands the things that we ought to have. Have the belief, the faith, and the vision to call, to speak to the thing that is dearest to your heart, which seems to elude you no matter what you do. Call it!

Call it into existence as though it were already in your life. Jesus tells us our heavenly Father has that kind of faith!

Now faith is the substance of things hoped for, the evidence of things not seen. —Hebrews 11:1

The Fall of Man

by Oral Roberts

Fourth of Seven Parts

When God created man and placed him in the Garden of Eden, it was a perfect paradise. He gave man everything that one could ever desire except for one thing. God would not allow him to eat of a certain fruit. Man couldn't stand it and committed high treason against God. The bottom line of that was, if he ate the forbidden fruit, man thought it would make him like God. In effect, he believed he would be God. That was Satan's temptation in the Garden of Eden.

Something in man yielded to that, and it is called the fall of man. In the Bible, particularly as the apostle Paul teaches it, that was called the fall of man from his first estate—from the way God created him, placed him in the Garden, and told him to multiply and replenish the earth.

Think back to what might have happened had he not fallen. Because when he committed that sin, it was so deep within him, so much a part of his being, that it was not like a little ordinary sin. It was a sin from the depths of his being where he would actually dethrone God if he could, and God is the Creator and will be forever.

Because of that sin, man was cast out of the Garden into a world that had been struck a devastating blow. And everything that is wrong with our earth today began happening because of that sin.

Every child that has been or ever will be born on this earth has been born with the seed of sin in his heart. One thing we don't have to learn is how to sin. It just seems so natural to do the *wrong* thing, when it should be natural to do the *right* thing. It should be more natural to smile than to frown, to say a good word rather than a blasphemous word or to curse, to lift someone up rather than to knock them down. It should be more natural for us to love God than to move away from Him, to want to go to heaven rather than lose our souls in hell. It should be more natural for us to be good people rather than bad people, but it seems to be easier to go the other way.

'The Seed of the Woman Will Destroy You!'

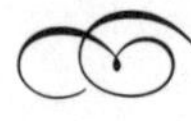

by Oral Roberts

Fifth of Seven Parts

Everything wrong in this world and with human beings, with our governments, with our businesses, with our families, is because of the seed of sin that has been dealt with and of which it is said, "It is good!"

I know how devastated I feel when something in my life or in the lives of my family lies in devastation. But that would be nothing compared to the way God must have felt when He saw the life of man—His greatest creation, made above all animals, the only one given the power of choice, the only one with an immortal soul—lying in ruins.

The fall of man brought the curse upon everything in the world—every living thing. God had to speak to Satan, who had come in the form of a serpent to tempt Adam and Eve. He spoke to him and put a curse upon him. He put a curse on him to take away some of his powers so that he didn't have the utter power of destruction for us. He put a curse on him so we, by our faith, can defeat the devil in our lives.

But Satan was in this earth then, and he is in this earth now. He is in the power of the air. He is called the prince of the powers of the air, the god of this world, and he will be that until Christ returns.

If it is possible for God to have taken the limits off His faith, this is what He did, and the Bible describes it well. He looked at the woman, and then He looked at the devil, and He said, "The seed of that woman, or the woman's species, shall bruise your head. You will have power to bring damage to the earth, but the seed of that woman ultimately will bruise your head and will destroy you!"

Abraham of Perfect Faith

by Oral Roberts

Sixth of Seven Parts

The first son, Cain, was born to Adam and Eve. The second son was named Abel, and Cain hated Abel. It was so easy for Cain to have hate, and he rose up and killed his brother, Abel, out of jealousy.

Then a third son, Seth, was born. The Bible says Seth worshipped God. That was the dividing line. From Seth came a line of people through sons and daughters and finally to a man named Abraham.

Abraham is the first man in the history of the world who had perfect faith in God, who said that God is the most high God, and that He delivered us from all of our enemies. And Abraham taught us to give one tenth of all we possess to God.

Abraham begat Isaac, who followed in his footsteps. Isaac begat Jacob, who had a lot of trouble in his life. Finally Jacob won the victory over himself and was able to take the limits off his faith and turn to his grandfather's God. God changed his name to Israel, and Israel had twelve sons and one daughter, named Dinah.

These twelve sons became the fathers of a family God was raising up in the world that would serve Him with faith. No matter what you have in life, no matter how great love is, I believe faith is the thing that is most important. For God says, "Without faith it is impossible to please him" (Heb. 11:6). You shall live by your faith or die by your doubts. So God created a faith line by raising up this family and believing that this family would become a nation.

God went to a young virgin girl in Israel, Mary, not yet married, and gave her the matchless privilege of bearing the humanity of the seed of God, the Messiah whom the Jews were looking for, who is Christ.

Mary took the limits off her faith and bore the humanity while God, by the Holy Spirit, put in the divinity. It was God in man—in order to sit where we sit, and feel what we feel, and go through what we go through.

'It Is Finished'

by Oral Roberts

Seventh of Seven Parts

Jesus taught, He preached, and He healed. That's the basis of how the Christian church was founded.

Jesus lived that life, and then He came to the defining moment of His existence in the Garden of Gethsemane on the evening of the last night of His physical life upon this earth. Judas betrayed Him, and the enemy came to arrest Him and prepare to crucify Him the next day. Before they came, Jesus had gone aside to pray. And for the first time in the life of His humanity, walked the earth as you and I do, He came face to face with the fact that He was going to have to die. He was going to die not just for Himself but for the sins of all the people who would ever be born. He was to rise from the dead and ascend to heaven. He would someday return and restore Eden, to bring a new earth, a new heaven, and a new humanity.

He had said on earth, "I and my Father are one" (John 10:30). In that Crucifixion, for the first time in eternity He would be separated from His Father for a little period of time. But He went to the cross in order to take our place, to bear our sins, and to redeem us from our sins so that we, when we die, can be raised from the dead and live forever and become part of that new world in eternity. To do that, He had to take our place, and our place had been separation from God.

In order to do it all, He had to be separated. And on the cross, we can hear His cry through these centuries: "My God, my God, why hast thou forsaken me?" (Matt. 27:46).

To really understand the cross and the Crucifixion, you've got to know what it really means to be away from God—the darkness of the soul, the failure to know that when we die we'll go to heaven.

Jesus went to the cross, taking the limits off His faith. And then came that great moment in history as He hung there, and John 19:30 tells us He said, "It is finished." And Luke 23:46 says He cried, "Father, into thy hands I commend my spirit."

You Have an Inheritance

by Jerry Savelle

Jerry Savelle Ministries International

I don't know too many Christians who would argue with the fact that they are redeemed by the blood of Jesus. Most Christians have been taught redemption, but not all of them know about their inheritance in Christ and are living in it.

Ephesians 1:7 says, "We have redemption through his [Jesus'] blood, the forgiveness of sins, according to the riches of his grace." Then verse 11 says, "in whom also we have obtained an inheritance."

The same people who identify with the redemption through Christ should also identify with the inheritance! Notice, neither of these is something that will happen someday—it's past tense, already done. In other words, that inheritance belongs to you right now just as much as redemption belongs to you right now.

Think about it. When do you get an inheritance? When you die, or when someone else dies? My earthly father, Jerry Savelle, Sr., went on to be with the Lord a few years ago. My mother is still living at this writing, and I hope she lives to see the appearing of Jesus! But if she should go by the way of the grave, my younger sister and I are joint heirs of my parents' estate. That means that everything my father and mother acquired in their lifetime will be inherited by my sister and me when they are both gone.

So many Christians are waiting to receive their spiritual inheritance when they die and go to heaven. But we have an inheritance now! Romans 8:17 says we are heirs with God and joint heirs with Jesus Christ. That means we have divine health, prosperity, and authority over the devil *now!*

Meditating on God's Word

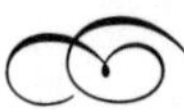

by Dr. Creflo A. Dollar
World Changers Church International

Ephesians 1:3 says that God has blessed us with all spiritual blessings in heavenly places in Christ. These blessings are on the inside of us. The question is, How do we get the blessings that are deposited in us to come upon us?

We do it the same way Jesus did it. From His early childhood Jesus spent time reading and meditating on the Scriptures. In essence, He clothed Himself in them. We know this because when Jesus was found in the temple in Jerusalem speaking to the teachers of the Law after His parents discovered He was missing, the Bible says, "All who heard Him were astonished at His understanding" (Luke 2:47 NKJV). And Jesus was only twelve years old at the time!

Also, because Jesus spent time studying God's Word, He became what it said. (Luke 4:17-21.) We, too, become what we meditate on. When we meditate on poverty, worry, distress, and sickness, that's what we yield to. On the other hand, when we meditate on God's Word day and night, we can expect the blessings that God has deposited in us to come upon us.

Joshua 1:8 NKJV puts it this way: "You shall meditate in [God's Word] day and night, that you may observe to do according to all that is written in it. For then you will make your way prosperous, and then you will have good success."

So how can you get the blessings that are deposited in you to come upon you? By meditating on God's Word day and night so that you may be sure to obey all that is written in it. This is God's plan for your success and prosperity.

A Life of Abundance

by Gloria Copeland
Kenneth Copeland Ministries

Have you ever noticed that you never hear, "Oh my, I have more money than I need"? Such words sound ridiculous in a world ruled by lack, yet as children of God, that is what we *should* be saying!

Jesus said that we're *in* this world, but we're not *of* it. (John 17:15,16.) We belong to the kingdom of God, and it has no shortages. It has an abundant supply of every resource you will ever need.

Years ago when the only abundance Ken and I had was an abundance of needs, the Lord quickened the text verse to me. In the face of our impossible-looking situation, we chose to believe God's Word and began saying, "God is able to make every earthly blessing come to us in abundance!" We started speaking prosperity instead of lack, and we began obeying the promptings of the Holy Spirit where our finances were concerned. Miraculously, eleven months later, we were completely debt free.

Financially, we had been total failures, yet simply because we believed God and obeyed His Word, God was able to supply us not according to the shortages of this world, but according to His riches in glory. If you will dare to believe God's Word and begin speaking it instead of your circumstances, He'll do the same for you and abundance will be yours.[1]

The Light of the World

by Richard Roberts

I remember hearing a story once about a father who awakened in the middle of the night during a storm, concerned that his young son might be afraid of the thunder and lightning. He picked up his flashlight and slipped into the boy's room, shining the light to see if everything was all right.

All of a sudden a clap of thunder exploded in the night and the little boy shot straight up in his bed and cried out, "Who is it?"

His father started to shine the light in the boy's face, but then he realized that would only make him more frightened. So he shone the flashlight on his own face so his son could see who was there. The little boy exclaimed with relief, "Oh, Daddy, it's you!" "It's all right, son," the father reassured him. "Everything is going to be all right."

To me, that story is a picture of God the Father taking the Light of the World, which is Jesus Christ, and shining it on His own face. When the storms of life come, God reassures us, "Don't be afraid. I'm here, and everything is going to be all right."

Jesus said, "I am the light of the world. He who follows Me shall not walk in darkness, but have the light of life" (John 8:12 NKJV). No matter how frightening the storm clouds look hovering all around you, the light of Jesus is shining in the darkness and His mighty power is there to bring you through the storm safely.

A Piece of Fabric

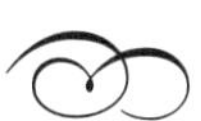

by Lindsay Roberts

Sometimes we don't obey God because it's inconvenient or because our flesh doesn't like what He's asking us to do. But 1 Samuel 15:22 says, "To obey is better than sacrifice." When God asks us to do something, He's trying to get a wonderful blessing to us. Yet sometimes we let the dumbest things stand between us and our obedience.

I'll give you an example. When I came to Oral Roberts University as a student, I knew God had called me here, but I didn't know there was a dress code. I came from a beach town in Florida where we wore sandals all the time. I mean, dressing up meant changing from old flip-flops to new ones. I didn't even own a dress, and I found out I was expected to wear one every day! As soon as I heard that news, I called my mother in Florida and said, "Mama, I'm coming home!" She said, "Why?" And I answered indignantly, "Because they say I have to wear a dress every day. I'm not using my hard-earned money to buy a dress!"

My mother, wise woman that she is, answered calmly, "Lindsay, do you mean to tell me that you're going to let a piece of fabric come between you and the call of God on your life?" Well, when she put it that way, what could I say? She mailed me some skirts and told me, "You just stay there and let God talk to you."

So I did. And it wasn't long before I met and married Richard, which was God's plan for me. Imagine how sad it would have been if I'd let dresses keep me from that plan. Don't let anything stand between you and obeying God. Obedience can bring God's marvelous blessings into your life.

An Ambassador of Love

by Terri Copeland Pearsons
Kenneth Copeland Ministries

You have been reconciled to God! And since you are born of His nature and love, it should be in you to take the message of reconciliation to those around you—to draw them close and love them.

Some might say, "Well, I couldn't possibly get close to *those* people! They're living in gross sin!"

Well, don't beat them with your judgment stick or try to punish them for their sin. Jesus already took the punishment for them! When we're tempted to be harsh or critical, we should ask ourselves, "Is this how Jesus would speak to this person? Is this the tone of voice He would use?"

Let God show you how to be loving to those people who give you the hardest time. He'll give you the power to do something nice for them. They will probably be ugly again, but the power of love will enable you to rise above it and it won't matter. What will matter, however, is that something eternal will have happened. The very love and presence of Almighty God will have come on the scene. And that love can do things that nothing else can do.

You can have the same awesome impact on your world that Jesus had. Love breaks chains. Heals wounds. Brings people together. Love makes the impossible possible, because love never fails.[1]

Atmosphere for Healing

by Keith Butler
Word of Faith International Christian Center

Recently our congregation has been studying God's Word regarding God's will for us to be healed. As a result, when someone ministers on healing and prays for the sick in our church, the two come together and we see results. The Word produces faith, and faith produces an atmosphere for healing.

The Word has a lot to say about healing. In Exodus 15:26 God tells the children of Israel, "I am the Lord that healeth thee." In Matthew 8:16 when the people came to Jesus, He healed all that were sick. Then 1 Peter 2:24 NKJV says that by Jesus' stripes you were healed. Psalm 107:20 says that God sent His Word, and healed them. That's what happened in Acts 14:7-10. As the apostle Paul was preaching the Word, he observed a crippled man. Perceiving that the man had faith to be healed, Paul said, "Stand upright on thy feet. And he leaped and walked" (v. 10). Where did that faith come from? It came from hearing Paul preach the Word. Paul's preaching established the atmosphere for healing.

I believe another element needed to establish an atmosphere for healing is will and determination, which we see in the Canaanite woman in Matthew 15:21-28. She begged Jesus to heal her daughter. Although He told her that He was sent only to the lost sheep of Israel, she would not take no for an answer. She continued to ask for healing. Her will and determination established an atmosphere for healing, and her daughter was made whole!

An atmosphere for healing can be established when the Word is preached and you have a desire and determination to be healed. This is the time to believe for and lay claim to your healing.

Unexpected Answers

by Vicki Jamison-Peterson
Vicki Jamison-Peterson Ministries

God has ways to answer our prayers that we may not have thought of. Often when we pray, we have in mind a certain way for God to answer. But He can give us answers that we may not have even thought about yet!

Jesus said in Mark 4:22 AMP, "[Things are hidden temporarily only as a means to revelation.] For there is nothing hidden except to be revealed, nor is anything [temporarily] kept secret except in order that it may be made known."

God wants to reveal unexpected answers to you! I've seen Him do it in the realm of healing, for example. I have a friend who started searching for answers after she was diagnosed with breast cancer, and as she did, things were *revealed* to her. The Spirit of God began to show her things about health and nutrition which led her to change the way she ate and took care of herself. She adopted a new and healthier lifestyle, believing God for healing, and today she is well.

After hearing her story, I began to use my faith to pray and ask the Lord to cause things to be revealed that I needed. I would pray, "Lord, I ask You to help someone find the answer to this need." Then, lo and behold, I would find it.

There have been times when I've prayed and not received an immediate manifestation, but an answer came eventually. God may choose to reveal the answer to your problem in a different way. Don't throw away your options or say, "It can't happen this way." It's so easy to overlook your answer just because it doesn't come the way you expect it. Ask God to bring to pass whatever you need. Then open the door to receive God's answer however He chooses to send it.

'Up With Good Seeds!'

by Evelyn Roberts

Several years ago, I was asked to speak to the children in one of the third-grade classes. I was going to speak on Seed-Faith, but it is a pretty big subject for a third grader to understand. Then the Lord gave me an idea. Somebody had given me a plant that had died. So I stirred up the dirt that was left in the little basket and planted some seeds in it.

I took the basket to school, and the children were very excited and curious. I told them that I had planted seeds in the basket. I said, "I brought this so I could talk to you about Seed-Faith. Seed-Faith is something you do, and when you do it, you do it as unto the Lord and you expect something to come back to you."

I explained, "When you go out on the playground and see a little girl or boy off in a corner and they have nobody to play with, you can plant a seed of faith in their life by saying, 'I'll play with you. I'll be your friend.' The Lord will bless you for that good seed you plant.

"But if you go over to a lonely little child and kick him, that is a seed too. It's a bad seed. When you plant good seeds, you'll get them multiplied back to you in the form of something good. When you plant bad seeds, you are going to get back something bad!

"I'll leave this basket here with you," I said. "If I planted good seeds, you will see them come up. If I planted bad seeds, nothing good will happen."

When I left, the teacher had each child write a sentence or two about what they had learned from my talk, and she sent them to me. I shall never forget what one little boy wrote: "Down with bad seeds and up with good seeds!"

That's what I'd like to say to you today: Down with bad seeds and up with good seeds! Sometimes you don't want to plant good seeds into the lives of people who aren't good to you, but your seeds will bless their lives, and God in turn will bless your life.

'A Comfort Zone'

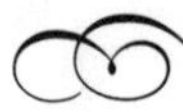

by Richard Roberts

The years that I've been President of Oral Roberts University have been full of struggle. I've often faced seemingly insurmountable odds, and there have been times when people were certain that I would fail and the university would close. But they overlooked the Holy Spirit who dwells in me. Now they pat me on the back and tell me what a great job I'm doing. Of course, it's not me; it's the Holy Spirit!

God didn't intend for us to face the world and its trials by ourselves. That's why Jesus said in John 14:16-18, "I will pray the Father, and he shall give you another Comforter, that he may abide with you for ever; even the Spirit of truth; whom the world cannot receive, because it seeth him not, neither knoweth him: but ye know him; for he dwelleth with you, and shall be in you. I will not leave you comfortless: I will come to you."

With the hectic lives most of us lead, we need "a comfort zone"—a haven of tranquility and rest, a place where we can escape the turmoil surrounding us. And God has provided such a place of power and restoration.

The Holy Spirit is your comfort zone! When everything seems to be crumbling around you...when you're in the middle of some hellish trial...by the miracle power of God, the Holy Spirit can give you the comfort and strength you need to pull out of the mess you're facing. Ask God for the comfort and power of the Holy Spirit, and see what a difference it can make!

The Hand of Faith

by Keith Moore
Faith Life Church

Part One of Two Parts

Many Christians believe that God heals. They believe Jesus paid the price for their healing and it is part of their redemption, yet they're not releasing their faith to receive it. The Bible shows us that we can have faith to be healed and still not be healed. When the apostle Paul was preaching in Acts 14, a man who had been lame from birth heard him and Paul looked on him, perceiving that he had faith to be healed. (v. 9.) Notice, the man was still sitting there crippled, even though he had faith to be healed. That story shows that healing must be taken or received, as we take the faith we have and release it to God.

Mark 11:24 says, "What things soever ye desire, when ye pray, believe that ye receive them." Faith is like the hand that reaches out to take hold of what God's Word says belongs to us. For example, if I bought you a Bible and handed it to you, you wouldn't beg me, "Oh, please, give me the Bible!" You'd reach out and take it. In the same way, your healing has been bought and paid for, and the Lord is offering it to you.

When we read in the Gospels about people who received their healing, it wasn't the passive ones who sat in a corner wishing and hoping for it. It was people like the woman with the issue of blood who pressed through the crowd to take her healing or like blind Bartimaeus who cried, "Jesus, have mercy on me!" (Mark 5; Luke 18). They reached out with the hand of faith to take the healing that they believed in...and you can too!

Condemnation Is a Faith-Killer

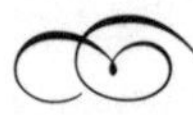

by Keith Moore
Faith Life Church

Part Two of Two Parts

Often we don't reach out to receive what God has promised us because we think, *I'm not a very good Christian.* The problem is that condemnation will keep us from acting on our faith. Many Christians have faith to receive a promise, but they won't act on it because of condemnation.

Condemnation is a faith-killer. It will make us fear and draw back from the promises of God. We might know we have authority in Jesus' name to rebuke cancer or some other disease, but we will put up with it instead because we know we've failed. We may say, "I am healed!" when we're around our Christian friends, but in our hearts we aren't really expecting healing to happen because the enemy is continuously reminding us of our mistakes.

Jesus paid the price for our sins so we could be clean and free. Even if we've blown it, 1 John 1:9 says, "If we confess our sins, he is faithful and just to forgive us our sins, and to cleanse us from all unrighteousness." I've had people say to me, "You don't know what I've done." And I answer them, "And you don't know how powerful the blood of Jesus is." No matter what you may have done, when you ask God for forgiveness, the blood of Jesus cleanses you so that it's as though you'd never sinned.

Romans 8:1 says, "There is therefore now no condemnation to them which are in Christ Jesus." When your faith is unhindered by condemnation, you can act on your faith to receive everything God has promised you in His Word!

God Gives the Ability

by Lindsay Roberts

In Webster's dictionary one of the definitions for the word *power* is "the ability to do or to act." Often we want to do certain things, but we don't have the ability to do them. For example, there's no way I could walk onto a basketball court and play with an NBA team. I don't have the ability!

When I was growing up, I loved to play tennis, and one of my idols was Margaret Court. She holds 86 major world tennis titles and has won Wimbledon three times. Today she is the pastor of a wonderful church in Australia, and we are friends. But the difference between Margaret and me on the tennis court is that she has more ability. She has a God-given talent. I can call myself a tennis player, but if I don't have the ability, it's a lovely fantasy, not a reality.

Jesus said in Acts 1:8 NKJV, "You shall receive *power* when the Holy Ghost has come upon you." That means when God sent the Holy Spirit into the earth, He gave us "the ability to do or to act." The Holy Spirit is the divine Paraclete——the One called alongside to help—the power source which gives us the ability to accomplish God's will. The Holy Spirit is the power that gives us the ability to lay hands on the sick and see them recover. When we get in a position where we don't know what to do, we can tap into God's power source. Through the Holy Spirit, God's ability is available to us to do whatever task He assigns us!

An Unshakable Declaration of Faith!

by Richard Roberts

In 2 Chronicles 20, King Jehoshaphat was about to face three marauding armies which were threatening to destroy every living thing in Israel. When word reached Jehoshaphat that a great multitude was coming against him from beyond the Dead Sea, he was terrified. In other words, he was a normal human being just like you and me. He got scared. But before Jehoshaphat made a move, he decided to seek God's help.

Notice that Jehoshaphat didn't call on all of his counselors and wise men first. He didn't ask his top military aides to devise a strategy. Before he consulted anyone else, he cried out to God for help!

I love what Jehoshaphat said! He declared, "If calamity comes upon us, whether the sword of judgment, or plague or famine, we will stand in your presence before this temple that bears your Name and will cry out to you in our distress, and you will hear us and save us" (v. 9 NIV). He was saying, "God, no matter how bad the situation looks, we're going to run to You, and You will deliver us." No ifs, ands, buts, or maybe sos.

What an unshakable declaration of faith Jehoshaphat made that day! He wasn't saying, "God, I hope You'll deliver us," or, "I pray You might deliver us," but, "You will deliver us!" And the armies were defeated!

God loves it when His children run to Him in times of trouble. When it looks as if your life is falling apart at the seams, I encourage you to exercise your faith and run to God as your Deliverer!

That's a Lot of Love!

by Oral Roberts

One day I was out on the golf course alone. It was a day when not many golfers were playing, so I was by myself, which gave me an opportunity to reflect.

I began to think about the family of God and how the triune God looked ahead and saw a family in the Garden of Eden with everything just right. And even though God knew that man, created in His own image and likeness, would be deceived by the devil and fall into sin, He still wanted a family.

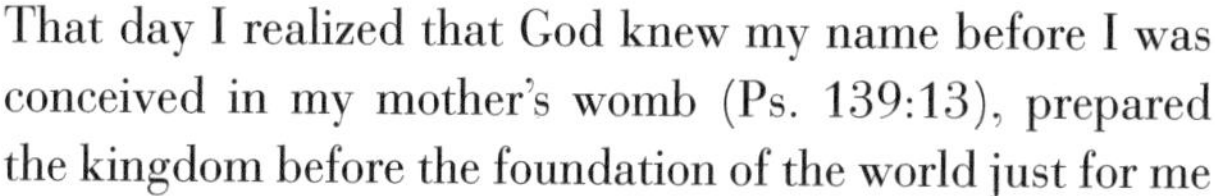

That day I realized that God knew my name before I was conceived in my mother's womb (Ps. 139:13), prepared the kingdom before the foundation of the world just for me (Matt. 25:34), and sent His Son to die on Calvary's cross for my sake (John 3:16). Then the realization hit me—*God loves me!*

This wasn't the first time I realized that God loved me. But this realization was particularly significant that day because it came at a moment in my life when I was in the pits, and God was telling me, "Oral, I love you!" Before I knew it, tears were running down my cheeks, covering my face. So I picked up the golf ball, put it in my bag, and went home.

"Oral, what's the matter?" Evelyn asked as I walked in the door. "Evelyn, God loves me!" I said. "Well, you know that," she answered. "I know I do," I said, "but I've never known it like I know it now. He *really loves* me!"

Has it ever occurred to you just how much God loves you? He loves you so much that He will incline unto you, hear you when you cry, bring you out of the pit, place your feet upon a rock, and put a song in your mouth. (Ps. 40:1-3.) And that's a lot of love!

Let the Weak Say, 'I Am Strong'

by Richard Roberts

The Lord promises again and again in His Word that He will strengthen us. He knows that, as human beings, we often feel our weakness to the point where we don't believe we *can* be strong.

In Joel 3:10 we read, Let the weak say, I am strong. Notice that strength is first something we confess with our mouths. We *say* to ourselves, *I am strong.* Note, too, that the Bible doesn't say we were strong or that we will be strong. It says we are to speak to ourselves in the *now* of our circumstances and say, I *am* strong! What a good word that is to us when we are feeling weak—unable to cope or to bear up under the pressure, to be patient or have courage. In that very moment—in that very circumstance—we can claim, by our faith, the provision of God to us: *I am strong!*

On what is our strength based? Our strength is not in ourselves but in Christ Jesus who lives within us by the power of the Holy Spirit. In Isaiah 40:28-29, the prophet said, "Hast thou not known? hast thou not heard, that the everlasting God, the Lord, the Creator of the ends of the earth, fainteth not, neither is weary? there is no searching of his understanding. He giveth power to the faint; and to them that have no might he increaseth strength." Our strength does not come from our own abilities or power, but from the wisdom and power of God, which is poured into us any time we admit our weakness and ask Him to replace our weakness with His strength.

The apostle Paul wrote, "Be strong in the Lord and in the power of his might" (Eph. 6:10). Take that as God's word to you today! You can be strong in any situation or circumstance you face today because the Spirit of God is strong within you!

Don't Be Deceived

by Jeanne Caldwell
Agape Church

Part One of Two Parts

It's so important that we stay free of deception in these last days. In Matthew 24, the disciples went to Jesus, asking, "What shall be the sign of thy coming, and of the end of the world? And Jesus answered and said unto them, Take heed that no man deceive you" (vv. 3,4). These were the men who knew Jesus best, but He obviously felt they could be deceived. So He instructed them. I want us to review some of the ways the Bible says we can be deceived so that we know what to watch out for.

#1 James 1:22—"Be ye doers of the word, and not hearers only, deceiving your own selves." We'll be deceived if we just sit in the pew and hear the Word but don't act on what we've heard after we leave the church.

#2 First John 1:8—"If we say that we have no sin, we deceive ourselves." We need to understand that all of us have sinned and fallen short of God's glory, and it's only by His grace that we're saved. (Rom. 3:23; Eph. 2:8.)

#3 Galatians 6:3—"If a man think himself to be something, when he is nothing, he deceiveth himself." God hates pride. We can keep from being deceived if we remain humble and teachable.

#4 First Corinthians 3:18 says that we are deceived when we think ourselves to be wise with the world's wisdom. God's ways are wise. When we think we're smart based on the world's standards, we can easily be deceived. Being open to God's instruction and having a teachable spirit can keep us from deception.

The Word Will Guard You

by Jeanne Caldwell
Agape Church

Part Two of Two Parts

The Bible tells us the ways the enemy tries to deceive us so that we can know what they are and can guard against falling into them. Here are more ways the enemy tries to deceive us:

#5 James 1:26—If any man among you seem to be religious, and bridleth not his tongue, [he] deceiveth his own heart. A tongue that isn't kept under control reveals a person's true condition.

#6 Galatians 6:7—Be not deceived; God is not mocked: for whatsoever a man soweth, that shall he also reap. We often use this Scripture in reference to finances, and it's absolutely true. But don't be deceived—we'll also reap if we sow anger or some other fleshly action toward others.

#7 First Corinthians 6:9—We are deceived if we think the wicked will inherit the kingdom of God. The only way we can enter heaven is by accepting Jesus Christ as Savior. He is the only way to God.

#8 First Corinthians 15:33 NASB—Do not be deceived: "Bad company corrupts good morals." We are deceived if we think that contact with sin will not have an effect upon us. We can't be a Christian and play with sin, because it will eventually affect us. We are called to be a holy people, separated for God's service.

Look into the truth of God's Word, and purpose in your heart to let it guide your life. The Word can guard you from deception so that you can live a good life, acceptable to God.

Seed Your Children's Minds

by Cathie Dorsch

Agape Church/*Kids Like You* Television Program

First of Two Parts

Recently I attended Lindsay Roberts Women's Conference, and while there, I felt so impressed that we were not seeding our children's minds enough about going to college. We wait until they're in junior high or senior high to start telling them to clean up their record. They need to get into some activities and get ready for college. We don't seed into our children that there is a preparation and a process to follow to enter the business world or any profession they choose.

I thought, *What better way to show them than to follow a day in the life of a student at Oral Roberts University.* We have a 15-minute clip on our *Kids Like You* program. The whole program is designed for children. We talk to kids and tell them things they might see at the university—what the university library looks like, the classrooms, the dormitories. We do some segments from some of the scenic locations on the campus just to give them the feeling of what it might be like to get geared up for college.

In Isaiah 28:9-10 God asks, "Whom shall he teach knowledge? and whom shall he make to understand doctrine? them that are weaned from the milk, and drawn from the breasts. For precept must be upon precept, precept upon precept; line upon line, line upon line; here a little, and there a little."

Human beings have the longest childhood of any of God's creations. We don't grow up and marry in the first five years. We have about eighteen to twenty years that is a process during which time our parents raise us, and hopefully it is with His Word and His Holy Spirit. Even Jeremiah 1:5 says that before we were formed in the womb, God knew us. He has our children in His mind even before they are born.

Speak Life to Your Children

by Cathie Dorsch

Agape Church/*Kids Like You* Television Program

Second of Two Parts

The words we say to our children are so important! They are death and life because you are the most important person in your child's life. Your child can have sports heroes, teachers, or spiritual leaders they respect, but the parent is the one the child will believe. Fifty other people, including wonderful children's ministers and pastors, can all say great things, but if the parent says something else, they're going to believe the parent.

It has always been God's design to have the child raised in a family unit, in the home. Children come and go from the family unit to activities, school, or community involvement being a light and a witness, because they are being coached, instructed, taught, and encouraged in meaningful ways by a parent. This is the greatest learning period of children's lives, and the family is the greatest role model they'll have in their lives.

Proverbs 4:20-22 says, "My son, attend to my words; incline thine ear unto my sayings. Let them not depart from thine eyes; keep them in the midst of thine heart. For they are life unto those who find them, and health to all their flesh."

Are we speaking life to our children and health to their flesh? We must, because our children will give attention to our words. While it takes many encouraging words to build your child's self-esteem, it can take only one negative word to undo them.

There are things you should be doing, such as spending an hour at night with your child doing homework, on just being involved in their lives. Don't wait until May to see if they are going to graduate, change classes, or be held back. Then you have only three weeks to undo the damage or find out why it happened. Your children are coming home with report cards to report to you what is going on. A parent should know every day what is going on with their children.

The Very Best Place To Be

by Lindsay Roberts

When we feel that God is calling us to do something, sometimes it is difficult because it may be contrary to what our human nature wants to do. And yet, at the same time, being in the will of God is the place of greatest fulfillment, protection, safety, and satisfaction in life. That's why it's so important that we discern God's will.

For example, when Richard conducts a crusade overseas, my flesh fights against it. His trips to countries that are not safe, his absence from home, and the long hours he puts in are unpleasant. Even as devout Christians, it's a sacrifice for our entire family. Yet we know that the very best place for Richard is in the will of God. The very best place for his wife to have her husband is in the will of God. And the very best place for our children to have their father is in the center of God's will.

Answering God's call to go to dangerous countries can be hard because some people understand and some don't. "You have a wife and kids," they say. "Isn't that being irresponsible for you to go?" But what is more important—our comfort, our reputation, or the Father's approval?

The truth of the matter is that when you're in the center of God's will, you have a peace which surpasses all understanding. (Phil. 4:7 NKJV.) As you step out in obedience to God and see Him prove Himself faithful, you grow and you learn. It's rewarding, and that makes life exciting. What really matters is that at the end of the day, the Father will say, "Well done, my good and faithful servant" (Matt. 25:21 NLT).

Who's First?

by Richard Roberts

Who or what do you put first in your life? Your spouse? Your children? Your job? The dictionary defines the word *first* as "preceding all others in time, order, or importance; the finest grade." What in your life would fit that description?

God wants us to put Him first and everything else in our lives second. He asks us to give Him our best—"the finest grade"—in every area of our lives.

Proverbs 3:9 NKJV says, "Honour the Lord with your possessions, and with the firstfruits of all your increase." *The Message Bible* says, "Give him the first and the best." Why? Read the next words: "So your barns will be filled with plenty, and your vats will overflow with new wine."

When God tells us to put Him first and give Him our best, He is not trying to take something from us. He's trying to give something back to us. Putting God first starts a chain reaction in the supernatural realm. God begins to work—often in miraculous ways. When we sow and obey God's laws, we reap a harvest according to those laws.

'The Facts Aren't Always the Truth!'

by Oral Roberts

I have found that worry often comes by looking at circumstances and conditions as they are...or seem to be. When viewed in this way, your problems always look bigger than the solution.

There used to be a TV show in which a detective, inquiring into a case, would always say, "Just the facts, ma'am, just the facts." It made good sense to a detective, but in the spirit realm the facts are not always the truth!

For example, while Jesus was hanging on the cross, He was forsaken, suffering, and dying. Those were the facts. But the truth is that He was overcoming sin, sickness, demons, and hell! And the suffering of His death resulted in the glory of His resurrection. He said, "Because I live, ye shall live also" (John 14:19).

The same principle is true for your life. The facts you face daily are not necessarily the truth. The fact may be that you are sick...but the truth is, by the stripes on Jesus' back you were healed. (1 Peter 2:24.) The fact may be that you're facing severe financial problems...but the truth is, when you plant your seeds of faith, God can multiply them back in a miracle financial harvest. (Luke 6:38.) The fact may be that you're confused and don't know which way to turn...but the truth is, the Holy Spirit knows exactly what the will of God is for your life, and He is interceding to the Father for you. (Rom. 8:26,27.)

I want to encourage you—to remind you—that God really is in control of this world...and He is in control of your life. He wants you to stop worrying and believe the truth of His Word instead of "just the facts."

Signs, Wonders, and Miracles

by Billy Joe Daugherty

Victory Christian Center Church and School

We were invited to a ministers' conference and were allowed fifty minutes to speak. Many of the ministers there were denominational, evangelical preachers who had not embraced healing, deliverance, or miracles. So I spoke on miracles, believing God for the healing of people in the church services.

Five minutes before the end of the service, the Spirit of God said, "Are you going to do it or just talk about it?" It was time to demonstrate it. If we believe in the full Gospel, there ought to be something for people to see with their own eyes. This was the hour!

So I said quickly, "Everyone who needs a healing miracle, lift your hand." Hands popped up all over that place. I had taught them about laying hands on the sick. I said, "The person next to you, who is full of the power of God, is going to lay hands on you." I said, "All of you who are receiving something, begin to move your body. Begin to act on your faith. All of you who have received an evident, obvious miracle, lift your hand."

Several hands went up. I said, "Those of you who have been healed, come quickly to the front." This all happened in about two minutes. I asked the man standing next to me, "What happened?"

"I can see now," he answered.

Surprised, I asked, "What?"

He repeated, "I can see now."

Then a man jumped up and said, "I'm a pastor of a denominational church. This is one of my chief elders, and he's been blind. We just laid hands on him, and he can see!"

We serve a risen Savior! He is alive!

A Sacrifice of Praise!

by Lindsay Roberts

There was once a six-month period during which it seemed as if Richard and I were experiencing every negative situation we could go through. Finally I had enough. "Lord," I said, "are we going to have to go through everything?" Immediately the Lord answered me, saying, "No, just the things you'll be ministering on. Until you've been there, you can't teach others about it."

During that six-month period, Richard and I went through some pretty rough times, yet the thing that God told us to do was praise Him until something happened. And that's what we did. Every time we were in the car you could see us with our hands raised high, praising the Lord. People thought we were waving at them, and they'd wave back. What we were doing was getting back to the basics. And because we focused on praising the Lord, guess what happened? Miracles started to happen!

Now, I understand what the term "sacrifice of praise" means. When you wake up in the middle of the night, worried, not knowing what to do, and you begin to praise God, that's a sacrifice of praise. When everything in you hurts and won't work, yet you continue to praise God, that's a sacrifice of praise. When your world is falling apart, and still you praise God, that's a sacrifice of praise. And God honors that! Psalm 22:3 says that God inhabits the praises of His people.

Richard and I learned an important lesson during those six months. When you're faced with a problem, don't try to work it out or analyze it. Praise the Lord and watch Him be God in the situation. I believe this is how you can position yourself to see turnarounds like you've never seen before. And when you've experienced a turnaround, you can minister to others who need one.

A Gift Opens the Door

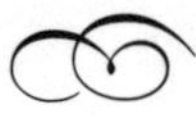

by Marilyn Hickey
Marilyn Hickey Ministries

Part One of Three Parts

Proverbs 18:16 NKJV says, "A man's gift makes room for him, and brings him before great men." When I first studied this Scripture, I thought, *If that means a material gift, isn't that like manipulating someone?* But the Lord told me I needed to think of giving in terms of blessing people who were blessed. If I wanted to receive their blessing, I needed to bring them gifts. Because gifts make what? Room for you, and they bring you before great men.

I knew a man who wanted to minister in a certain town, but the mayor wouldn't let anyone use the town square for Christian meetings. My friend prayed about it, and the Lord said, "Give him a gift."

My friend found out that many people in the town needed eyeglasses, so he got 2,000 pairs of glasses donated. He wrote to the mayor and asked if he could go to the town square and bless the people by handing out 2,000 pairs of glasses. The mayor called my friend and said, "It's wonderful that you want to do that. I can't thank you enough." My friend said, "While we're giving out the glasses, we'd also like to preach and pass out tracts. Could we do that?" The mayor said, "Of course." The man was able to start a church in that city because he gave a gift!

Some might feel that my friend was manipulating the mayor with his gifts, but I believe he was honoring him. In the same way, when we give tithes and offerings to the Lord, we know He doesn't need them. He already owns everything on earth, according to Psalm 50:10-12. But we give to honor Him, and in turn we receive His abundant blessings.

The Power of a Gift

by Marilyn Hickey
Marilyn Hickey Ministries

Part Two of Three Parts

The Queen of Sheba knew the power of a gift. She'd heard of the wisdom of King Solomon, and she wanted to receive his wisdom. She didn't just make an appointment to see him. She went with gifts. First Kings 10:2 says that she came to Jerusalem with...camels that bare spices, and very much gold, and precious stones.

The queen knew she wasn't the only person who wanted to meet Solomon. She also knew that he already had riches—he didn't need the items she gave him. But by bringing him gifts, she found favor, and it brought her before the wisest and richest man in the world.

God's Word says, "When the queen of Sheba had seen all Solomon's wisdom, and the house that he had built, and the meat of his table...and his ascent by which he went up unto the house of the Lord; there was no more spirit in her. And she said to the king, "'It was a true report that I heard.... Thy wisdom and prosperity exceedeth the fame which I heard. Blessed be the Lord thy God, which delighted in thee, to set thee on the throne of Israel: because the Lord loved Israel for ever, therefore made he thee king, to do judgment and justice'" (1 Kings 10:4-7,9).

The queen learned that Solomon's wisdom and abundance came from the Lord. She learned the Source of it all! And she went home with God inside her. She touched her nation with God's wisdom, and they turned to the living God. But this wouldn't have happened if it hadn't been for her gifts that got her in the door.

A Gift Keeps Giving

by Marilyn Hickey
Marilyn Hickey Ministries

Part Three of Three Parts

A gift keeps on giving. It doesn't stop. According to Proverbs 17:8 NKJV there is continuous prosperity in a gift: A present is a precious stone in the eyes of its possessor; wherever he turns, he prospers. So after you give a gift, it keeps on working and prospering. That's what happened with my mother.

Over 40 years ago my mother became a Partner with Oral Roberts Ministries. I remember this because at the time I couldn't understand it. "He's wild!" I told her, speaking about Oral. "He prays for the sick and tells people to put their hands on the television to get healed!"

My mother totally ignored me, thank God! She believed in the ministry and sent her Seed-Faith gift each month. Once she had a tumor and prayed in agreement with Oral as she placed her hand on the TV. And God healed her.

Did my mother know that when she sowed seed into the ministry her gift would make room for me? Did she know that her gift would open doors so I could go before great men? Did she know that her gift would make a way for her granddaughter to attend Oral Roberts University and then be called into full-time ministry? She didn't know any of that. But that's exactly what her gifts did, and her gifts are still working, still giving as I travel around the world, bringing God's message to all people.

Just like my mother, we have no idea what our gifts will do in the future. But if God's Word is true—and we know that it is—our gifts can keep prospering and working after we sow them.

Controlling Your Thoughts

by Richard Roberts

God gave us a mind to use, but there are times when we have to get out of our mind, so to speak, and into the Spirit. How do you set your mind aside in those times when you need to operate in the Spirit? By getting your mind in shape. And you get your mind in shape by bringing it under the control of the Holy Spirit.

It's important to get your mind in shape because if Satan can defeat you in your thought life, he can separate you from your faith and what you believe.

You can keep your thoughts under control by doing what the Bible says: "Casting down imaginations, and every high thing that exalteth itself against the knowledge of God, and bringing into captivity every thought to the obedience of Christ" (2 Cor. 10:5).

We can't stop our thoughts, of course. They come. But once ungodly thoughts come, we have to say, "No! Down, flesh! I will not entertain that thought." Then you put on the mind of Christ by renewing your mind with the Word of God.

Romans 12:2 NKJV says, "Do not be conformed to this world, but be transformed by the renewing of your mind, that you may prove what is that good and acceptable and perfect will of God." Think of it as washing yourself in the Word—of taking a bath in it. When you immerse yourself in God's Word, the truth of the Word wells up within you and you can effectively come against the attacks of the devil in your mind.

God Is Concerned

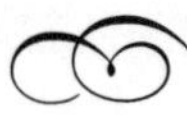

by Lindsay Roberts

One of the most amazing verses in the Bible is found in Matthew 10:30 NKJV where Jesus said, "The very hairs of your head are all numbered." Think about that! God knows us better than we know ourselves. He doesn't just love us in a general sort of way. He's concerned with the intricate details of our lives.

Knowing how much God cares about even the little things in our lives helps us to pray more effectively. Some people think, *Oh, my problem is too small to pray about.* But in this passage of Scripture Jesus explains the value God places on His children and His concern for small things that affect us. He notices when a sparrow falls to the ground, and He assures us that we are of more value than many sparrows. (v. 31.) God wants us to talk to Him about the ordinary needs of our daily lives. He is concerned with our cares whether in the workplace or in our families.

My first thoughts when I get out of bed each morning are to pray for my children. I pray about what they are facing that day. If a child has a dentist appointment, I pray about that. If a child has a ballgame, I pray about the ballgame. Now if we as earthly parents are concerned about these things for our children, how much more is our heavenly Father concerned about their needs—and ours? First Peter 5:7 NLT says, "Give all your worries and cares to God, for he cares about what happens to you." That includes every need and every problem you have, big or small!

The Pieces of the Puzzle

by Taffi L. Dollar
World Changers Church International

Sometimes life can seem like a jumble of mismatched puzzle pieces, and we are left wondering how they all fit together. But God has specific plans for each of our lives, and He sees the finished picture even when we can't.

In order to know God's plans for us, we must learn to hear His voice. The Lord doesn't just speak to the pastor, the teacher, and the prophet. He wants to speak to each one of us—to mothers and fathers, to secretaries and construction workers, to the well-to-do and the down-and-out. The desire of God's heart is that whoever we are and whatever we do, we learn to hear His voice.

You can hear the voice of God and know His heart through His Word: "Now therefore hearken [or listen] unto me O ye children: for blessed are they that keep my ways.... Blessed [happy, fortunate] is the man that heareth me, watching daily at my gates" (Prov. 8:32,34).

It's important that we practice walking side by side with God every day of our lives. He wants to be the friend we confide in. The Lord says if we "watch daily at His gates" we are happy and fortunate. We are to be envied if we wait on God daily, listening to His voice and doing those things which we hear. It is then that the pieces of the puzzle of our lives begin to fall into place, and we are better able to understand what the will of the Lord is for us individually.

God Is Good

by Evelyn Roberts

When Oral was seventeen and dying of tuberculosis, some people would visit him and pray, "Lord, if it be Your will, heal this boy." But Jesus never hesitated to heal anyone. When a leper approached Him, saying, "If thou wilt, thou canst make me clean," Jesus replied, "I will," and He did (Mark 1:40,41).

If you were to say to someone who had never heard of Jesus, "I want you to serve my Jesus, but He won't heal you or meet your needs," how many people do you think would want to serve Him? Not many! But our God is not like that. Matthew 14:14 NKJV says, "Jesus...saw a great multitude, and was moved with compassion toward them, and he healed their sick." I believe it's when people hear that God is good and they learn that He loves them and wants to meet their needs that they will want to serve Him.

Protected by the Blood of Jesus

by Kellie Copeland Kutz
Kenneth Copeland Ministries

Shortly after my cousin Nikki, an on-fire-for-God believer, was killed in an accident involving a drunk driver, I began to seek the Lord to find out how we could make sure this never happened again. That very week, I heard Billye Brim teach on the blood of Jesus, stressing, "We have to plead the blood of Jesus over our families every morning and every night."

As I began to study the Bible on the subject, I read about God supernaturally protecting the Israelites from the plagues sent against Pharaoh and his people for refusing to let God's people go. In Exodus 12, God instituted the Passover to protect the Israelites from the final judgment on the Egyptians: the death of every firstborn.

In Exodus 12:7 KJV, God instructed the Israelites to "take of the blood, and strike it on the two side posts and on the upper door post of the houses." Those who obeyed were protected behind the blood and escaped death. Today, we can apply the blood of Jesus to the "doorposts" of our lives by speaking words of faith.

God is offering us assurance that our loved ones will be protected. We do this by walking in the light of God's Word and appropriating His promise of protection through the blood of Jesus.[1]

Overgrown Cucumbers

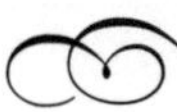

by Lindsay Roberts

Recently I gathered a bushelful of cucumbers I'd planted in my garden, but they were not very impressive. They were overripe and all tangled up with overgrown vines. I asked my mom to cut one open, but she said, "No, these cucumbers are not good." We couldn't even eat them.

I could have picked the cucumbers when they were ready, but I procrastinated. I said, "It's hot; I'll wait a little while." Then the rains came, and I said, "When the ground dries up, I'll go out and pick them." But by the time I finally went to the garden, the weeds had grown up and my cucumber crop was ruined.

Then it hit me! God multiplied my seed and gave me a beautiful harvest, but I failed to receive it because I didn't go out and bring in the harvest when it was ripe! I missed the harvest season!

Similarly, we can miss our harvest from the seeds of faith we have planted if we're not looking for it and expecting it. Many people say, "I give, but I don't expect anything back from God." The Bible says, "God... gives the increase" (1 Cor. 3:7 NKJV). He causes the seeds we plant to grow. Our part is to watch for the harvest season and reach out and receive the increase when it comes. Like a gardener, we can reap the rewards and blessings of our labor and our investment in God's work if we live in expectancy and gather up the harvest.

How God Sees You

by Richard Roberts

When you look at your reflection in the mirror, you don't see the same thing that God sees. You see your exterior, but God sees your heart. (1 Sam. 16:7.) That's how God saw Gideon when He found him cowering from the Midianites and chose him to be Israel's deliverer.

The angel of the Lord appeared to Gideon and said, "The Lord is with you, O valiant warrior" (Judg. 6:12 NASB). Why would the angel call Gideon a mighty warrior? He was a frightened farmer, threshing wheat in a winepress—an unusual place—hoping the Midianites would not find him. But God did not see Gideon as weak and fearful. The Lord looked at him and said, "Go in this your strength and deliver Israel from the hand of Midian" (v. 14). Suddenly Gideon recognized that he had strength he didn't know he had, and he was able to subdue the Midianites.

You, too, have strength from God that you don't know you have! The same strength that God put inside Gideon He has put inside *you.* You are "strengthened with might through His Spirit in the inner man" (Eph. 3:16 NKJV). God operates in the supernatural realm, and He doesn't see you the way natural eyes do. He sees your potential! Just as He told Gideon, "Go in this your strength," that's what He wants you to do also.

God doesn't see you as weak, ineffective, or fearful. He sees you as you *can* be because He's given you the strength to become just that. He sees you the way He created you, and He wants you to see yourself that way, too, through the eyes of faith. When you see yourself the way God sees you, you can conquer life's battles!

Good Luck? Bad Luck? Yeah, Right.

by Kenneth Copeland

Kenneth Copeland Ministries

"It doesn't matter how hard I try, everything still turns out wrong!"

Have you ever felt that way? I have. There was a time in my life when everything I tried fell apart. Back then, I chalked it up to "bad luck."

I've found out since then that there's no such thing as luck—good or bad. It's not luck that determines how things turn out in our lives—it's choices. When we make good ones, things go well for us. When we make bad ones, things go wrong.

There is only one way you can be absolutely sure you've made the right choice, but it is not according to how things operate in this world. You have another, far more powerful option.

Take the record in Mark 4:36-41 for example. The disciples were in a boat, facing a raging storm. No doubt they were doing everything in the world to keep their boat afloat. They were bailing; they were paddling.

They didn't say a word to Jesus, even though He was right there in the boat with them! They didn't ask Him for help until the boat was full of water and they were about to sink. Why? They made a wrong choice. They chose to look to natural solutions instead of supernatural ones. Putting their faith in Jesus never even entered their minds until they were about to drown!

Many well-meaning Christians make that same mistake today. Jesus is right there in the boat with them, but they're depending on natural resources to get them through. They're making wrong choices, and chalking it up to bad luck.

If you're living like that, stop! Get in the Bible. Start living according to His promises. Then, when the storms of life come, you'll know what to do.[1]

Don't Fear! You've Got Power!

by Oral Roberts

Years ago I rode on a plane beside a man who, for the first fifteen minutes of the flight, had a queasy stomach—not because we were in turbulent weather, but because he felt the turbulence of fear in his inner being.

"I can't talk," he said. "I can't collect my thoughts because the first fifteen minutes I'm in a plane, my stomach just turns, and I get sick."

We may all feel fear differently, but we all feel it at times. That's why Paul reminds us in 2 Timothy 1:7 that God has not given us a spirit of fear, but of power and of love and of a sound mind.

One time when the Lord revealed a new direction for my ministry, it was so beyond what I thought I could do that I asked God to "uncall" me. "God, I can't do this," I said. "I've done what You called me to do so far, but this one I can't do."

All of us have times when we don't know what to do, and the burdens get heavy. We let down our faith in God, and we feel fear. Fear is the absence of the spirit of power, love, and a sound mind that God promises us.

Why are we sometimes afraid of doing what God tells us to do? Sometimes we're operating in our own spirit instead of God's. Our own spirit is never equal to the occasion. But, oh, what mighty things we can do when we move into God's Spirit! When we let God's Spirit work in and through us, we can face anything! There's no way we can be afraid! We can look at what we're called to do and boldly say, "Let's go, Lord! Let's start yesterday!"

Talk the Word

by Jerry Savelle

Jerry Savelle Ministries International

Do you ever feel like God blesses some people more than you because He loves them more? That's not true! Blessings and miracles are coming your way every day. You either attract them or you repel them.

I once asked the Lord how we can attract His blessings, and He simply said, "Through your words and actions." Our words and actions either cause blessings to be attracted to us or to pass us by. Some parents tell their children, "You'll never amount to anything. Your daddy didn't amount to anything. He was poor, and you're going to be poor too." So the children grow up saying and believing that about themselves. The blessings and miracles that God sends their way pass them by because God can't agree with that kind of language. It's contrary to His Word.

If you want God's blessings and miracles in your life, talk the Word of God. Start saying what the Bible says and acting like it's true, whether you see the evidence of it or not. If you obey God's commands, Deuteronomy 28:2 says, "All these blessings shall come on thee, and overtake thee." You may be saying, "I don't see any blessings overtaking me. Where are they?"

Don't be moved by what you see. If you've been saying, "Nothing good ever happens to me," then miracles are going past you and on to someone who is saying what the Bible says. Start saying that your miracles are on the way. They're hunting you down right now. If you believe and say what God says about you, then His blessings can find you, and miracles can come to your house!

Amazing Grace

by Bridget Hilliard

New Light Christian Center Church

Part One of Two Parts

When I was growing up, I used to sing, "Amazing Grace! How sweet the sound that saved a wretch like me." I thought God's grace was only about His unmerited favor and His power to save. But then I did a study on the word "grace," and I discovered that it is so much more than that! There is grace for any situation we face. Here are some things the Bible says about grace:

God's grace is more than enough for any problem or need. "My grace is sufficient for thee: for my strength is made perfect in weakness" (2 Cor. 12:9). When you face weakness or obstacles, God's grace is available and more than enough to help you overcome.

God's grace includes everyone. "Grace...was given to each of us individually [not indiscriminately, but in different ways]" (Eph. 4:7 AMP). God gives grace to each of us without discrimination.

God's grace empowers you. "We are fellow workmen.... According to the grace (the special endowment for my task) of God" (1 Cor. 3:9,10 AMP). Whatever assignment God has given you, His grace is a special endowment to help you carry it out.

God's grace brings you the people and the knowledge you need to know for your success. "God is able to make all grace abound toward you; that ye, always having all sufficiency in all things, may abound to every good work" (2 Cor. 9:8). When your heart is right, God can raise up people to use their power, ability, and influence to help you.

Grace Is Accessed by Faith

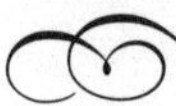

by Bridget Hilliard

New Light Christian Center Church

Part Two of Two Parts

God's grace is accessed by your faith. And Mark 11:23-24 is the model for how you operate in faith to tap into God's grace. Verse 24 NKJV says, "Whatever things you ask when you pray, believe that you receive them, and you will have them." To operate in faith and live the victorious, overcoming life God wants you to live, do these things:

1. Ask the Father, in Jesus' name, to give you the grace you need to do the task He has assigned you. (John 15:16.)
2. Believe the moment you pray that you receive the grace promised in God's Word.
3. Declare or confess what you believe you've received when you prayed. Begin to say, "Thank You, Father, that Your grace is operating in me."
4. Demonstrate or live out what you asked for. Walk with the confidence of someone who has God's grace working in them.
5. Endure and stand steadfast until you see the manifestation of what you're believing God for.

God's grace isn't earned. It has been freely given to us, but it's received by faith. For example, I use a security code to get in the gate surrounding my house. When I'm punching in my code, I'm not trying to earn my way through the gate—the house is already mine. I'm just operating the principle that makes the gate open up to me. In the same way, you're not trying to earn grace when you operate the principles of faith according to God's Word. Grace already belongs to you. His amazing grace begins to work in your life when you operate the principles of faith!

God Believes in You!

by Eastman Curtis
Destiny Church

Have you ever made a huge, industrial-strength boo-boo that looked as though it could never be fixed? Isaiah 59:19 says, "When the enemy shall come in like a flood, the Spirit of the Lord shall lift up a standard against him." That word *standard* literally means "a flag of victory." No matter what your past is, what you're going through, or how badly you've messed up, I have good news for you: God still believes in you!

When trouble comes into your life like a flood, God doesn't turn His back or say, "Okay, you got yourself into this mess. Now you're going to have to get yourself out of it." No! Psalm 46:1 says that God is a very present help in times of trouble. He rolls up His sleeves, grabs hold of the flag of victory, and runs it to the top of your flagpole. He says, "You're not going under; you're going over!"

It's one thing for you to believe in God, but it's another thing to understand that God believes in you. He always expects the best of you. If you've gotten into sin or fallen away from Him, He believes you're coming home. If you're in the middle of a financial mess, He believes you're coming out of it. If you've strayed away from His plan, He believes you're getting it right with Him.

Romans 11:29 NKJV says that the gifts and callings of God are irrevocable. God hasn't changed His mind about you. You may have given up on yourself. Your family or your friends may have given up on you. But God has not given up on you! He believes you're going to make it!

We're Not Civilians!

by Gloria Copeland
Kenneth Copeland Ministries

A soldier in boot camp will jump out of bed before dawn every morning to run and do push-ups. He may not like it, but he'll do it because his commanding officer has ordered him to do it. He endures the discomfort because he knows it's an inescapable part of military life.

A civilian, on the other hand, might start an exercise program, but when the going gets tough, his muscles feel sore and his schedule gets busy, he'll just quit exercising. If someone asks him about it, he might just shrug and say, "I tried exercise, but it didn't work for me."

Some Christians are like that. They hear the Word of faith and they think, *Well, I'll try that.* Then when the hard times come, they give up.

But that's not how it should be. After all, we're not civilians! We're soldiers! We don't *try* faith; we make it our lifestyle. We walk by faith, whether it's hard or easy. We don't do it so we'll be blessed. We do it because we're determined to be pleasing to Jesus. He is our commander-in-chief, and the Bible says without faith, it is impossible to please Him.

Of course, we will end up blessed if we'll walk by faith. We'll end up healed and delivered and prospering in every area of life because God promised we would. That, however, is not our motivation. We're motivated by our desire to serve the Lord. That's what makes us believe His Word, stand fast, and endure when the hard times come.[1]

Your Magic Moment

by Oral Roberts

Every time I encounter a bumblebee, I think of how scientists say it's a scientific impossibility for a bumblebee to fly. The size of its body is too big and too heavy for the size of its wings. But the fact is, the moment that bumblebee stretches out those little undersized wings, it *can* fly. It defies all the scientific impossibilities.

We, too, come against impossibilities in our lives. But the Bible says, "With God nothing is ever impossible" (Luke 1:37 AMP). In every hopeless-looking situation there is a defining moment when we can make the choice to take our little, undersized faith and turn it toward our oversized God, defying all impossibilities. That is our magic moment.

But magic moments don't just happen. They happen because of an act of faith. There have been situations in my life when I've had a lot of faith. But more often I've had to use my "little faith." However, if I start by taking just that first small step of faith, I find that the closer I get to Jesus, the more confident I become. And as I keep on believing God, He starts moving on my behalf in ways I never expected.

Just as the bumblebee stretches forth its inadequate-looking little wings to do the impossible, you can stretch forth your faith—even though it may seem too small to do the job—and open the door for God to do the impossible for you. That's your magic moment, your time for miracles from God!

Medicine for Our Souls

by Joyce Meyer
Joyce Meyer Ministries

What we say is so important because words are containers for power—they can carry either creative or destructive power. They either heal or hurt. They influence the way we act and feel. Our words help determine our attitude and outlook. So much can be learned about a person by what he says—about himself, about others, about everything in general. The Bible says, "Out of the abundance of the heart the mouth speaketh" (Matt. 12:34). You will quickly discover that you must not be led by feelings, speaking out your anxieties, fears, and worries. Rather, you must order your conversation aright, claiming God's promises and calling "those things which be not as though they were" (Rom. 4:17).

The apostle James teaches us that no man or woman can tame the tongue. I had such a battle trying to control my tongue! I could not keep from popping off, and I never seemed to know when to keep still!

As James 3:5-6 points out, "Even so the tongue is a little member, and boasteth great things. Behold, how great a matter a little fire kindleth! And the tongue is a fire, a world of iniquity; so is the tongue among our members, that it defileth the whole body, and setteth on fire the course of nature; and it is set on fire of hell."

We definitely need God's grace to help us watch and control our mouths! One of the ways He helps us is by reminding us of how we should talk. As the old proverb says, "If you can't say something good, don't say anything at all." That is good advice!

Speak every positive thing you can think of out of your mouth—to yourself and to others. Not only will you begin to feel better personally, you will also see some dramatic changes in your life for the better. The Word of God is medicine for your soul, and I believe you can be healed from the sickness of misery brought on by the mouth. God has done it for me, and He'll do it for you.

Today We Remember

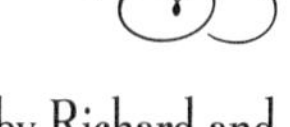

by Richard and Lindsay Roberts

Memorial Day in the United States is the day we remember the men and women who have sacrificed their lives in service for this country. This is a time when we remember and thank God for them.

In John 15:13 Jesus told His disciples, "Greater love hath no man than this, that a man lay down his life for his friends." He willingly laid down His life for us. It seems so unbelievable that someone would sacrifice themselves in our behalf. Yet our servicemen and servicewomen do it—every day.

Although we set aside only one day each year to honor those who have died in service to our country, we should honor them every day. Thank God for our servicemen and servicewomen who are willing to walk out our freedom. We need to continually pray for them and for their families and lift them up every day. Thank God for our freedom, and for the ones who have done so much to create and protect it!

Will you say this prayer with us today?

Father, in the name of Jesus, we pray a prayer cover over our armed forces and the leaders of our nation. We pray for them and we ask in the name of Jesus for divine protection over all of our servicemen and servicewomen. For those who have lost loved ones serving our country, Father, we lift them up before you in the name of Jesus. We pray for the peace that passes all human understanding to enter into their hearts and their lives. We pray a harvest into their lives for what their family members have done, in Jesus' name. Amen.

The 'Perfect' Job

by Lindsay Roberts

After I graduated from college, I planned to go to law school at Oral Roberts University. But first I wanted to take off a year to earn some money. I landed my dream job—a high-paying, prestigious position with opportunity to advance quickly. The firm would even pay my way through law school. It seemed like the perfect job for me.

When I told my mother, she said, "You're not supposed to take the job." "But Mom," I replied, "it's the job of a lifetime!" She said, "No, you're not supposed to take it." The goal I had worked toward through high school and college had finally come to pass, and my mother was saying no!

I had a decision to make: Did I trust the world's lure of money, or did I trust the Holy Spirit who was working in my mother? My mom had a track record of listening to the Lord, and in my heart I knew she was right. I turned down the job. Just a week later, armed robbers invaded the firm's building, and the area where I would have been working was shot up. People were killed.

When my mother told me no, it sounded wacky because the job seemed to be everything I needed. But I knew she was listening to the Lord. Deuteronomy 28:1-2 MESSAGE says, "If you listen obediently to the Voice of God, your God, and heartily obey.... All these blessings will come down on you and spread out beyond you because you have responded to the Voice of God, your God."

The world may be telling you the words you want to hear, but they may not be God's words. No matter how good the situation looks, place your trust in the Lord. Ask for His guidance, then listen for His voice and obey. You'll be glad you did!

'Be Pliable in His Hands'

by Evelyn Roberts

Each one of us has a calling in our heart. Yours is different from mine, and mine is different from yours. But your calling is what you are supposed to do in life. You are not supposed to try to be like anybody else. You are to be like God wants you to be because He chose you for your particular calling.

I prayed all of my life, "God, call me to be a missionary!" But, you know, He never would call me. All the girls around me were getting called. But I wanted to go!

You see, God had a different plan in mind for me. His calling on your life may be different from what you expect. But each one of us has to go with the calling God has put on our heart. Sometimes when He calls you to do something, He doesn't tell you how many years you're going to have to do it. And sometimes He moves you in and out of various situations. The main thing is to be pliable in His hands.

I like to tell the students at Oral Roberts University that God didn't call me to be a missionary, because He wanted me to wash Oral Roberts' socks instead. And, believe it or not, I still do!

When I was growing up, the Pentecostal Holiness people had a camp meeting once a year, and everyone would set up tents and stay for a week or so. One year I took along my guitar to play at a youth meeting, and on my first night there the only vacant seat was next to this tall, young man with black hair and blue eyes. Oral Roberts was the most gorgeous human being I had ever laid eyes on. I thought, *Now he is exactly what I've been hoping for. Exactly!*

We began to talk, and he asked, "Where are you from, and what do you do?" I said I was from Westville and that I was a schoolteacher. When I asked him what he did, he said, "I'm a preacher."

About that time, the Lord whispered in my heart, *Yes, and you're going to marry that young man.* And I did!

JUNE 2

God's Divine Insurance Policy

by Mark and Janet Brazee
Mark Brazee Ministries

No doubt all of us would agree that we are living in dangerous times. But nothing that is happening today has caught God by surprise. The Bible says in 2 Timothy 3:1, "This know also, that in the last days perilous times shall come." God has known about these times all along, and He has provided us with a divine insurance policy—His Word—so we can live in supernatural protection!

In the natural, insurance policies pay off when something has already happened. But God's policy covers us before things happen! Psalm 91:1 says, "He that dwelleth in the secret place of the most High shall abide under the shadow of the Almighty." The "secret place" is a place of protection. To dwell there is to believe that God is big enough to take care of you, and you follow His inward urgings as He speaks to you. As you go about your day, something inside you may say, *Don't leave right now*, or, *Take another route.* That is the built-in compass you have from God—the leading of the Holy Spirit—that makes His divine insurance policy work in your life.

We have a missionary friend who called us one day shortly after September 11, 2001. He said, "What do you think about my returning to the mission field? I'm standing at the airline counter right now, but I have a check in my spirit about going." We told him, "Then don't get on that plane! Follow your inward leading." So he didn't go. You may ask, "What happened?" Nothing happened, because he obeyed the Spirit's inward leading and didn't get on the plane.

Romans 8:14 says, "For as many as are led by the Spirit of God, they are the sons of God." We can expect to be led by God's Spirit, and when we listen and obey Him, we can walk in the protection of His divine insurance policy.

Seize the Moment

by Cathy Duplantis
Jesse Duplantis Ministries

First Peter 1:4 NLT says, "God has reserved a priceless inheritance for his children." This inheritance consists of the wonderful promises in God's Word that are rightfully ours as believers! God has already given them to us. But we have to seize the moment and lay hold on them.

That brings to mind the story of the birth of Esau and Jacob found in Genesis 25:24-26 NKJV, which says, "Her [Rebekah's] days were fulfilled for her to give birth, indeed there were twins in her womb. And the first came out red. He was like a hairy garment all over; so they called his name Esau. Afterward his brother came out, and his hand took hold of Esau's heel; so his name was called Jacob."

As Jacob was being born, he grabbed hold, or seized, Esau's heel. If a newborn baby could reach out and seize what would become his inheritance—Jacob would receive Esau's birthright when they were older—how much more should we grab hold of what we need from God?

As believers, we have received an inheritance from God that provides everything we need and more. His Word says in John 10:10 AMP, "Jesus came that they [His believers] may have and enjoy life, and have it in abundance (to the full, till it overflows)." But, like Jacob, it's up to us to seize the moment and grab hold of what God has for us. There is no need to go without when God has given us an inheritance that can transform our circumstances!

The Secret of Life

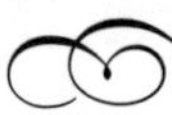

by Oral Roberts

Through the years I've had people tell me, "I don't believe in miracles." And my reply has always been, "You will when you need one." I believe the secret of life is not only believing in miracles, but expecting to receive them.

Acts 3 tells the story of a lame man who was expecting to receive. "A man crippled from birth was being carried to the temple gate called Beautiful, where he was put every day to beg.... When he saw Peter and John about to enter, he asked them for money.... Peter said, 'Look at us!'" So the man gave them his attention, expecting to get something from them. That's a powerful statement.

Then Peter, knowing that the man might not be looking at them and expecting to receive what he could give him, said, "Silver or gold I do not have, but what I have I give you. In the name of Jesus Christ of Nazareth, walk" (vv. 1-6 NIV).

Peter was saying, "A miracle is coming toward you. It's here! Now seize it with your faith." The lame man's expectancy caused his faith to rise, and instantly the man's feet and ankles became strong. He jumped to his feet and began to walk. (vv. 7-8 NIV.) He entered the temple walking, jumping, and praising God. The miracle changed his life forever. He had found the secret of life!

God is a God of action, and unless we throw up some type of resistance, He's continually moving toward us with His miracles. The secret of life is to expect God's miracles and rise up in faith and receive them!

Seek Him

by Richard Roberts

Many people today are seeking after "things"—fame, fortune, and personal pleasure. They find themselves working hard to achieve what they feel is important, but they never feel complete or at rest. Perhaps they are overlooking the most important thing—seeking after the Lord.

God is not hard to find if you seek Him. Deuteronomy 4:29 NIV says, "If from there you seek the Lord your God, you will find him if you look for him with all your heart and with all your soul." Psalm 9:10 NIV says, "Those who know your name will trust in you, for you, Lord, have never forsaken those who seek you."

Are we to seek the Lord only when it's convenient? I believe God is saying, "Seek Me with your whole heart, with your whole soul. Seek Me in every area of your life. Seek Me in the morning. Seek Me at noon, in the afternoon, and in the midnight hour."

The psalmist shows us how to seek God:

"O God, you are my God, earnestly I seek you; my soul thirsts for you, my body longs for you.... Because your love is better than life, my lips will glorify you. I will praise you as long as I live, and in your name I will lift up my hands. My soul will be satisfied as with the richest of foods; with singing lips my mouth will praise you. On my bed I remember you; I think of you through the watches of the night.... My soul clings to you; your right hand upholds me" (Ps. 63:1,3-8 NIV).

The rewards for seeking God are innumerable. To name a few—He never forsakes you, He upholds you, and He gives you rest and peace of mind. What rewards!

Inspiration From the Almighty

by Marilyn Hickey

Marilyn Hickey Ministries

I remember when our fifteen-year-old daughter, Sarah, came to us and said, "Mother, next year I will be sixteen. You know, everybody in our school, when they turn sixteen, their parents buy them a car. Are you and dad going to buy me a car?"

I thought, *I don't even want to think about your getting a driver's license and certainly not a car.* But I said, "Well, Sarah, we'll pray about it."

My husband, Wally, and I prayed about it for a couple of weeks, and God gave us an inspiration from the Almighty when Sarah came to us and asked, "Well, Mother, what did God tell you and Dad?"

"Well," I answered, "He told us a way that you can buy your own car, and you can be the first person at Lutheran High who buys her own car." Oh, how her face dropped! But I continued, "Here's what He told us. You have saved $1,000. You always work every summer," because she worked in the ministry and did data processing. "Next summer you could save another $1,000. Then usually you work over spring break, and you work over Christmas break. That gives you some extra money. Sometimes you get some money for Christmas. You would have enough money to buy a used Volkswagen. By the time you're sixteen you could buy a Volkswagen, and you would have paid for it yourself! Sarah, you are a high achiever. I never want to hurt that. I always want to help it. This is what God showed me."

She bought it. I mean, she worked and worked and bought a little orange Volkswagen. She drove it all through her senior year. She told me once, "You know, kids come up to me at lunchtime wanting to borrow my car, and I say, 'You can't borrow my car. I worked hard to get this car, and I'm not letting anybody borrow it!'"

God Fights Our Battles

by Lindsay Roberts

Second Chronicles 20 tells the story of a great and miraculous victory King Jehoshaphat of Judah won when he was threatened by three enemy armies. They were so big and powerful that he knew he couldn't beat them. But then he received this word from the Lord:

"Do not be afraid or discouraged.... For the battle is not yours, but God's.... Take up your positions; stand firm and see the deliverance the Lord will give you.... Go out to face them tomorrow, and the Lord will be with you" (vv. 15,17 NIV).

When Jehoshaphat and his army gathered for battle the next day, he appointed singers to go ahead of the troops, singing praises to God. And as they began to sing, the Lord caused the enemy armies to turn on themselves and destroy one another. They were totally defeated!

Notice, the first thing God told Jehoshaphat was, "Don't be afraid or discouraged. The battle is not yours, but God's." There are times when we do have to go to battle, whether it's for our country, our family, our finances, our health, or whatever. But God does not want us to be afraid. Our job is to take our position of praise and look to Him to back us. As we put our full trust in God, His promise is that He will be with us and fight our battles for us!

'Junk Food Christians'

by Jerry Savelle
Jerry Savelle Ministries International

My foreign friends tell me that America has the best junk food in the world. And we do! But we know we can't live on junk food alone. Our bodies need nutrition. You can't survive on spiritual junk food either. Yet many Christians want a "comfortable" Christianity, one where they don't have to make any kind of sacrifice and there are no demands on their lives. I call them "junk food Christians."

This is not a new phenomenon. Everywhere Jesus went people followed Him, but not always for the right reason. Many of them just wanted to see the miracles and signs and wonders that Jesus wrought. But when He began to talk about discipleship and tell them how they should live their lives, He was stepping on their toes, so they moved on.

Second Timothy 4:3,4 NLT says, "A time is coming when people will no longer listen to right teaching. They will follow their own desires and will look for teachers who will tell them whatever they want to hear. They will reject the truth." I think that time is now.

The Message translation says, "People will have no stomach for solid teaching, but will fill up on spiritual junk food." Some people want to see the spectacular, but they don't want to hear a message that would require them to change their lifestyle to line up with God's Word. Change is important. It's a part of growth. If we are satisfied to remain as we are, we are going to miss out on God's best. But if we are willing to change and make an unwavering commitment to walk with Christ, there is no limit to how He can bless us!

Love Responds Lovingly

by Lindsay Roberts

The Bible tells us in 1 John 4:7 NKJV, "Beloved, let us love one another, for love is of God." It's easy to love someone who's loveable. I don't know about you, but I know some people who make walking in love hard! However, the good news is that we don't have to love the unlovable in our own strength. Romans 5:5 NKJV says, "The love of God has been poured out in our hearts by the Holy Spirit who was given to us." So we can draw on the love of God that came to live in us when we were born again.

We are able to love because we have been loved by God. First John 4:9 NKJV goes on to say, "In this the love of God was manifested toward us, that God has sent His only begotten Son into the world, that we might live through Him." He loved us so much that He sent Jesus to die for us, and we can love people through Him!

The love of God that's in us can cause us to respond lovingly to others if we let it. When we think of it like that, love is more than a good feeling. It's not an option. It is supposed to be demonstrated. Love is an act of our will.

God is love, and the closer you get to God through His Word and through a relationship with Him, the closer you get to love. And the closer you get to love, the more you can let that love flow through you even to those who are hard to love. It's all about establishing a relationship with God.

'I Am Happy!'

by Joyce Meyer
Joyce Meyer Ministries

One of the greatest things anybody can give you is a blessing. The Bible says the blessing overtakes the curse. No matter what has been done to you, said about you, spoken over you, or happened to you, it is finished because we are the blessed of the Lord.

You are precious in His sight. To be blessed is to be happy. I can remember a lot of years in my life when I said, "God, I just want to be happy." I was sitting here this morning, and I thought, *I am happy! I am happy! Everything in my life may not be perfect, but I'm happy!*

There are too few people in this world who are satisfied. They wander from thing to thing, trying to fill the hole they have inside them and can't find anything because it's a God-shaped hole that only He can fill. The Bible says it is wonderful to have godliness with contentment. When you have that, you can have that contented feeling no matter what your circumstances. That is what it means to be blessed, to be happy, to be envied, to be spiritually prosperous.

I am spiritually prosperous, which means I can hear from God. I can be led by the Holy Ghost. I've got discernment. I've got the news ahead of time. I'm not living in deception. With life, joy, satisfaction, and God's favor and salvation, regardless of my outward conditions, I am blessed.

I bless you now. And now that you know what it means to be blessed, you can get more excited about it!

Frustrating Decisions

by Richard Roberts

Perhaps you have heard about the man who complained about how hard he had to work. When a friend asked him what he did for a living, the man said, "I sort potatoes."

"That doesn't sound too difficult," commented the friend.

"Oh, it isn't the work," replied the man. "It's all those decisions!"

The illustration is humorous, but the fact remains that decisions can be most frustrating. They can sap your strength, your vitality, and your joy. But God did not leave you to wander aimlessly...searching...and never knowing His will. He has left a simple biblical formula to guide you in Proverbs 3:5-6 NKJV:

1. Trust in the Lord with all of your heart.
2. Lean not on your own understanding.
3. In all your ways acknowledge Him.

What happens if you do these three things? He shall direct your paths! Do you have a decision to make that is troubling you? Instead of fretting and worrying, why not try God's plan?

An Act of Committal

by Evelyn Roberts

Are you troubled over a problem for which there seems to be no answer? Are you bent under a burden from which there seems to be no rest? If you are, take heart in this story from 2 Kings 4:8-37:

God gave a barren Shunammite woman a son, fulfilling a prophecy given to her by the prophet Elisha, a frequent visitor to her home. One morning the boy fell ill, and by noon he was dead.

The woman's heart was broken. What was she to do? Her thoughts flew to the consecrated room in her home that she had set aside for Elisha. Because he was a man of God, to her this room meant the presence of God.

Carrying her precious burden to the room, the woman laid the child on Elisha's bed. Then she went out, shutting the door behind her. With that act, she committed her son entirely to God. No wonder she received him back to life!

This is a beautiful picture of committal—laying our problems, our burdens, and our afflictions before the Lord and leaving them there. Our greatest temptation is not to shut the door but keep committing and recommitting our problems to Him, thinking that God needs our help.

We should know that God's power is more than sufficient for any problem we face. It takes faith to "shut the door" and go out, leaving our burden entirely in God's hands, but when we do, we give Him control of the situation and allow Him to fully work in our lives.

A Thousand Times More

by Oral Roberts

First of Five Parts

The Lord gave me a poem, and I really think that Moses said it. To his people, I think he said, "You're a book not yet written. You're a poem not yet composed. You're a song not yet sung. You're a future not yet fulfilled. You're a miracle not yet happened." But I want to say to you, "You are a book that God is writing. You are a poem that God is composing. You are a song that God is singing. You are a dream that God is dreaming. You are a destiny that God is completing. You're a future that God is fulfilling. You're a miracle about to explode."

We once invited a couple to our house. The woman was a real woman of God, and while we were talking after dinner, she said, "Oral, have you ever seen this verse?" She opened her Bible to Deuteronomy 1:11 and read about *God making you a thousand times more.* She said, "My husband and I accepted this dinner invitation because God told me to show you this Scripture." (And I have been running with that Scripture ever since!)

I asked God, "What does this mean? It really can't mean what it says because Jesus promised us thirty-fold, sixty-fold, and a hundredfold. That is all we've ever claimed." And He answered, "Take your pen and paper and write." Then He began to explain to me, "Write these nine things down, and I'll tell you what the thousand times more is."

The first was, "You shall possess the land. The devil doesn't own anything. He was kicked out. He's a renegade. He's bound for hell. And you have no right to let him steal from you one inch of ground, one piece of lumber, one piece of furniture, one car, one dollar." He continued, "You shall possess the land. Tell the people they are to have land. They are to have a house. They're to have a car. They are to have money in their pockets. I'm not pleased with their being sick and tired and broke all the time. I can't run My kingdom with people who are sick and broke all the time. You tell them to possess the land."

Introduced to America

by Oral Roberts

Second of Five Parts

Evelyn and I started this healing ministry in 1947. We were living in Enid, Oklahoma, when the call from God was revealed that we were to move to Tulsa. A preacher there had set up a big thousand-seat tent. He had been trying to fill it but hadn't been able to because of the weather and other things. He had heard I was entering the healing ministry and wanted me to preach on Tuesday and Wednesday nights and pray for the sick.

I preached to a couple hundred people, and the Lord began to save and heal. I was asked to stay until Sunday, then was asked to stay the next week—and I stayed nine weeks!

During that time, a very angry young man stood across the street with a revolver aimed at my head. My associates said to me, "Reverend Roberts, we cannot permit you to go on this stage tonight. We have just learned that there is someone who is going to shoot you tonight."

Suddenly, these words came from my mouth: "It is just as near heaven from this spot as it is anywhere else on this earth." I walked out on the stage and could almost feel the bullets hitting me as I walked toward the microphone. The moment I began to speak, I forgot someone was there to kill me. The man pulled the trigger, but the bullet missed me by twelve inches. He was put in jail, and when asked why he shot at me, he said, "I wanted to kill him!"

The next morning the headline in the Tulsa papers and across the nation was: *Young Evangelist Is Shot At!* Oral Roberts was introduced to America in one day. Everybody knew about me—a man who prayed for the sick.

When God's presence comes into me, something happens. He separates me from myself. He fills me with His presence and glory so that when I speak, it's like the Lord speaking. It illumines my mind and puts strength in my body. The world looks different and heaven looks brighter. Jesus looks sweeter. Everything changes with the anointing. It bears the burden.

It Is Our Land!

by Oral Roberts

Third of Five Parts

We walked into a little house that a preacher friend had been living in, and the Spirit said, "This is your house." But my friend told us he had sold the house to a man who was coming that evening to close the deal.

When I thought our little house might be sold to another man, I got into my car and drove to a nearby park. I laid my head on the steering wheel and began to cry and pray. I told God that I had no place for my wife and children, and I reminded Him that He had told me I was to take the healing power of Jesus to the uttermost bounds of the earth. It was then that I felt a deep settled peace go down into my stomach. I knew that I knew that I knew.

That night my friend said the buyer did not show up, and he offered to sell the house to me for a $3,000 down payment. The problem was that I had only $25 to my name.

The next morning the owner went with me to the savings and loan company to sign papers to buy the house. I was handed a pen to sign the papers to buy the house, when much to my surprise the man said, "Oral, wait a minute. My wife and I are going to build a new house next year, and we don't need this $3,000 now. If it's alright, you can wait a year to pay it." That was one of the narrowest escapes my faith ever had!

God wanted us to possess the land. It was in that little house that this ministry was born. During the next nine weeks, there were hundreds of letters from people from different states. Preachers from coast to coast were calling to ask us to come and pray for the sick. It all happened on that little piece of land in that little five-room house which we turned into an office until we could afford to build a new office.

God said, "You are to possess the land! You are to rescue it from the devil. It is your land. It is your property." God said we are to own this earth. We are to own the wealth of this world. It's laid up for us, and it's time that we reached up and pulled it down.

A Trick of the Devil

by Oral Roberts

Fourth of Five Parts

The Lord said, "You shall be the head and not the tail. You shall lead and not follow. Tell My people that I am not happy with their borrowing habits, for they are to lend and not borrow. They can give and receive back so multiplied that one day the people of God will have the biggest loan service the world has ever known, and we can take care of our own."

God continued, "No weapon formed against you shall prosper." The devil has lots of weapons, and we get worried to death because he does. But the Bible says that God has weapons that are mighty to the pulling down of strongholds.

When I began my healing ministry, my song leader, who was my age, was my buddy, my best friend. But in a matter of days, he became my worst enemy. He came to me insisting he wanted in on my "racket."

I asked, "What racket? What do you mean?"

"This healing racket! People are getting healed. They're going to give you a lot of money, and I want my part of it."

"Sir," I answered, "I've never thought about being rich in my whole life. It has never entered my mind."

I went home and said, "Evelyn, I'm not going to stay in the healing ministry. People are going to think it's a racket."

Oral," she answered, "that's a trick of the devil. And you just put it aside."

Suddenly the people in the church were becoming cold toward me. I knew that man had spread the word that my healing ministry was a racket.

Evelyn and I prayed, "Lord, when this man eats, don't let the food digest. When he sleeps, give him no rest. When he works, give him no fulfillment until he makes this right and takes his hand off God's anointed." Later this man repented before the people, and today he's one of my best friends.

Learning Seed-Faith

by Oral Roberts

Fifth of Five Parts

We were conducting a crusade in the big tent in Seattle, Washington. A man named Mr. Skrinde was sitting in the audience one night, an immigrant from Sweden. He was in his sixties and had invented something for the Jeep. The Jeeps had been greatly used during the war, but something was wrong with the axles. After the war, they were trying to solve this problem in the Jeep. Mr. Skrinde came up with an invention, but it was turned down. When he received that rejection, he just shriveled up in his body. He worked in a rest home, making only a few dollars a month.

This particular evening, I was telling my audience about building ORU and talking about Seed-Faith. This precious man decided to give me $10 as Seed-Faith. Mr. Skrinde came up to me, and as I looked at him, the Lord gave me an idea. While I was talking about Seed-Faith, I said, "Now when you people get home, if you have a basement, go down there and look around. If you have an attic, go up there and look around. And be expectant for new ideas." God only knows why I said that, because it just came into my mind.

A light came on in Brother Skrinde's mind because he knew what was up in his attic in the trunk. It was the drawings he'd made for the Jeep company. He went into the attic, got those plans, made a few changes, and sent them back to the company.

Soon the company called him, saying, "This fits exactly. You're going to get an override on all the Jeeps that are made, because we've been losing millions of dollars on recalls."

Brother Skrinde became a multimillionaire overnight! He began to give to his church and built a new sanctuary. He became one of the largest supporters of the building of Oral Roberts University.

God said, "You tell the people I'll never leave them nor forsake them. Tell them to read Romans 4:17, which says, "Call those things that be not as though they were." God explains His own faith nature, and He tells us to have faith. One translation of Mark 11:22 says, "Have the faith of God," which means have the God-kind of faith.

An Easy Yoke

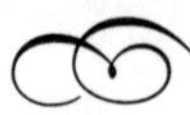

by Lindsay Roberts

The Bible says in 2 Corinthians 6:14, "Be ye not unequally yoked together with unbelievers: for what fellowship hath righteousness with unrighteousness?" So it matters whom you spend time with and connect yourself to.

What does "unequally yoked" mean? My grandfather was a farmer, and he taught me about yokes. If a yoke doesn't fit oxen right, it's called "uneasy." If it's a proper fit, it's called "easy." Jesus said in Matthew 11:30, "My yoke is easy, and my burden is light." Being yoked or connected together with Jesus is a good fit for you, but being yoked with someone who isn't a Christian or doesn't have the same spiritual values is not a good fit.

If a yoke is easy and fits properly around the ox's neck, the burden will be light, and the yoke will not break the ox's neck. But if the yoke is not easy and it is not properly balanced, the burden will be heavy, and the yoke will break the ox's neck.

Ironically, if you put a strong ox beside a weak one, the weak one isn't going to be the one that gets hurt. The stronger one that is doing all the work and pulling the load will get dragged down by the weaker one. The stronger one can even end up with a broken neck!

That's why God tells us, "Don't be unequally yoked." You may be the one out front working hard for God and pulling the spiritual load in a relationship, but if your yoke doesn't fit, you'll feel the results. Be careful about being unevenly yoked to unbelievers or spiritually weak people. Of course, reach out and help them all you can, but don't get yoked together with them. God wants your yoke to be easy and your burdens to be light!

A Triple Miracle!

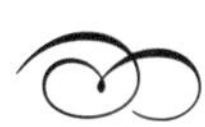

by Richard Roberts

A while back we had a need in the television department at ORU. We discussed the need among ourselves and figured out what it would cost to take care of it. Although we had a real need and we had exactly the amount of money it would take to resolve it, we decided it was not the time to take care of it. Rather, we would sow that amount of money as an extra seed into the lives of others.

The next day we got a group of our employees together, and I said, "Let's not look at what we have need of. Let's not even focus on that right now. Let's sow into others' needs." We sowed our seed, using the money that would have taken care of our own need.

Now giving is an eternal principle. Everything in life can be looked upon as a seed—your love, your time, your prayers, and, yes, your money. And when you sow your seed, God says in Luke 6:38 that He will multiply it back to you. And that's what He did. By the time I arrived at the television studio that evening—less than twenty-four hours after sowing our seed—the need in the television department had been met *three times over!*

Now you cannot figure out something like that in the natural. It's God, and He will not be figured out! Isaiah 55:9 says, "As the heavens are higher than the earth, so are my ways higher than your ways, and my thoughts than your thoughts." We sowed the seed, and God provided a triple miracle!

As you sow your seed and plant it against your need, expect God to multiply it back to you—*good measure, pressed down, and shaken together, and running over* (Luke 6:38).

Sitting on the Edge of His Seat

by Kenneth Copeland
Kenneth Copeland Ministries

All my life, my mama said, "Kenneth, Jesus is coming this year."

I would say, "Is that right, Mama?"

"Yes," she'd say, "He's coming this year, so you had better get yourself straightened out!"

Even though Jesus didn't come when Mama said, she was right—JESUS IS COMING! I don't know when, but I do know He's coming—sooner than most people think.

We are living in a whole new time frame. From the very beginning, God has given us the time frame in which He will work with mankind. It's a seven-day time frame—where a day is as a thousand years. For example, we see in Genesis that God created the earth in six days, and rested on the seventh. Then He gave mankind a 6,000-year lease on the earth. Jesus was born 4,000 years into that time frame—or on the fourth day. For all practical purposes, 2,000 years have come and gone since Jesus' ministry—which is 6,000 years since Adam was created.

Where does that put us on our spiritual clock? We have entered that sliver of time between Adam's lease on earth and the period of time we read about in today's verses. You and I are being squeezed between 6,000 years of time behind us and another 1,000 years ahead of us. The 1,000 years facing us is the time when Jesus will reign over the earth, which is the first time since Adam's fall that humanity will be totally and completely out of contact with Satan.

I'm telling you, Jesus is coming! He's about to rise off His heavenly throne and return to earth. He may not have stood up yet, but I guarantee you, He is on the edge of His seat![1]

Jesus Has Time

by Evelyn Roberts

As I've studied the life of Jesus, I've come to this conclusion: Jesus always had time for a healing miracle. No matter where He was going...what He was doing...how tired He was...or how difficult the need...Jesus took time to heal all who came to Him. If someone in need crossed His path, He stopped to help them.

There was the time when Jesus was about to enter the city of Nain just as a funeral procession was leaving the city. As He approached the town gate, a dead person was being carried out—the only son of his mother, and she was a widow.... He went up and touched the coffin, and those carrying it stood still. He said, "Young man, I say to you, get up!" The dead man sat up and began to talk, and Jesus gave him back to his mother. (Luke 7:12,14,15 NIV.)

There was the time when a woman with an issue of blood made her way through the crowd, determined to touch Jesus' garment, and He stopped and took time for her. Jesus turned and saw her. "Take heart, daughter," He said, "your faith has healed you." And the woman was healed from that moment. (Matt. 9:22 NIV.)

There was the time when a centurion asked Jesus to heal his servant, and He quickly responded. (Luke 7:1-10.)

And there was the time when Jesus was on His way to Jerusalem and a blind man named Bartimaeus shouted out to Him, "Son of David, have mercy on me!" And Jesus stopped to heal him. (Mark 10:46-52.)

Jesus was never too busy to heal those who were hurting in Bible days, and He isn't too busy to heal you today.

Are You Willing To Pray and Believe for a New Life?

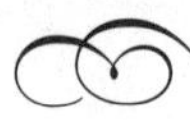

by Lindsay Roberts

What is it in your life that has you in a beggar's robe today? Are you like Bartimaeus—sitting in despair by the side of life's road, hoping against hope that something or someone will have pity on you?

Today is your day to start taking action—to become so dissatisfied with the condition the devil has put you in that you start crying out to God with a loud, persistent cry until you get the miracle you need!

Are you in need of a physical miracle? A financial miracle? A healing in your emotions? A healing in your mind? Is there something in your family or something in your past that has you down? Are you wrapped in a cloak of guilt or shame? Then hear these words from the Bible:

"Knowing the time, that now it is high time to awake out of sleep: for now is our salvation nearer than when we believed. The night is far spent, the day is at hand: let us therefore cast off the works of darkness, and let us put on the armour of light" (Rom. 13:11,12).

Let's pray together for this to be the day in which your deliverance begins:

Heavenly Father, I come to You in the name of Jesus, and I ask You to hear my cry. I don't want things in my life to go on as they are. I want You to come into my life, into my situation, and to work the miracle that only You can work. I trust You to do that, and I make a decision today to cry out to You for this miracle until I receive Your answer. I cast off my beggar's robe right now. I'm setting it in my mind and heart as of this moment and this prayer that I'm never going back to the way things have been. I'm expecting a change in my life and circumstances. I'm expecting old things to become completely new. I pray this in the name of Jesus. Amen.

Heavenly Vision

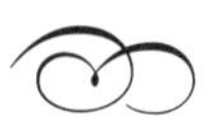

by Richard Roberts

When Paul stood before King Agrippa to give a defense of his faith, he made this bold declaration: "I was not disobedient unto the heavenly vision" (Acts 26:19).

What a powerful statement that is! First, Paul knew that there was a heavenly vision for his life. He knew that God had a plan, a dream, a goal, a purpose for his life. Second, Paul had made a decision in his life to follow the heavenly vision and not his own.

What is the vision of your life today? What are your hopes, your dreams? What's on the "back burner" of your thinking? Is it a heavenly vision, or is it your own? Are you even aware that there is a heavenly vision for your life?

I know what it's like to try to live my life according to my own vision. I grew up reading what the newspapers said about my father. I'd read in the Bible what happened to some people who believed in God. And I thought, *If that's Christianity, I don't want any part of it.* I made my own plans, left home, and rejected God, my family, and the heavenly vision. I pursued my vision—to be a nightclub singer and a professional athlete.

The day came when I found myself flat on my back in a hospital bed, sicker than I ever knew a young person could get. I was alone and without friends in a place miles away from home. And as many people do when they get desperate, I began to call out to God.

The good news is that when you do call out to God, He answers! Step by step, God healed my body, led me back home and to Oral Roberts University. And the day came when I chose heaven's vision for my life instead of my own. I chose to be God's man, and when He called me to preach, I chose to accept that call.

Are you traveling down the wrong road in your life? Trade your vision in for God's heavenly vision for your life! There's no better way than His!

Get Out Your Umbrella!

by Eastman Curtis
Destiny Church

Nothing is too difficult for God. You may be thinking, *God would never help someone like me.* But He truly wants to set you free from whatever is hindering you from receiving His blessings. He wants to give you His very best.

There is a powerful Scripture found in James 1:5 NKJV. It says:

"If any of you lacks wisdom, let him ask of God, who gives to all liberally and without reproach, and it will be given to him."

Now, read that Scripture again, and substitute for the word "wisdom" whatever it is that you lack. For example, *If any of you lacks* finances, *if any of you lacks* health.... The Scripture is saying that when you have a need, take it to God, who provides His blessings in abundance. And He will not scold you for asking.

God doesn't play favorites, yet many of us disqualify ourselves from His blessings because we dwell on our shortcomings. But here is the good news: God is not a faultfinder! In fact, the whole reason that Jesus went to the Cross was to cleanse you, wash you, and set you free from all guilt and condemnation so that you can receive everything that God has for you!

God isn't sitting in heaven with an eyedropper, waiting to give you just a drop or two of His blessings. He's the God of more than enough, "able to do exceedingly abundantly above all that we ask or think, according to the power that works in us" (Eph. 3:20 NKJV). Ezekiel 34:26 says that He sends down *showers* of blessings. So take your needs to God; then get out your umbrella!

Stay Focused on God

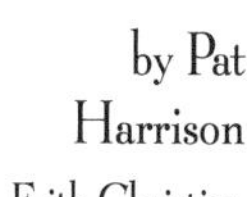

by Pat Harrison
Faith Christian Fellowship International

All of us face situations at times that can easily distract us from what we're called to do for God. I was facing a distracting situation one day, and I thought, *Lord, I don't know if I can do this.* But God told me, "Yes, you can." Then He began to talk to me about staying focused. He said, "But you must stay focused on Me to be able to do what I have asked you to do."

How do you stay focused on God? You abide in Him through His Word. Jesus told His disciples, "If you will abide in Me, I will abide in you." (John 15:4.) Abiding in God means developing a relationship with Him through prayer, the Holy Spirit, and studying His Word.

Jesus went on to say, "If you abide in Me, and My words abide in you, you will ask what you desire, and it shall be done for you" (John 15:7 NKJV). That's basically what the Lord was saying to me: "Stay focused on Me. Speak what I speak. Do what I do. Then you become a magnet that draws everything to you that you need."

Staying focused on God and abiding in Him are choices that you make. It's a matter of deciding, *Okay, I'm going to stay focused. God's Word says I can, so I can.* When the Word of God is your foundation, you can go to the Word before your difficulties become distractions so that you remain focused on God.

I have found that it takes no more effort to focus on God's Word than it does to focus on worry. In fact, focusing on God is a lot easier, because when you get into worry, you become anxious. The "what ifs" start, and your mind begins to race. But peace comes when you focus on God's Word. You can relax and say, "God's Word is truth, and it's working in my life!"

Dream...and Make No Excuses!

by Richard Roberts

Have you been holding on to a dream, a vision that God has given you, but in the natural it appears there's no way it will come to pass? This isn't the time to quit. It's the time to believe that the seeds you've sown and the vision God has given you are both going to come to pass.

I recently heard from a man who saw us on TV back in 1988. He said, "I was living in a little efficiency apartment in Nashville, thinking my dream of being a songwriter was about to die. I turned on the TV and your program was on. You said, 'There's someone watching who's about to give up on their dream. Don't do it!'

"That sparked something in me," he told me. "Over the next few days a song began to germinate in me, and a few weeks later I finished it." That song eventually became a No. 1 hit for country singer Randy Travis, and he has written fifty-five hits since then!

Now that man could have given up his dream of writing songs, but he heard the word of knowledge from God, believed it, and acted on it. Some people hear a word from God and say, "That's not for me. That's baloney!" Those people make excuses for why their dream doesn't come to pass. But others hear God's voice and say, "I stretch my faith, I release my faith, and I go into agreement with God." They put action to what they believe, and God honors their faith.

Do you have a dream or vision that needs to be restored? Jesus said, "Be not faithless, but believing" (John 20:27). Use your faith and believe God!

God Is Against Sickness

by Oral Roberts

Did you know that God never made anyone sick? He is against sickness! In no place in the Bible will you ever find that Jesus was for sickness. He was against it. That means God doesn't go around giving people cancer or other terrible diseases. He doesn't go around seeking to hurt people. Everything that is good is from God. Everything that is bad is from the devil. "And every good and perfect gift is from above, coming down from the father of the heavenly lights, who does not change like shifting shadows" (James 1:17 NIV).

I respect doctors, and one reason is that they have grasped this eternal truth and are against sickness and for health. Consciously or unconsciously, they have a pretty good theology of healing. Sometimes I wish we Christians had such a good theology of healing. Then we might be less inclined to argue about whether it's God's will to heal or not. We would approach people who have hurts and ills with Christ's own positive attitude of wholeness for them.

I speak out of experience when I make that statement, for I know that healing begins in this life. You have this wonderful claim upon the very real promise of God, which is intended personally for you and your loved ones in the *now.* God is against sickness in your body, and He is for your healing. Believe that, and reach out to Him with your faith to receive the healing you need today!

Wimps Don't Witness

by Billy Joe Daugherty

Victory Christian Center Church and School

What motivates you? What is your passion? What stirs your life? Now ask yourself, "Why did Jesus give His life on the cross?" There's only one answer, and that is that Jesus loves people, and His passion is for them to become part of His family.

In Matthew 4:18-19 Jesus saw Peter and Andrew casting their nets into the sea. He said to them, "Follow me, and I will make you fishers of men." And they left their nets and followed Him. Do you have a passion for leading people to Jesus?

In Luke 15:3-7 Jesus talks about a man who had a hundred sheep, and one of them became lost. Not wanting to lose even one, the shepherd left the ninety-nine sheep to search for the lost one. When he found it, he called everyone to rejoice. That's also the will of our Father. He doesn't want even one soul to perish. He said, "There is more joy in heaven over one sinner who repents than over ninety-nine righteous people who need no repentance."

Luke 15:11-32 tells of the father who had two sons, and the younger son said to him, "I want the money that's coming to me." He received his inheritance, wasted it on wild living, and ended up in the pigpen feeding pigs. There he remembered his father and said, "I'm going home!" His father saw his son coming at a distance and ran to embrace him. He said, "Get a robe and shoes, and a ring for his finger. Kill the fatted calf! Let's have prime rib and barbecue tonight, for my son has returned!" Likewise, Jesus says, there is joy when one sinner comes home.

Wimps don't witness. It takes a man or a woman of God with passion to witness boldly to others. And this is the hour when God is speaking to us to be witnesses for Jesus Christ.

June 29

The Love Walk

by Joyce Meyer
Joyce Meyer Ministries

I believe one of the biggest reasons for most of our unhappiness is just plain old-fashioned selfishness. "What about me?" we ask. If we're always dissatisfied, always needing another miracle, and thinking, *Oh, this will do it!* we're living in the flesh. Living in the Spirit produces peace and joy.

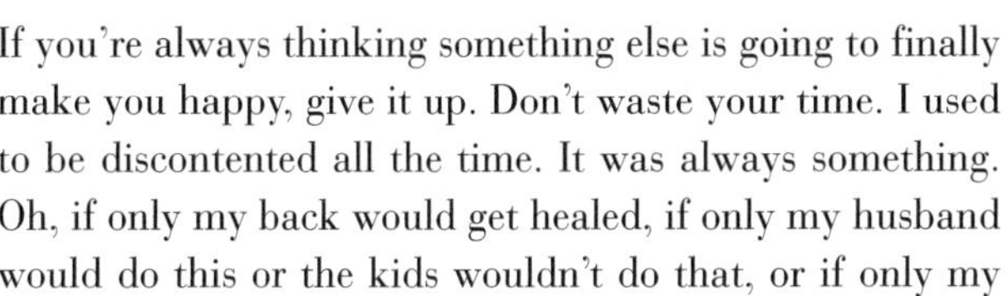

If you're always thinking something else is going to finally make you happy, give it up. Don't waste your time. I used to be discontented all the time. It was always something. Oh, if only my back would get healed, if only my husband would do this or the kids wouldn't do that, or if only my ministry would grow....

To make a long story short, I discovered that if I'm not satisfied, it must be that I'm not hooked up right with God's system, because Jesus says, "I give you living water. If you drink this living water, you shall *never* thirst again" (John 4:14).

I found out that I didn't have a love walk. I spoke in tongues, but I didn't walk in love. I wanted miracles and I wanted the gifts of the Spirit, but I was more interested in the gifts than the fruit. The Bible doesn't say you'll know Christians by their gifts but by their love. Jesus said in John 13:34-35, "A new commandment I give unto you, That ye love one another, as I have loved you.... By this shall all men know that ye are my disciples."

The Bible tells us that if we have a strong love walk, the other things we seek and desire will just come together. Jesus said, "Seek ye first the kingdom of God, and his righteousness; and all these things shall be added unto you" (Matt. 6:33). When we get a strong love walk, the devil is going to run from us and take our unhappiness with him. He is afraid of people who walk in love.

'My Mountain Was Removed!'

by Lindsay Roberts

The first time I really discovered the power of God was when the doctors discovered a tumor, a very large tumor, larger than an orange, on my right ovary. They were concerned about what would happen to me if surgery didn't take place immediately.

This was discovered on Friday, and surgery was scheduled for Saturday morning. But the entire faculty, staff, and student body of ORU were gathered together for a seminar that weekend before school began to help get the school year started on the right foundation.

I asked the doctor if I could wait until Monday and spend the weekend at the seminar laying hands on others and praying for them. I told him I needed to plant a seed of my prayers to receive a miracle harvest in return. He approved and I went to the services all weekend as planned.

Sunday night I was admitted to the hospital and scheduled for surgery at 7 o'clock Monday morning. That night the doctor explained that the tumor was so large he would have to remove whatever it had attached itself to, which included my right ovary. In explaining my problem to me, the doctor said, "Compared to the organs in your body, the tumor is so large it is like a mountain squeezing the life out of a little molehill, and it has to be removed."

His words were like God had lit a rocket inside me, and I began to praise Him. I knew that I was in for a miracle! Richard prayed and agreed with me that God was in control and this would be our miracle. I turned in my Bible to Mark 11:23-24, and I read, "Whosoever shall say unto this mountain, Be thou removed, and be thou cast into the sea; and shall not doubt in his heart, but shall believe that those things which he saith shall come to pass; he shall have whatsoever he saith."

I started praising God because the explanation the doctor had given me was that the tumor was like a mountain. I went into surgery, and as soon as they made the incisions, the operating room began to buzz. God had removed the tumor! My mountain was moved!

Who Am I, Who Are You, and Who Is God?

by Richard Roberts

First of Two Parts

Have you ever asked God, "Who am I?" I have. I asked God, "Who am I that I should begin a live daily television show?"

I thought back to the thousands of people who have shared how God has used our television programs to turn their lives around and bring them the miracles they needed. And I thought to myself, *Why is it that so many times we see our humanness and wonder who in the world we are to attempt the things God tells us to do?* We seem to forget that God has promised us that we can do all things through Christ who strengthens us. (Phil. 4:13.)

Moses was someone who asked God, "Who am I?" He had failed, and his failure was far from small. He had killed an Egyptian in an attempt to deliver God's people in his own strength. He had fled Egypt for his personal safety, and then on the backside of the desert he had an encounter with God.

God appeared to Moses in a burning bush and told him He was going to send him to deliver His people. Moses looked at himself and his failures and asked, "Who am I, that I should go unto Pharaoh, and that I should bring forth the children of Israel out of Egypt?" (Ex. 3:11).

And how did God answer Moses? He said, "Certainly I will be with thee" (v. 12).

Those are great words for you and me!

But then Moses said to God, "Behold, when I come unto the children of Israel, and shall say unto them, The God of your fathers hath sent me unto you; and they shall say to me, What is his name? what shall I say unto them?" (v.13).

'I Am That I Am'

by Richard Roberts

Second of Two Parts

MOSES WANTED TO KNOW NOT ONLY WHO HE WAS BUT ALSO WHO GOD WAS. THIS IS NOT UNLIKE THE SITUATION PEOPLE FIND THEMSELVES IN TODAY. MOST PEOPLE DON'T KNOW WHO GOD IS.

Who is God to you? Is God just someone whose name is used as a curse word? Or if you have received His Son as your Lord, who is this One who by the power of the Holy Spirit is living in your heart?

God Himself has answered the question: "And God said unto Moses, I AM THAT I AM: and he said, Thus shalt thou say unto the children of Israel, I AM hath sent me unto you" (Ex. 3:14).

God says, I AM THAT I AM. That means He is whatever you lack in your life. If you lack health, God is your Healer. If you lack salvation, God is your Savior. If you lack finances, God is your Source of supply. If you lack freedom from fear, God is your Deliverer. With that knowledge, Moses led God's people out of Egypt.

Who is God? God is Noah's rainbow, He is David's slingshot, He is Samuel's horn of oil, He is Hezekiah's sundial, He is the Rose of Sharon, He is the King of kings and Lord of lords! He is all anyone needs!

What do you need today? God can meet that need. He doesn't say "I was," or, "I used to be," or, "I will be." God says, "I AM. I AM right now in the very present moment that you live." Release your faith to Him for the miracle you need. He is able to bring it to you!

Exodus 3:15 tells us, "And God said moreover unto Moses, Thus shalt thou say unto the children of Israel, the Lord God of your fathers, the God of Abraham, the God of Isaac, and the God of Jacob, hath sent me unto you: this is my name for ever, and this is my memorial unto all generations."

Cooperating With God

by Oral Roberts

Often I look back upon the many healings I've experienced, both through prayer and medicine, and I try to find out what I did to cooperate with God in the healing process.

What was my relationship with God during those times? What did I do to release my faith to Him?

If you need to be healed, you can cooperate with God in your healing process by asking yourself similar questions. Have you put God first in your thoughts and asked for His help? Have you focused your faith on Him for the continued provision of your health? Are you continuously directing your mind to think positive thoughts about your life and your situation?

Maintaining a positive attitude is so important in cooperating with God in the healing process. When negative thoughts try to enter your mind, concentrate on scriptural truths like, "I am the Lord that healeth thee" (Ex. 15:26), and "I will never leave thee, nor forsake thee" (Heb. 13:5). If you begin to feel discouraged—and we all do at times—pick up your Bible and immerse yourself in God's Word.

Declare the Word over yourself and your loved ones. There is something about hearing yourself speak God's Word on a constant basis that causes faith to rise in your heart to claim His power to make you whole.

Independence Day for You

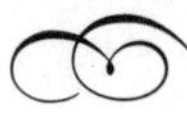

by Richard Roberts

Today the United States celebrates its independence from England. On that day in 1776, our forefathers drafted a Declaration of Independence to establish a free nation based on godly principles. And Psalm 33:12 says, "Blessed is the nation whose God is the Lord."

I believe Luke 4:18 NKJV is our spiritual declaration of independence. Jesus said, "The Spirit of the Lord is upon Me, because He has anointed Me to preach the gospel to the poor; He has sent Me to heal the brokenhearted, to proclaim liberty to the captives and recovery of sight to the blind, to set at liberty those who are oppressed."

I thank God that Jesus was anointed to preach, because it is the preaching of the Gospel that calls men and women to repentance. When Peter preached to the crowd on the Day of Pentecost, the people were pricked in their hearts and asked, "What must we do to believe?" Peter preached and 3,000 people were saved! (Acts 2:1-38.)

Jesus was anointed to heal and proclaim freedom to those in bondage to sin, sickness, fear, and poverty—anything that is not like God. His healing power can break the chains that are binding you. If you haven't given your heart and life to Jesus, today is the perfect day to do it by praying this prayer:

O Lord, I renounce the devil and all of his works. I repent of every sin. I am truly sorry. I ask You to save me, heal me, deliver me, and set me free. From this moment I am going to serve You with everything that is within me. This is my independence day! In Jesus' name. Amen.

A God of Miracles!

by Sharon Daugherty
Victory Christian Center Church and School

The first time I ever heard that God was a miracle-working God was when I went to Oral Roberts University as a student. I grew up in church, but there had never been an emphasis on the God of miracles. It was at ORU that I began to hear and understand that miracles still happen today. I learned that you can pray and believe, and God can intervene in your life. He can turn things around supernaturally if you believe His Word. Ever since I got that truth down into my heart, there has been a steady stream of miracles in my life.

Billy Joe and I have four children, and all of them have experienced the miracle power of God. When our second daughter, Ruthie, was just six months old, she became very ill and went through a battery of medical tests to find out what was wrong. Doctors diagnosed three different diseases, but they finally agreed on leukemia because her white blood count was so high. I remember praying for Ruthie, speaking the Word over her, and refusing to agree with the diagnosis. We said what God's Word said about her. And from January to November we watched her white count slowly go down to normal. By the time Christmas rolled around that year, she was completely healed!

All through the Bible there are examples of God working miracles. Psalm 77:14 NIV says, "You are the God who performs miracles; you display your power among the peoples." God is still a God of miracles today, and He wants to work miracles in your life as you stay in faith and believe Him!

Put It On!

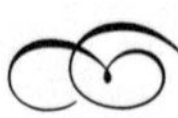

by Keith Moore
Faith Life Church

The book of Philippians is an amazing book. It was born out of much suffering. Although the apostle Paul was in prison when he wrote it, he said, "Rejoice in the Lord always. Again I will say, rejoice!" (Phil. 4:4 NKJV). And in verse 11 he said, "I have learned in whatever state I am, to be content."

I believe Paul was saying that we don't just live in a geographical location—we live "inside." In other words, we live in our spirits and in our minds. We could be on a beautiful tropical island and still be depressed if we were dark on the inside. Paul was in a gloomy, stinky jail cell, but because he was full of fellowship with God, he was rejoicing and content.

Our circumstances don't have to dictate to us whether or not we are joyful. We can decide. Some people, when faced with that choice, say, "I'm not a 'put-on.' If I don't feel happy, I'm not going to act like I do." But Ephesians 4:24 tells us to put on the new man. It's up to us to put on a new garment of praise and worship whether we feel like it or not. If you refuse, it's like it would be if I offered you my jacket when it was really cold outside, but you said, "Oh, no thanks. I'll just be cold." You have to put on the coat to be warm.

You may feel like crying over your circumstances. But as you put on the cloak of rejoicing, the darkness begins to be dispelled by the light of God that shines brighter in your heart.

How We Learned To Live by Faith

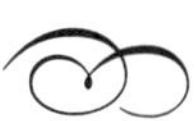

by Gloria Copeland
Kenneth Copeland Ministries

Over thirty-five years ago, Ken and I began living by faith. We were living in Tulsa and had absolutely nothing! At thirty, Ken was Oral Roberts University's oldest freshman as well as a copilot for Oral Roberts.

One day Ken came home proclaiming, "We are going to become Oral Roberts' partners and send ten dollars a month as seed-faith offerings!"

"Where in the world will we get ten dollars?" I asked.

I hadn't heard the faith sermons Ken had been hearing, and I didn't have the supernatural revelations that he had been receiving. But as we began to sow our seed, we began to increase. Unexpected money began to come our way. We had also begun to tithe. The more we went after the Word of God, the more God manifested Himself. He wants to increase us, and that requires us to walk by faith.

The only way faith comes is by hearing, believing, and acting on God's Word. Faith sees ahead as though it were today. It sees the answer in the Word of God.

We don't have to pray for grocery money anymore, but we still have to study God's Word and believe Him to help us fulfill His call. We will always have to live by faith, but after thirty-five years of doing so, we wouldn't want to live any other way.[1]

'I Embrace Healing!'

by Lindsay Roberts

Jesus went to the cross and paid the price for whatever it is in your life that's broken or needs to be healed. Whether you need healing in your mind, in your emotions, in your marriage, or in your physical body, He fixed it at Calvary. He went to the cross for the very thing you're asking Him to heal in your life.

Why would Christians ever be skeptical of healing? That would mean we accept sickness and disease! Why would we accept the very thing that Jesus Himself went to the cross to defeat? The Bible says in Isaiah 53:5, "He was wounded for our transgressions, he was bruised for our iniquities: the chastisement of our peace was upon him; and with his stripes we are healed." We know He died for our salvation, but He also went to the cross for our healing.

One of the words for "healing" in both the Old and New Testaments is *sozo.* It is the same root word as the word for salvation, and it means the same thing: "deliverance; to preserve from sickness, to save, make whole, save from disease and its effects." Jesus went to the cross for our salvation and our healing! Another way of saying it is that He died for our wholeness and completeness—that means our spirits, our souls, our emotions, and our bodies.

The terms "Christian" and "skeptical of healing" should never be used in the same breath. If we accept that Jesus died for our salvation, then we can also accept that He went to the cross for our healing. Thank God, instead of being skeptical, we can read the Bible and say, "I embrace healing!"

'When in Need, Plant a Seed'

by Evelyn Roberts

Not long ago I was asked to speak to a group about dealing with the death of a loved one. One of the things I talked about was the struggle we all have with bitterness when we've suffered any kind of loss. And I shared with the group the motto Oral and I have when we suffer a loss: "When in need, plant a seed."

I told them the way we found to get grief out of our hearts and keep bitterness from creeping in was to reach out and help somebody else.

When I'd finished, one of the ladies said to me, "Oh, Mrs. Roberts, I wish my mother could have heard you." She went on to say that after her father died, her mother shut herself up in her home for two years and wouldn't let anybody in and wouldn't go out.

"I know what you're talking about," the lady said. "You can become so self-centered and bitter that you're no good to yourself or anybody else."

When we lost our son, Ronald, in a very tragic death, I went through a terrible struggle. Oral and I prayed and sought the Lord. Oral asked, "Lord, what shall we do? What would You like us to do to plant a seed of faith that will reach out to help people?"

God spoke to him and said, "I want you to read the New Testament out loud on tape with your comments." And that's what Oral got busy doing. I stayed right with him day after day, working the tape recorder and helping to edit out the parts that were too long to fit on the tapes. Oh, that was hard to do! I wanted to leave in every word of his teaching.

It took us a year and a half to complete the project. But do you know what? That brought a healing on the inside of me! You can't read God's Word out loud every day, day after day, without something good happening.

When we reach out to others with our lives, even in our hurt—and especially in our hurt—the harvest comes back to us in the form of our own need.

'What Wilt Thou That I Shall Do Unto Thee?'

by Oral Roberts

First of Two Parts

Read with me Luke 18:35-43. "And it came to pass, that as he was come nigh unto Jericho, a certain blind man sat by the way side begging: And hearing the multitude pass by, he asked what it meant. And they told him, that Jesus of Nazareth passeth by.

"And he cried, saying, Jesus, thou son of David, have mercy on me.... And Jesus stood, and commanded him to be brought unto him: and when he was come near, he asked him, saying, *What wilt thou that I shall do unto thee?* And he said, Lord, that I may receive my sight.

"And Jesus said unto him, *Receive thy sight: thy faith hath saved thee.* And immediately he received his sight, and followed him, glorifying God: and all the people, when they saw it, gave praise unto God."

This religious crowd that was following Jesus had not asked for one miracle. They had been following Him, whereas the poor blind man had been sitting there by the side of the road all those days that Jesus had been on the earth. Day after day they carried him, and he sat on the side of the highway where the people passed by, so they could see his beggar's cup and the beggar's robe that he wore.

The other people were more fortunate. They could see. They could hear. They could walk. They could follow Jesus. They could travel to wherever He was. They were not the spiritual people of Israel. They were the religious people of Israel who didn't expect a miracle, who followed to catch Jesus in His words, to criticize Him, and finally to deny Him and see to it that He was nailed to a cross. This was the religious crowd which was following Jesus.

The crowd stopped and rebuked the beggar, saying, "Shut up! You're bothering this meeting." But the blind man cried that much louder: "Jesus, thou Son of David, have mercy on me!"

'Thy Faith Hath Made Thee Whole'

by Oral Roberts

Second of Two Parts

There is only One who can heal. We start with God when we've lost our job, our business, our family, our home, or our health, because if God does not do it supernaturally, He may have a natural force out there that He can direct you to. He knows where there is a better job for everyone who has lost a job. He knows there is better health for everybody who has lost their health. He knows there is sight for everyone who is blind. He knows there is hearing for everyone who has lost their hearing. He knows there are walking legs for all legs that cannot walk. He knows there is money for all people who don't have any money. He came to preach the Gospel to the poor.

Many people will say, "Lord, I want a blessing." Did you ever notice that when you say, "I want a blessing," you usually don't get what you ask for? Have you ever thought about what Christ said—to be specific, to say exactly what you want God to do?

Do you know that most people would rather give up anything than their sight? If they had to make a choice to give up anything, it would not be their sight. Jesus wants to know precisely what is wrong in your life. Doesn't He know? Yes. But He wants you to say it.

It was a big moment for the blind man, Bartmaeus, sitting there, expecting a miracle. Jesus was passing by. The miracle was coming. He believed it would come to him someday, and he recognized it when it approached. He reached out to get it, and Jesus said, "What do you want?"

The blind man said, "Lord, that I might receive my sight. And Jesus said unto him, Go thy way; thy faith hath made thee whole. And immediately he received his sight" (Mark 10:51,52). The people following, who had just rebuked him, now broke out into praise!

Your Very Best Friend

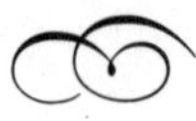

by Lindsay Roberts

When my nephew was six years old, he walked into the kitchen one day, just chattering away. His mom wasn't paying close attention to what he was saying until he offered "Dave" something to eat.

"Who's Dave?" his mom asked, not seeing anyone else in the kitchen but her son.

"Oh, he's just the guy I play with," he said of his imaginary friend.

"Have you ever played with him before?" she asked.

"No," my nephew answered. "Usually I play with Jesus, but He's too busy."

Intrigued, his mom asked, "Oh? What's He doing?"

"Mom, you know what Jesus does!" he said. "He's out doing those miracles and such!"

You know, we could all take a lesson from my little nephew. He usually plays by himself because he has little siblings, so he asks Jesus to play with him.

What if we thought of Jesus as our favorite friend? What if we invited Him into our homes, our marriages, our families, our businesses? What if we expected Him to enter into our lives in the most personal way and do miracles because we knew that is what "He's out doing" all the time? Wonderful changes could happen in our lives if we cultivated that kind of relationship with Him.

If you don't know Jesus as your best friend, all you have to do is open the door of your heart and invite Him to come in. He says, "I stand at the door and knock; if anyone hears and listens to and heeds My voice and opens the door, I will come in to him" (Rev. 3:20 AMP). Jesus is a friend who sticks closer than a brother. (Prov. 18:24.)

You're Already the Winner!

by Jerry Savelle

Jerry Savelle Ministries International

One time I was watching a boxing match between two well-known fighters, and one of them took a severe beating. The other guy knocked him out in the eighth round. Now when that knocked-out fighter was lying there on the mat, unable to even lift his arms, I would have signed a contract for $30 million to fight him right then. You know why? Because someone had already stripped him of his ability to harm me! I would have been sure to win.

Our enemy, the devil, schemes and plots against us. But we don't have to be afraid of his wiles, because Jesus has already defeated the devil! Colossians 2:15 says, "Having spoiled principalities and powers, he made a shew of them openly, triumphing over them in it."

In the good fight of faith, you have already been declared the winner in Christ! I don't know about you, but I can endure anything when I know in advance that I'm going to come out on top.

On the cross, Jesus stripped Satan of his ability to harm you! Sometimes we give up too quickly when our adversary looks big and strong. But everything he is and everything he uses against us has already been defeated! Yes, you've been called to fight the fight of faith, but remember, when you believe what Jesus has done for you, you're already the winner!

Faith in Gilgal

by Richard Roberts

First of Four Parts

Second Kings 2 tells us that when the time came for the Lord to take Elijah to heaven in a whirlwind, Elijah and Elisha left the little town of Gilgal, which was where the Israelites went after they came out of the wilderness. It is where the pillar of cloud guided them by day, and the pillar of fire gave them light and direction by night. They came every day. But when they got to Gilgal, the pillar of cloud, the pillar of fire, and the manna stopped.

Gilgal is where you have to use your own faith. It is where you have to believe. It's where you have to stop depending on somebody else's faith. Gilgal is where you make the decision, "I am going to believe God." It's where you believe Him for yourself.

Elisha was tested at that place. And you and I are tested at that place when we make the decision, "God, I'm going to believe You with my whole heart, with my whole strength, with my whole mind, with everything that's within me."

As they were leaving Gilgal, Elijah said to Elisha, "You stay here. I'm going to Bethel." But Elisha refused, saying, "I won't leave you!"

If you study Bethel, you'll find that it is the place of change. It's where Jacob received a vision—a change. It was here that Jacob's name was changed from Jacob to Israel. He had been a liar and a thief. He had been a supplanter, a trickster, and had stolen his own brother's birthright. But at Bethel Jacob's entire nature changed.

Most people fear change, but it is in change, in your willingness to be pliable and flexible in the hands of the Master, that you can fulfill the vision that God has laid on your heart.

Jericho—a Place of War

by Richard Roberts

Second of Four Parts

When they got to Bethel, Elijah said to Elisha, "You stay in Bethel, for the Lord has sent me to Jericho." But Elisha refused. Now Jericho is a place of war. This world is a battle zone. And we are in warfare—spiritual warfare.

Ephesians 6:10-18 says that our battle is not against people. It's not a flesh-and-blood fight, but a faith fight. Our battle is against principalities and powers, against the rulers of the darkness of this world, and spiritual wickedness in high places. If there ever was a time when we needed the armor of God to stand against the tricks of the devil, it is now!

Each morning when our family gets up, we put on our spiritual armor. First, we put on the helmet of salvation to protect our minds and what we believe. Then we put on the breastplate of righteousness to protect our hearts, for with the heart man believes. Your most vital organ is your heart.

Next, we put on the belt of truth because Jesus is the way, the truth, and the life. And, above all, we take the shield of faith because with the shield of faith we're able to quench the onslaughts of the javelins, spears, and darts of the devil.

Then we take the sword of the Spirit, which is the Word of God. Acts 20:32 says that the Word is able to build us up and give us our inheritance. What soldier would go into battle without his sword?

Then we put on our gospel shoes of peace to walk over the devil's roughest territory because it's rough out there, and Satan has set traps and lures for us. And finally, we pray in the Spirit, which I believe is the seventh piece of our spiritual armor—praying in tongues.

The devil is our adversary. He is defeated, but he is not destroyed. And you and I need the covering of the whole armor of God over our lives. This is how we are victorious!

Follow Jesus

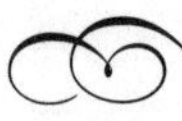

by Richard Roberts

Third of Four Parts

At Jericho Elijah said to Elisha, "Please stay here, for the Lord has sent me to the Jordan River." But again Elisha refused.

As Elijah and Elisha walked along the Jordan, Elijah said, "Ask me what I shall do for you before I am taken away." He knew in his heart that the moment of his going up to heaven was near. Elisha, quick as a wink, said, "I want a double portion of the spirit that has rested upon you!"

Elijah said, "You've asked a hard thing." Notice he did not say, "You've asked an impossible thing." But he said, "Thou hast asked a hard thing: nevertheless, if thou see me when I am taken from thee, it shall be so unto thee; but if not, it shall not be so" (2 Kings 2:10).

Elisha was acquainted with hard things because God had allowed tests to come into his life. I've often wondered why God allows us to go through tests. I know that God does not put bad things on us. God is not the author of sin, sickness, disease, fear, doubt, worry, or dread. Those come from the devil. But for some reason, God allows certain things to come into our lives. Jordan is symbolic of crossing over and leaving everything behind.

Several months ago, my dad and I were talking on the phone. He was in California, and I was in Tulsa. We were in prayer, and we were sharing as a father and son. I said to him, "Dad, I want a double portion of the spirit that's rested upon you." And on the other end of the line, I heard him say, "Well, son, if you see me when I go...."

I believe God gave me a revelation. He was saying what Elijah was saying to Elisha: "Son, keep your eyes on Jesus. Follow Him. If you keep your eyes focused on Jesus, you'll have what you're praying for." My father has always taught me, "Follow me, as I follow Christ."

Focus on Jesus

by Richard Roberts

Fourth of Four Parts

Elijah and my father were not saying we were to keep our physical eyes on them. I don't think that was what Elijah was saying to Elisha, and I don't think that is what my father was saying to me. I believe that what they were saying was, "Son, keep your focus on Jesus."

Paul said, "Follow me, as I follow Christ." In other words, "As long as you can see Jesus over my shoulder, follow me." That is what my father has said to me all of my life. I've been able to see the Lord Jesus Christ over the shoulder of my father, Oral Roberts. I believe he was saying, "If you keep your eyes on Jesus, if you focus your gaze upon Him, you'll have what you're praying for." My father said, "There have been a lot of men who have come to me and asked me to give them a double-portion blessing. But I've never done it once. I'm saving that for one man."

I didn't have to ask who it was. I knew!

"Son, you've asked a hard thing, but if you see me when I go...."

As Elijah and Elisha walked along, Elijah took his mantle, which represented the power of God, and he struck the waters. Everybody saw it. He put the mantle back on, and the next thing you know, the whirlwind and the chariot came down. God's first heavenly space shuttle! Elijah stepped on board and began to go up.

Meanwhile, the mantle came floating down and landed on the ground, and Elisha reached down and picked it up. He knew that the power was not in Elijah, but in Elijah's God!

If you study the Bible, you'll find that twice as many miracles were done under the ministry of Elisha. He got what he believed and asked for!

I want a double-portion anointing of the Holy Spirit, because in my own strength I cannot do what God has commanded me to do. No matter what you are doing, you can't do it to its fullest potential without the anointing of the Holy Spirit.

Dare To Step Out

by Gloria Copeland
Kenneth Copeland Ministries

God can take the most simple person in the world who will dare to believe what is written in the Word, and empower him to do any job he is called to do.

I know this because God did that for me. The reason I'm so blessed today is because I am so simple that I believe God is smarter than I am. When I see something in the Bible that doesn't agree with what I think, I change what I think and believe the Word of God.

Jesus admonished us to come as little children. So do that. Humble yourself and just take the Word as it is written. If God says you'll do the works, don't argue, just agree with Him and get busy!

Say, "Father, Jesus said, *'He that believeth on me, the works that I do shall he do also'* (John 14:12). I don't know how to do the works, but Your Word says I will. So I place myself at Your disposal. I expect to do the works that Jesus did!"

Then step out boldly and act on your faith. The bolder we are, the more power there can be released through us. Did you know that? It's when we hesitate and are afraid of what people might think that nothing happens. So make up your mind now to be bold—whether you want to or not.

That's how it works. But you have to take the first step. Do what the Bible says to do whether you feel like it or not. That's called ACTING ON THE WORD! And that's called FAITH![1]

Forgiveness...Your Path to Freedom

by Lindsay Roberts

In Numbers 12 the Lord tells us what we should do when people do us wrong. Verse 1 says that Miriam and Aaron spoke against Moses because of the Ethiopian woman he had married. Now frankly, it was none of their business whom Moses married, and they even went so far as to say, "Has the Lord indeed spoken only through Moses? Has He not spoken through us also?" (v. 2 NKJV). They were treading on dangerous ground, and the Bible says in verse 9, "The anger of the Lord was aroused against them." As a result, Miriam was struck with leprosy.

Now when somebody decides to judge you and stick their two cents' worth into your business, your human instinct might be to say, "Let's take 'em down!" Moses could have easily said, "It serves you right for talking about my wife that way!" But look at verse 13: Moses cried out to the Lord, saying, "Please heal her, O God, I pray!" Instead of crying out for vengeance, Moses prayed for mercy! So God healed Miriam and blessed Moses for his forgiving spirit.

It takes a big person to pray for someone who is coming against them. But God is saying, "Release that person. Don't hold it against them." We've all been hurt, lied to, or made fun of. But when you forgive those who have done you wrong and pray for them, it does two things: First, it allows them to see the love of God in operation, and they may get saved as a result. Second, it releases you from the terrible bondage of unforgiveness, and nothing will be held against your account. Forgiveness can be your path to freedom!

The Good Shepherd

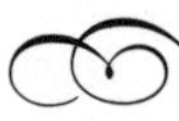

by Oral Roberts

First of Four Parts

Jesus said, "Verily, verily, I say unto you, He that entereth not by the door into the sheepfold, but climbeth up some other way, the same is a thief and a robber.

"But he that entereth in by the door is the shepherd of the sheep.

"To him the porter openeth; and the sheep hear his voice: and he calleth his own sheep by name, and leadeth them out.

"And when he putteth forth his own sheep, he goeth before them, and the sheep follow him: for they know his voice.

"And a stranger will they not follow, but will flee from him: for they know not the voice of strangers.

"This parable spake Jesus unto them: but they understood not what things they were which he spake unto them.

"Then said Jesus unto them again, Verily, verily, I say unto you, I am the door of the sheep. All that ever came before me are thieves and robbers: but the sheep did not hear them" (John 10:1-8).

Do you ever think about the people who come to Christ and those who don't? Jesus said, "I am the door: by me if any man enter in, he shall be saved, and shall go in and out, and find pasture"(v. 9).

In verses 14-15 Jesus goes on to say, "I am the good shepherd, and know my sheep, and am known of mine. As the Father knoweth me, even so know I the Father; and I lay down my life for the sheep."

With these verses as background, let's read from Psalm 23: "The Lord is my shepherd; I shall not want. He maketh me to lie down in green pastures: he leadeth me beside the still waters. He restoreth my soul: he leadeth me in the paths of righteousness for his name's sake. Yea, though I walk through the valley of the shadow of death, I will fear no evil: for thou art with me; thy rod and thy staff they comfort me. Thou preparest a table before me in the presence of mine enemies: thou anointest my head with oil; my cup runneth over. Surely goodness and mercy shall follow me all the days of my life: and I will dwell in the house of the Lord for ever."

The Nightingale of the Psalms

by Oral Roberts

Second of Four Parts

They say the little bird, the nightingale, never sings so sweetly as on a dark night. The darker the night, the sweeter the song of the nightingale. And when life is rough, things aren't going right, and there seems to be no way out, the Twenty-third Psalm is the nightingale of the Psalms. It is a psalm written by David in the last years of his life, when it was nighttime for him.

Not only was David coming to the end of a great forty-year reign in which he had brought Israel together and brought peace to the land after it was virtually destroyed by Saul, its first king. But it was a time when his enemies were coming against him in a way that was different than he had ever known. One of his sons had committed incest with one of his daughters, and his oldest son, Absalom, was now trying to kill him and take his throne.

The people who were his enemies were coming in at night and coming in during the day. And as he was coming to the end of his great reign, David, from whom comes our Savior, Jesus Christ, needed to hear the song of the nightingale. He needed to be the sweet singer of Israel. He needed to know something about the shepherd and the sheep that would be real to him in that time of life.

There is always a time when you and I need the special voice of God to come to us in the darkness of night and whisper the right words to our spirits and our minds.

I visualize David sitting on the throne as he's getting old. There is not much time left, and his enemies are coming from every side. The palace fades, and he goes back in memory to the pastures of Bethlehem and once again becomes the shepherd boy of his father, Jesse.

The Door of the Sheepfold

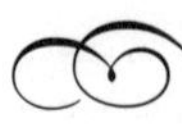

by Oral Roberts

Third of Four Parts

David could see himself out in the field with his sheep, reliving the days when he had led them from one pastureland to the other, where the grass was greener, down by the still waters, when he had led them through the valley of the shadow of death, where he had fought off their enemies, and when he had built the sheepfold and become the door himself.

When he would return in the evening, he would count the sheep and call them by their names, for he knew their names. They knew his voice, and they wouldn't follow a stranger. They would run from a stranger, but they would come to David.

When he had gathered them all in the sheepfold and they lay down, he then lay down in the doorway and became the door.

All these things came to David's memory, but he knew that now he was no longer a shepherd. He was one of those sheep. He was no longer David, the shepherd boy; he was David, the sheep boy. We read about this in the tenth chapter of John.

I want to share with you about your being a sheep and about Jesus being the Shepherd, the door of the sheepfold, the Good Shepherd, the One whose voice we know, the One who knows our names.

They tell us that a shepherd and his sheep have the closest relationship of any human and animal on the earth because they are more dependent upon one another. The sheep are particularly dependent upon the shepherd because they are defenseless. They must depend upon the shepherd, upon his rod and staff, upon his voice, and upon his ability to beat off the enemies.

And ye my flock, the flock of my pasture, are men, and I am your God, saith the Lord God. —Ezekiel 34:31

'The Lord Is My Shepherd'

by Oral Roberts

Fourth of Four Parts

Sheep have a way of eating grass and following their noses, not looking up, and just walking right over a cliff. They have a spirit of straying because they just follow whatever they are eating.

The shepherd has to watch where the sheep go. When he finds that one has strayed, he has to dare to leave the other sheep and take his rod and staff and go after the one that strayed. When he finds it, he reaches down with the crook of his staff, puts it around the neck of the sheep, pulls him to safety, takes him in his arms, and carries him back and puts him inside the sheepfold. He calls the wandering sheep by name and calms him down. They are both so dependent upon each other that it's as if they were one.

David, remembering his life as a shepherd boy, now switches his thoughts to that of a sheep. The nightingale begins to sing in the dark night, and David writes for us the Twenty-third Psalm. We can hear him as he sings and talks to those sheep, and says, "The Lord is my shepherd; I shall not want."

Not Guilty

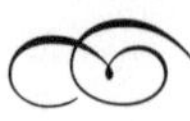

by Kenneth Copeland

Kenneth Copeland Ministries

All of us struggle with bad habits at some time or another. We work hard to change them. There may be some things in your life today where it's a little hard to get control. You may have to resist Satan in those areas. You can take God's Word and put him out of commission.

In the meantime, do not allow yourself to be harassed by him or made to feel guilty. It's dangerous.

Don't let yourself or anyone else say things like, "I'm so messed up. I'm so bad. I'm so worthless." That's directly opposite of what God says. If Jesus walked through the door and stood right there for the next 20 years talking every minute of every day, He would never call you worthless. It's proven in Hebrews 2.

Jesus is not ashamed of you. Therefore, you don't have any business being ashamed of yourself!

Start believing what the Bible says. Believe that you're God's special workmanship, created in Jesus. Start saying that. Instead of talking about what a messed-up person you are, start agreeing with what God says and know that you are in right-standing with God. (2 Cor. 5:21.) Practice seeing yourself that way. Practice seeing yourself without those bad habits. After all, Jesus has already beaten them for you. So believe it today by faith![1]

Turning Your Nothing Into Something

by Jesse Duplantis
Jesse Duplantis Ministries

The definition of a *miracle* is turning nothing into something. There are many instances in the Scriptures where Christ changed nothing into something. In Luke 5:3-7 Jesus borrowed Peter's boat. Before Jesus came on the scene, Peter and the other fishermen had toiled all night and caught nothing. After Jesus used Peter's boat to teach the people, He told Peter, "Cast out your net!"

Now let's go into Peter's mind. *Look, Jesus, You're a carpenter; I'm a fisherman. I'm telling You that there are no fish in this lake!* What Peter missed was that God will not ask you for something that He will not reward you for. Jesus asked Peter for his boat, and God will not be a debtor to any man. He turned Peter's nothing into something, and miracles took place!

Jesus also turned nothing into something for a woman named Mary, a prostitute out of whom Jesus cast seven devils. While others saw her as someone to be conquered, Jesus saw her as a great spiritual being. After Jesus rose from the dead, He revealed Himself to Mary before anyone else. (Mark 16:9.) Then she gave a proclamation that's still ringing today—"He's alive!"

God turns our nothing into something when we sow our seed. I'm on over 1,800 TV stations, and they're all paid for. How did I do it? By sowing seed and believing in something that some people don't believe in—the 100-fold return. And money is only a small facet of the work of God. I love the peace of God. You have the peace of God when you possess adequate resources, and you get that by sowing your seed and expecting God to turn your nothing into something.

See What God Says

by Marilyn Hickey
Marilyn Hickey Ministries

Part One of Three Parts

Are you facing major trouble in your life? If so, I want to give you three keys that can help you get through to victory.

The first key is to see what God says in His Word. Once one of our staff members went by himself to camp in the mountains. His wife and children were away visiting, and he wanted some prayer time. When he didn't show up for a scheduled meeting on Monday morning, we became concerned. We checked his home, but he wasn't there and his vehicle was gone. I began to worry, thinking, *What could have happened to him? Why did he go alone? Why didn't he take a cell phone?* Then I said, "Lord, I need to hear from You!"

I went to the Word and was led to Psalm 66:12, which says, "Thou hast caused men to ride over our heads; we went through fire and through water: but thou broughtest us out." While the search for our staff member continued by helicopters and on horseback, I kept returning to that Scripture. I said, "God, I'm not going to look at the problem. I'm going to keep believing Your Word." In the end, the staff member returned home safely. He had gotten lost while chasing his dog down the side of a mountain.

God once told me, "When you're going through a hard time, you need more of My Word than in normal times. You need to fasten your vision on what I'm saying and not on your problem." So the first key to victory in a time of trial is to get into God's Word. Look at what He says, and ask Him to give you revelation on how to apply His Word to your problem. God's Word works!

Watch What You Say

by Marilyn Hickey

Marilyn Hickey Ministries

Part Two of Three Parts

The second key to overcoming problems is to watch what you say. The story is told in Numbers 13 and 14:6-8 about the twelve men Moses sent to spy out the land of Canaan. They all returned with stories about a wonderful country, but ten spies said, "We can't conquer the land. The cities are fortified and the people there are much stronger than we are." But the other two spies disagreed and told Moses that they could do it.

The first group said they couldn't...and they didn't.

The second group said they could...and they did.

Now look at the story of Joseph in Genesis 37 and 39. Wow! His brothers sold him into slavery, the wife of one of Pharaoh's officers tried to seduce him, and he was put into prison for a crime he didn't commit. But Joseph spoke the words God gave him to interpret Pharaoh's dream about surviving the coming famine, and in one day he went from being a prisoner to being prime minister! Joseph didn't look at his problem and say, "I can't." Because he let God provide the words he spoke, Joseph not only saved his own life but also the nation of Egypt and the nation of Israel—the nation that produced the Messiah!

What are you saying in your time of trial? Are you saying that you don't have a chance or that you can do all things through Christ who strengthens you? (Phil.4:13.) If you will see what God's Word says, then say what His Word says, God can begin to do great things in your life.

Endure With Joy

by Marilyn Hickey
Marilyn Hickey Ministries

Part Three of Three Parts

The third key to overcoming your problems is to endure with joy. Hebrews 12:2 NKJV tells us to keep our eyes on Jesus, the author and finisher of our faith, who for the joy that was set before Him endured the cross, despising the shame, and has sat down at the right hand of the throne of God.

Jesus endured the greatest trial of His life by looking at the joy of the prize that lay ahead of Him, rather than the pain. If He had looked at how hard the ordeal of the cross was going to be, He might have said, "Father, I can't do it." But He kept His eyes on the joy that awaited Him.

We are all going to endure trials. But 2 Corinthians 4:17-18 NKJV says, "Our light affliction [trouble], which is but for a moment, is working for us a far more exceeding and eternal weight of glory, while we do not look at the things which are seen, but at the things which are not seen. For the things which are seen are temporary, but the things which are not seen are eternal."

Knowing that your troubles have eternal value and are small and will not last long in the light of eternity can give you strength to overcome with Christ's joy.

What Is Stewardship?

by Dr. Creflo A. Dollar
World Changers Church International

Stewardship is more than just obeying God in giving money. Stewardship is not being a cheapskate and never spending. A good steward is a manager who knows how to take orders from the boss. When the boss says do, you do. When the boss says don't, you don't. That's good stewardship.

First Timothy 6:10 says, "The love of money is the root of all evil." A wrong relationship with the material realm is the root by which Satan can do everything he wants to do in this earth. Luke 16:11 NKJV says, "Therefore if you have not been faithful in the unrighteous mammon, who will commit to your trust the true riches?" God is saying, "Love Me with your money instead of operating in the love of money. If you will be faithful with worldly wealth to do what I tell you to do with it, then I will trust you with the true riches of heaven."

Will you obey God with your money? Or will you live in fear and say, "God, I would like to give, but I can't. I have bills to pay." Don't you think God knows you have bills to pay? He's trying to run you over with material wealth that you've never seen before.

It's not until you get to the place that you do what God tells you to do with money and you have proven to all of heaven that money and materialism are not your god that you will see the harvest come into your life.

What I'm telling you will help you not to be broke another day in your life. It will help you get out of paycheck-to-paycheck living. And this is what it takes: plain, simple, childlike obedience to do what God tells you to do with your money!

A Debt of Love

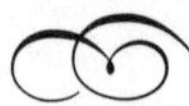

by Billy Joe Daugherty

Victory Christian Center Church and School

When people ask me when and how I started in the ministry, I tell them that I got started in January of 1971 as a college student, not long after I had been saved. While I was sitting in my dorm room studying, the thought hit me, *What have you ever done for anyone else?*

I began to think about my life, and I started to cry. I was suddenly overwhelmed with the thought that everything I had done in my life had been for myself, and I began to wonder what I could do. Then I recalled how I always loved going to the boys' club and participating in their athletic programs. So I thought, *I can coach a boys' basketball team!* And that's what I did! I started coaching nine fourth-grade boys with all I had. I'd pray with them and talk to them about the Lord every chance I got.

That's how I started in ministry. I had a revelation of how much God had done for me, how selfish I had been, and how I needed to share His love with other people. Then I acted on it.

The apostle Paul wrote in Philippians 1:9 NLT, "I pray that your love for each other will overflow more and more." I believe that if we can forget the need for titles and recognition and keep in our hearts all the wonderful things Jesus has done for us, we'll realize that we have a debt to pay. The thing is, we can never really repay that debt because it's a debt of love. It's a gratitude we have in our hearts to God for the great things He has done for us. When we realize that, we'll start looking for our place of service.

And how do we find that place? By saying, "God, how can I do something for someone else?" When God tells you how, act on it, and you'll be in the place God wants you to be.

Pressure Develops Character

by Bob Yandian
Grace Fellowship

A friend of mine used to work on offshore oil rigs in the Gulf of Mexico during the summer to make money for college. He tested all the pipe for the pipeline that came into the rig. Pipes were rated to take a certain amount of pressure, but the drillers never took the manufacturer's word for it. My friend tested each pipe with water pressure to be sure it would not spring a leak under water.

One day he was cranking up the pressure to test a section of pipe when suddenly a stream of water shot out of an unseen crack. When it happened, he told me the Lord spoke to him and said, "The pressure did not create the crack. The pressure revealed it." My friend said that revelation changed his life forever.

In the same way, pressure doesn't create our weaknesses—it exposes them. But that's when God's strength can flow through us. Character is developed through pressure.

In 2 Corinthians 12:10, the apostle Paul wrote, "I take pleasure in infirmities, in reproaches, in necessities, in persecutions, in distresses for Christ's sake: for when I am weak, then am I strong." Paul wasn't saying that when he was at his weakest, he was his strongest. He simply meant that when he realized his weakness, then he could rely on God's strength.

We all hate to be put under pressure. We want to run from it. But God sees our tests and trials as valuable. The apostle Peter described the trials of our faith as being "more precious than gold" (1 Peter 1:7). So don't run from pressure. This is how character is developed.

God's Wisdom

by Evelyn Roberts

Many people I meet view God as a harsh judge who is just waiting to pronounce a sentence upon them. If we think of God like that, we'll not have His wisdom. Wisdom is rooted in having the right understanding of God, which is knowing that God is a good God who does everything for the ultimate good of those who love Him.

The Bible teaches that wisdom—knowing what to do in every situation and how to discern every spirit—begins when we have a reverent and worshipful fear of the Lord. This type of fear is not the same as being scared. This kind of fear is a deep respect and awe of the Lord...being overwhelmed before Him because He is so wonderful, so powerful, so good, and so loving.

Proverbs 1:7 AMP says, "The reverent and worshipful fear of the Lord is the beginning and the principal and choice part of knowledge [its starting point and its essence]."

Are you facing a problem or circumstance and you don't know which way to turn? Ask God for wisdom. James 1:5 NIV says, "If any of you lacks wisdom, he should ask God, who gives generously to all without finding fault, and it will be given to him."

What a comfort it is to know that God wants us to have His wisdom. He is just waiting for us to turn to Him and ask for it. Believe that God not only wants you to have His wisdom, but that He is going to give it to you just when you need it. Ask Him for wisdom, then expect to receive it!

'Look at a Different Light'

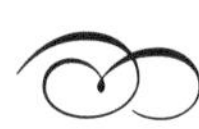

by Eastman Curtis
Destiny Church

Proverbs 11:27 NLT says, "If you search for good, you will find favor; but if you search for evil, it will find you!" Isn't that an amazing Scripture? If you're looking for good things in life, then you'll find the favor of God. But if you're looking for bad things—by being critical or expecting the worst—then those things will find you!

I can remember one time during a service in our church, I was singing and praising God during the worship time. My hands were raised, my eyes were closed, and my face was raised toward heaven. But then I opened my eyes, and I was startled to see a big bug stuck in one of the lights on the sanctuary ceiling.

I thought, *I can't worship God with that bug up there!* I reached over and tapped my wife and whispered, "Honey, look! There's a big bug up there. We can't worship God with that thing up there!"

My wife looked at the bug, then she looked at me and said calmly, "Eastman, look at a different light."

That was a revelation to me! I didn't have to look at the light with the bug in it. I could look at a different light!

You and I can look at "a different light" every day. We can decide to look for the good in things, because there are good things happening all around us. The Bible says that if we look for the negative—the depressing, discouraging things—they will find us. That's not what we want! If we will quit focusing on the negative and look for the positive, uplifting things in life, the favor of God can surround us like a shield!

The Miracle That You Have in Your Hand

by Richard Roberts

Do you remember the story in Mark 12:41-44 of the little widow who came and cast in her offering? The Bible tells us that Jesus was sitting against the treasury that day. He watched those who were rich come and cast in their offerings. Then He saw a certain widow come and cast in her two mites—what we today would call a couple of pennies. She used what she had in her hand.

Jesus said to His disciples, "She's given more than them all." They probably asked, "How could she have given more than them all? She gave so little, and they gave so much." Jesus answered, "Ah, because she gave out of her want." In other words, she gave out of her need. She used what she had in her hand.

That's what David did when he used his slingshot and his faith to battle the giant Goliath, although he had been offered Saul's armor. He used what he had. He knew and understood the mechanics of how a slingshot worked. He had gathered five smooth stones. He used what he had in his hand. (1 Sam. 17:38-40.)

Acts 3:1-10 tells us that one day Peter and John were going to worship, and they saw a man by the temple gate who had been crippled from birth. He was about forty years of age and had been carried there every day throughout the years to beg for alms. He looked at the disciples, expecting them to give him money. But Peter said, "Silver and gold have I none." He was not saying, "We don't have any money." What he was saying was, "It's not money that you need." Then he said, "Such as I have give I to thee." Then Peter took him by the hand and lifted him up, and the lame man was healed!

The man had asked for money, but what he really needed was healing. What did Peter have in his hand? He had the most powerful force on the face of the earth—the name of Jesus. And when he spoke that word, what he had in his hand was activated by his faith, and the lame man was healed!

God Is on Your Side

by Lindsay Roberts

Some words have double meanings. Take the word *contend*, for example, which means fight. It's a word that God uses when He fights against people, and it's a word He uses when He fights for people. In Isaiah 49:25 NKJV God says, "I will contend with him who contends with you." Notice that God doesn't say He will fight for them. Nor does He say He will contend against them. He simply says He will contend with them.

What does that mean? It means God fights with those who fight alongside you. But it also means He fights against those who fight against you and mean you harm.

A Christian has to fight spiritual battles every day. That's why the apostle Paul tells us in 1 Timothy 6:12 to fight the good fight of faith. There's a time to contend. And the good news is that as you fight, God fights with you on your side! And Romans 8:31 says that if God is for you, who can be against you?

'Your Name Is Not Oral'

by Jerry Savelle
Jerry Savelle Ministries International

When I first surrendered my life to the Lord in 1969, I knew nothing about the Bible. But I had a hunger for God and a great desire to live by faith.

There was a woman in my church who had been filled with the Holy Spirit for over 40 years. So I asked her, "Would you teach me about faith?" She said, "I know what's on your mind. You want faith like Oral Roberts, don't you?" That thought hadn't crossed my mind, but I had great respect for Oral Roberts, so I said, "Is there a problem with that?" She answered, "Yes, there is. You can't have it. The reason he has great faith is because of his name. Names reveal people's destinies, like Abraham, whose name means 'father of nations.' The name Oral means 'the spoken word,' and that's why he has great faith. You got stuck with Jerry."

I drove home with tears streaming down my face. There I was, just three weeks old in the Lord, and I'd been told that I couldn't have great faith because my name wasn't Oral. I cried out to the Lord, "You gave me the wrong name! How will I ever have great faith?" The Lord said, "Son, your name has nothing to do with it. I gave every man the same measure of faith. (Rom. 12:3.) Oral Roberts took his measure and did something with it until it grew and became great. You can do the same thing."

Acts 10:34 says, "God is no respecter of persons." He doesn't give one person more faith than another. If you'll use your measure of faith by studying and being a doer of the Word, your faith can grow until it becomes great also!

Let the Main Thing Be the Main Thing

by Joyce Meyer
Joyce Meyer Ministries

So much is going on in our lives that if we're not careful, we can forget the main thing that God has called us to do. We get into trouble when we center our attention on little things that don't make that much difference, and the main things don't get done. We call that majoring in the minors.

One of the things we have to do as believers is stay focused on the high calling from God that is on each one of our lives as believers. Otherwise, our lives can become very confusing. We can become too preoccupied with finances, health concerns, our children's education, and job security.

Mark 4:19 says that the cares and anxieties of this world, the distractions of this age, and the deceitfulness and the glamour of riches steal the Word from us. And that's right where Satan wants us—in a weakened position where we are not strong in the Word so that he can come in and hit us. Satan's goal is for us to be so busy running around putting out his fires that we stay caught up in trying to take care of our problems ourselves, rather than casting them on God and trusting Him to handle them while we reach out to others in need.

For many years, I thought I couldn't answer the call of God on my life or reach out to anybody else until I got my problems fixed. Then I finally got enough sense to realize I couldn't fix my problems; only God could. What I needed to do was put my problems in His hands and go ahead and help as many people as I possibly could. Somehow, when I stopped trying to fix myself and I let God's Word and purpose be the main thing in my life, I got fixed.

God Is a Life-Changer!

by Eastman Curtis
Destiny Church

Never quit praying or believing for God to save your loved ones. I know a young man who, as a teen, was kicked out of three schools for using drugs and alcohol. Talk about breaking a mom's heart! He was the kind of guy that parents warned their children, "Don't hang around with him—he's a bad influence." Then a little grandmother told him about Jesus, and in the twinkling of an eye that teenager moved from being a druggie to being an honor roll student. He was even elected senior class president and received a scholarship at a college preparatory school for his leadership capabilities and exemplary conduct! I know this story sounds too amazing to be true, but it is. I was that young man!

If an encounter with Jesus Christ could work that life-changing miracle in someone as far gone as I was, He's able to change your loved ones too. The Bible says, "When someone becomes a Christian he becomes a brand new person inside. He is not the same anymore. A new life has begun!" (2 Cor. 5:17 TLB.) And this miracle can happen in the twinkling of an eye.

Let's agree together in faith for our loved ones and believe God for miracles right now:

Father, in the name of Jesus, I ask You to move upon the hearts of my loved ones and place Your hand upon them. I thank You, Jesus, that You came to save to the uttermost, and that's what You are doing right now. I pray that You will send forth Your angels and bring laborers across the paths of my loved ones to share Your love and Your goodness with them wherever they are. From this day forward, I declare by my faith that my loved ones are returning home to You, in the name of Jesus. Amen.

Count It All Joy

by Lindsay Roberts

Proverbs 18:21 says, "Death and life are in the power of the tongue." That means our words are connected to power. God says, "I have set before you life and death, blessing and cursing: therefore choose life" (Deut. 30:19).

If death and life are in the power of the tongue, then we have a choice. We can allow the words of our mouth to snare us, or we can speak blessing.

The choice has been set before us, and God urges us to choose life. It seems like the obvious answer, so why does He have to tell us to choose life? I think it is because Satan makes the wrong choice look so absolutely appealing that if we don't consciously choose what we should, we may walk along the road to death without realizing where we're headed.

Often when we choose life, we must change a lot of things. One of those things is our speech. The psalmist prayed, "Let the words of my mouth, and the meditations of my heart, be acceptable in thy sight, O Lord, my strength, and my redeemer" (Ps. 19:14). When our words line up with God's words, then He becomes our strength and our Redeemer. The words from our lips and the meditations, or concerns, in our hearts should mold to God's perfect plan.

James tells us, "My brethren, count it all joy when ye fall into divers temptations" (James 1:2). Let the words from your mouth conform to God's plan for you. Whatever it is that's hurting you, choose to count it all joy! If you can't do it in your own strength, it's okay. Hook up to God's. Be a partaker of His strength. You can do all things through Christ who strengthens you. (Phil. 4:13.)

Healing Power

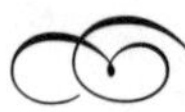

by Kenneth Copeland

Kenneth Copeland Ministries

Not so long ago it was just as tough to get people to make decisions for Jesus as it is to get them healed today. Religious tradition had convinced people that salvation just couldn't be obtained by the average person. Then, a man named Dwight L. Moody started preaching something new. He started telling people that Jesus took their sins upon Himself, and if they'd simply receive the gift of salvation, He would be their Lord!

Whole denominations preached that message to anyone who'd listen. You'd hear it in every church service. If you walked in the door and admitted you weren't a Christian, somebody would grab you and tell you that Jesus died for your sins! They would tell you to trust Him and He will change your life forever.

Well, what do you think would happen if everyone picked up on the truth about healing in the same way? I can tell you what would happen. Healing would become as easily received as salvation, and we'd wonder why we had so much trouble with it for so long!

If you're sitting there right now wishing such a move of God would begin, stop wishing and start your own! Dig into the Bible. Study and think about God's promises about healing. Listen to messages by men and women who understand healing. Then start sharing the healing power of God to others who need to hear it.

I'm not saying all this will be easy. It won't be. Not in this world. No, you'll have to stand strong for it in order to win. When you stand strong in faith, you will see God's healing power touch through you![1]

None of These Things Move Me

by Gloria Copeland
Kenneth Copeland Ministries

If you want to rob persecution of every last scrap of its power, adopt the attitude Paul had in 2 Corinthians 4:17-18. He wasn't concerned about the pressure he was experiencing down here on the earth. And, believe me, he was under tremendous pressure.

He'd probably laugh at us talking about persecution these days, we've had so little of it.

Paul's thoughts weren't centered on this natural life. He was thinking about that eternal weight of Glory. He was looking ahead to spending eternity in the presence of Jesus.

So he didn't grow weary. He didn't faint under persecutions, tribulations, or threats. In fact, in Acts 20:24 he said, *"None of these things move me, neither count I my life dear unto myself, so that I might finish my course with joy."*

Once you adopt that attitude, the devil won't be able to control you at all. He won't be able to find any persecution that will stop you.

You'll have your eyes so fixed on running your race and finishing your course, you won't even pay any attention to his junk. Instead of fussing and fuming over all the ugly things people are saying about you, you'll be busy looking forward to the day when you will stand face to face with Jesus and hear Him say, "Well done, thou good and faithful servant."[1]

Ordinary People Doing Extraordinary Things

by Oral Roberts

First of Two Parts

John 1:29-30 tells us, "The next day John seeth Jesus coming unto him, and saith, Behold the Lamb of God, which taketh away the sin of the world. This is he of whom I said, After me cometh a man which is preferred before me: for he was before me."

Verses 32-34 continue: "And John bare record, saying, I saw the Spirit descending from heaven like a dove, and it abode upon him. And I knew him not: but he that sent me to baptize with water, the same said unto me, Upon whom thou shalt see the Spirit descending, and remaining on him, the same is he which baptizeth with the Holy Ghost. And I saw, and bare record that this is the Son of God."

"One of the two which heard John speak, and followed him, was Andrew, Simon Peter's brother [somebody lesser, the little brother, the ordinary one]. He first findeth his own brother Simon, and saith unto him, We have found the Messias, which is, being interpreted, the Christ [the Anointed One]. And he brought him to Jesus" (vv. 40-42).

I want you to look at this ordinary man who made one of the greatest sales recorded in the New Testament. He was there when John the Baptist saw the Holy Ghost come in the form of a dove and light upon Jesus' head and remain there. He had heard John say, "Behold the Lamb of God, which taketh away the sin of the world. And he shall baptize you with the Holy Ghost." And the Bible says he went and found his brother and brought him to Jesus!

'I Have Found the Messiah!'

by Oral Roberts

Second of Two Parts

Andrew—who found the Messiah, who knew that he had found the One the Bible had prophesied about, who had found the Christ, the Son of the living God—found his brother, Simon Peter, and said to him, "Remember, they taught us in synagogue that the Holy Spirit was upon the prophets and different ones in Israel. This Messiah, the One we've been looking for, will baptize us with the Holy Ghost and fire. Peter, I have found the Messiah. I have found the Son of God!"

Do you remember the day, the night, the hour, or the moment you found Jesus Christ to be your Messiah, your Christ—the Anointed One, who washed away your sins, who didn't roll them back for one year but who saved your soul for time and eternity? Do you remember the time when salvation came into your soul?

Simon Peter opened the door to all of us Gentiles. The Day of Pentecost would not have had a spokesman without Simon Peter. Nobody before him had cried, "Thou art the Christ, the Son of the living God!" But behind Simon Peter was this little ordinary guy named Andrew, who said, "I have found the Messiah!"

God Really Does Love You!

by Terri Copeland Pearsons
Kenneth Copeland Ministries

"God is love" (1 John 4:8). But be honest. Is God really love to you?

Most people think God is following them around with a big stick, ready to smack them every time they sin. Yet when you look at the life of Jesus, He went to extreme lengths to prove to us the love of God. Ultimately, He even went to hell for us.

God loves you with an amazing love! He didn't have you born again just so He could get you off His conscience. Religion has taught people that God saves us just so we can praise Him and live for Him forever. In other words, to satisfy His own egotistical, selfish need to have people tell Him how great He is all the time.

No! God isn't like that! Ephesians tells us that He redeemed us in order to restore our fellowship with Him—both now and throughout the ages. His heart cries out to those who are in bondage to or have been hurt by sin. He knows how wonderful He can cause their lives to be. His driving compassion moves Him to be with us and to bless us.

If you haven't really experienced this love in a personal way, ask God to reveal the full scope of His marvelous love for you. He will...because He loves you.[1]

Dealing With Fear

by Lindsay Roberts

Every one of us has had an occasion to be afraid of something for some reason. But if you look at circumstances, you're sunk, because circumstances can get you into a spirit of fear. You can be afraid of riding in a car or airplane, or of slipping and falling in a bathtub. If you've known someone who fell down a flight of stairs and died, you can be fearful of ever going down stairs again. If you've lost a child, like my husband, Richard, and I have, you can fear losing another child. Whenever you have had a frightening experience, the spirit of fear can come in through that weakness and attach itself to you.

If we focus on the incident, which may be horrific, we have good reason circumstantially to live in fear. But if we look at the whole scope of the Bible, we see that God has not given us the spirit of fear that causes us to be afraid of circumstances! Second Timothy 1:7 says, "God has not given us the spirit of fear; but of power, and of love, and of a sound mind." That Scripture tells us that there is a spirit of fear, but it's not from God!

Look what God has given us. He has given us three counterbalancing measures to the spirit of fear: the spirit of power, the spirit of love, and the spirit of a sound mind. Power to take authority over the spirit of fear. Love—the perfect love of God—which is totally complete and which casts out all fear. (1 John 4:18.) And, last, a sound mind.

Have you ever tried to make a logical decision when you felt as though you were going crazy from fear? Those kinds of decisions are of no value. God has given you a sound mind to help you operate rationally, logically, and practically in times of trouble. He has given you everything you need to have victory over fear!

Giving Ourselves Away

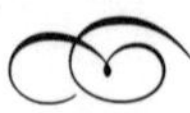

by Billy Joe Daugherty
Victory Christian Center Church and School

When I was a student at Oral Roberts University, Coach Bernis Duke led the tennis team to top national rankings for several seasons. Last year, he was inducted into the Intercollegiate Tennis Association Hall of Fame.

But what I remember most about Coach Duke is not the great tennis teams and the acclaim it brought ORU. I remember that every week he loaded the back of his car with groceries and gave them to poor people in Tulsa. Though he was busy with his duties on campus, Coach Duke made the time to give of himself to people who were hurting.

Jesus said we will find our place in the kingdom of God by being servants—by giving ourselves away. When two of His disciples were arguing over their place in the kingdom, Jesus told them, "Whoever desires to become great among you shall be your servant. And whoever of you desires to be first shall be slave of all. For even the Son of Man did not come to be serve, but to serve, and to give His life as a ransom for many" (Mark 10:43-45 NKJV).

Jesus set the example of servanthood. He took a towel and washed the disciples' feet. (John 13:4,5.) He left heaven's glory and came to earth to give Himself to free hurting people. He forgave and pardoned. Even at this very moment, He is still serving at the right hand of the Father praying for us. (Rom. 8:34.) Jesus has called us to follow that example. No matter what walk of life we may be in, every one of us can do something for others. We can all give ourselves away.

'Speak the Word Only'

by Richard Roberts

First of Three Parts

Wherever Jesus went, people interrupted Him. It would have been easy for Him to say, "Now just wait a minute. Let Me finish this message." In Matthew 8:5-13, when the centurion came to Jesus, perhaps He was in the middle of preaching. The centurion said, "My servant, my military aide, is grievously tormented with the palsy, a terrible paralytic condition."

Jesus turned to him and said, "I will come and heal him." That settled the issue. Healing is God's will. He said, "I will come. I don't have to pray about it. I don't have to think about it. I don't have to seek the elders. I will come, and I will heal him."

The centurion answered, "Lord, it's not necessary for You to come. Speak the word only, and my servant shall be healed. For I am also a man under authority. I speak to this soldier and tell him to go, and he goes. Or I tell this soldier to come, and he comes. My authority comes from Caesar in Rome. But I recognize that You have authority over all authority."

I believe the centurion fell down on his knees that day and worshiped the Lord, and he transferred his allegiance from Caesar to Jesus.

Jesus turned to the crowd and marvelled, "I've not seen this kind of faith before—such great faith!" Only twice in the Bible did He refer to faith as being great faith—once to this Roman army captain and once to a little Syrophoenician woman who came to Him in behalf of her demon-possessed daughter. (Matt. 15:21-28.) This story demonstrates that faith is where you find it. It's not always where you think it is.

Then Jesus turned to the centurion and said, "Go your way. And as you go, your servant will be healed." The Bible says his servant was healed in the same hour!

Believe That God Will Do What He Said He Will Do

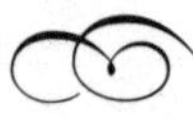

by Richard Roberts

Second of Three Parts

I believe that God is who He says He is. Believe Him when He says He is a healer. I believe that He is the almighty God. I believe that He flung the stars from His fingertips, piled high the mountains, dug deep the gorges, scooped out the beds for the oceans, traced the rivers with His fingernails, and created every living thing.

Believe that God is who He says He is—not what the world says He is. The world will tell you that things are God, but God is not a thing. God is not a person. God is not a man that he should lie. God is a Spirit, and we worship Him in spirit and in truth. (John 4:24.)

My God is an "I am" God. He is always in the now of our lives. I choose to believe that God is who He says He is.

Believe that God will do what He said He will do. Mark 11:23 illustrates this beautifully: "For verily I say unto you, That whosoever shall say unto this mountain, Be thou removed, and be thou cast into the sea; and shall not doubt in his heart, but shall believe that those things which he saith shall come to pass; he shall have whatsoever be saith."

As Jesus and His disciples left Bethany, Jesus felt hungry. He looked at a fig tree, hoping to get some figs, and found nothing as it was not yet fig season. The Bible says that He said to the tree, "Never bear fruit again!" They went on into the town, and when they left the city, they saw the fig tree dried up from the roots. And Peter remarked, "Jesus, look! The tree that You cursed only a matter of hours ago has now dried up from the roots."

Jesus answered, "Have faith in God." In other words, "Believe that I can do what I say I can do. For verily I say unto you, if you will believe in your heart and say it with your mouth, and if you refuse to doubt what you say and what you believe, then you can have whatsoever you believe."

Reach Out by Faith and Receive What You Are Believing For

by Richard Roberts

Third of Three Parts

Reach out by faith and receive what you are believing for. Mark 11:24 reads, "Therefore I say unto you, What things soever ye desire, when ye pray, believe that ye receive them, and ye shall have them."

When you are praying about a desire that God has placed in your heart and you know that it is in harmony with His will and with His Word, believe that you will receive, and you shall have it.

Sometimes the answer is not instantaneous. Most of the healings that I have seen in my life have come as a process, where someone receives a touch from God and there is an immediate change. But sometimes it takes a while, a period of time, for the process to work.

This was particularly brought to my attention back in the late seventies when I was a guest on a national television program. Through a word of prophecy, I was told by the Lord that I was going to have a healing ministry.

The Lord said to me, "Your father has laid hands on the sick, but you will speak the word." I was not aware that it was going to be a word-of-knowledge ministry as it is now. But God said to me, "You will speak the word, and people will be healed."

I had a choice as to whether I was going to believe that or not. But I began to pray and set my faith in agreement with that word.

God's word to me didn't happen instantaneously. For three years I stood in faith, and I would not let go of the word God gave me. By faith I believed it was on the way, and I received.

Marked for Blessing

by Jerry Savelle

Jerry Savelle Ministries International

Psalm 68:19 says, "Blessed be the Lord who daily loadeth us with benefits. The God of our salvation! Selah." Notice that word *selah*, which means "stop and think about that." That verse is saying God is such a good God that He wants to bless us every day of our lives, twenty-four hours a day! Jesus said in Matthew 6:11, "Give us this day our daily bread." God wants to bless us on a daily basis.

Psalm 67:7 says, "God shall bless us; and all the ends of the earth shall fear him." *The Message Bible* says, "You mark us with blessing, O God." I love that phrase! Recently when I read it in that translation, it just exploded in my spirit. I stopped and said, "I'm a marked man!"

I'm marked by God to be blessed, and so are you! Let me define the word *marked*. One meaning is "a sign of distinction." When someone has been marked, it means there is a sign of distinction on their life—something by which they are known. For example, Oral Roberts is known for healing and miracles. His life is marked with that distinction.

God wants the mark of distinction on our lives to be blessing. When someone sees you, they ought to think, *There goes a blessed man or woman.* There should be evidence in your life that you are marked for blessing. Now that doesn't mean you don't have challenges. Being marked for blessing doesn't exempt you from adversity. What it does exempt you from is being defeated by those challenges. When you are marked for blessing, you can't lose for winning!

Promise and Power

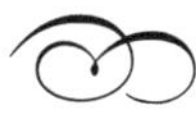

by Lindsay Roberts

Early in our marriage, I wrote in my Bible beside Mark 11:23-24, "Richard and Lindsay to have children." I wrote that when I was facing surgery for a tumor on my ovary which meant I would never be able to have children.

That tumor was like a mountain, but I knew Mark 11:23-24 said I could speak to that mountain, and it would have to obey. I could have the things that I desired, which was to have children, so I claimed the promise and the power of these two verses.

The tumor was miraculously healed, and today Richard and I have three beautiful daughters!

There is power in the Word of God. We can stand upon His promises, speak to our mountains of need, and receive the things we desire from the Lord!

The Only Job You've Got

by Jesse Duplantis
Jesse Duplantis Ministries

According to the Bible, if you're a Christian nothing is impossible to you. In Matthew 19:26 Jesus said, "With men this is impossible; but with God all things are possible." The only job a Christian has is to believe that God can do His job—that He can do what He has promised in His Word.

You see, God is not asking you to do His job. That's why He said, "With men, it's impossible." He's just asking you to believe. I know in my own life, everything that God ever asks me to do is impossible. Do you know why? Because He doesn't want me doing it! He just wants me to believe that He can do it.

Our trying to do God's job is why many of our prayers are delayed or never get answered. He wants us to get our hands off His job and let Him do what He has promised to do.

When God first told me to go on worldwide television, I said, "I can't do that!" He said, "I didn't ask you to do it. I asked, 'Are you willing to believe that I can put you on worldwide television?'" When He wanted me to believe for a multimillion-dollar jet, I said, "Lord, do You know how much money those cost?" He said, "You have an airplane now, Jesse—did you pay for it?" I answered, "No, Lord, You did." He said, "I'm not asking you to pay for the jet either; I'm just asking you to believe Me for it."

That really set me free, because then I knew that the only job I had was to believe that God could do His job. And He did. Our job is to focus on God's Word and believe what it says.

He's Given You Peace

by Kenneth Copeland
Kenneth Copeland Ministries

Some people have the idea that if you live by faith, you can float through life without any problems. Forget it. It will never happen.

Just look at Jesus. If anyone should have been able to float through life, it was Jesus. He had perfect faith. Yet, He had the toughest time of any man who ever walked on earth. He was persecuted, criticized, and plotted against. He was tempted with every sin mankind has ever known. Yet He resisted it all.

If you think that's easy, think again. There's nothing tougher than feeling the pressure of sin or sickness, and then standing, refusing to let it take over. There's nothing tougher than standing up at those times and saying, "No! I won't receive this sickness on my body. I won't give in to this circumstance! I've been set free by the blood of Jesus, and I will live free by faith in Him!"

If you want to see just how much pressure such a stand of faith can bring, look at Jesus before He went to the cross. The pressure of the temptation He faced put such a strain on His physical body that drops of blood poured through His skin like perspiration. Even then, sin could not conquer Him.

None of us will ever face that much trouble. We'll never have to stand against that much pressure. Yet we have available to us the same power and peace that took Him not just through the pressure, but through the whipping, the mocking, and the Crucifixion. We have the peace that took Him all the way through!

"Peace I leave with you," He said. "My peace I give you.... Do not let your hearts be troubled and do not be afraid."

He's given you His peace—far more than you'll ever need. So don't rehearse the problem over and over in your mind. Instead, receive the peace He provided for a day like today.[1]

That Is the Way Love Is!

by Oral Roberts

First of Four Parts

Before the foundation of the earth was laid, God the Father, the Son, and the Holy Ghost were lonely and wanted a family. Why? Because God is love. When you have love, you have to give it away. You can't hold love. Love has to be given. God is love, and He had this great love but had no one to love. He wanted a family. He decided to create man so He could pour His love out upon man. But He had to make that man so he could choose to return the love or not return it. That was a fearful thing. But otherwise, he would have been like the animals.

So to be a man, he had to be given choice. God had foreknowledge that man would go away from Him and mutiny against Him in the Garden of Eden, and He would lose that family.

The Bible says that Jesus was the Lamb slain before the foundation of the world was laid. (1 Peter 1:20; Rev. 13:8.) God had such love, knowing the family would go away, that He gave His only Son to be slain. Before Jesus was ever killed on the cross at Calvary, He was killed in eternity past.

Jesus said, "I'll go down to earth, and then I'll even die on the cross." And the Holy Spirit said, "I'll go down and watch over Him."

God had all that love, and that's the way love is!

There is no fear in love; but perfect love casteth out fear. —I John 4:18

The God-Kind of Faith

by Oral Roberts

Second of Four Parts

I was called to build Oral Roberts University. I had no money, no land, no buildings, no teachers, and no students. My own men mutinied against me, saying that if I built it, they would leave me. They thought I was going to leave the healing ministry. My life felt like nothing. But when you come to that point, there is an answer. This is when you do as God did. You call those things which be not as though they were. (Rom. 4:17.)

When God's Son was slain before the foundation of the world for man's sins, God had called that which was not as though it was going to be. That is to say, God knew man was not going to stay true to Him, that man was going to fall. He knew the great curse was coming upon mankind, but God had already called that which was not as though it would be.

Today there are millions and millions of people who are restored to God. We're no longer away from God. We're not strangers and foreigners. We are children of the kingdom because God's faith operates by calling that which is not as though it were.

I'm learning about faith. Sometimes even my wife says, "Oral, where is your faith? Oral, I know you to be a strong man of God. Why are you letting this get you down?" And that is what she should say to me when I'm like that. Just because you are a preacher doesn't mean that you don't make mistakes and say things you ought not say.

Matthew 18:18-19 is the faith agreement. We have the Word of God preached to bring up our faith. If it doesn't come up, we can't release it to God. If faith stays in our hearts, it's like love staying in our hearts.

We must learn to call that which is not as though it were. This is the kind of faith God has, and we can have the faith that God has too—the God-kind of faith!

'I Give You My Name'

by Oral Roberts

Third of Four Parts

God recently gave me a revelation concerning Matthew 18:19. It says, "Again I say unto you, That if two of you shall agree on earth as touching any thing that they shall ask, it shall be done for them of my Father which is in heaven."

Many times over these years of healing ministry, I have met people who were distraught because God hadn't healed them. But they had never asked Him to heal them. They thought He already knew. He does know, but for whatever reason He thinks is best, He tells us to ask.

Apparently we have to get into the action as nothing is automatic. Jesus says, "Any thing that they shall ask, it shall be done for them of my Father which is in heaven." When the Father in heaven does it, it's done. Nobody can stop the Father when He starts working. And if God is for us, who can be against us? And Jesus said, "Again I say." He evidently had been saying this over and over. Psychologists tell us that you have to hear something seven times to hear it once.

Notice in verse 20, He said, "For where two or three are gathered together in my name, there am I in the midst of them." Jesus never gave His name to His disciples until the last night of His life. In John 16:24 He said, "Hitherto have ye asked nothing in my name: ask, and ye shall receive that your joy may be full." In other words, He was saying, "I give you My name." And we pray in the name that He gave us. He gave us the name that is above every name, and the name before which every knee shall bow and every tongue shall confess.

Seed-Faith Is God's Way of Meeting Our Needs

by Oral Roberts

Fourth of Four Parts

Jesus says if two of you come into a prayer of agreement, "There am I in the midst of them" (Matt. 18:20). Notice He used His name, I AM. Do you remember that God told Moses His name was I AM? Jesus stretched all the way back to God speaking to Moses at Mount Sinai. He was saying, "When two people pray in agreement, I AM not at Sinai or out in the desert, but I AM in the midst of them."

Visualize Jesus standing in your midst when you pray in agreement with someone. Now if Jesus were with you in the flesh, you would jump and shout. You would worship Him. I'm talking about a now God who does now things!

When the disciples asked Jesus why they could not cast out a devil, "Jesus said unto them, Because of your unbelief: for verily I say unto you, If ye have faith as a grain of mustard seed, ye shall say unto this mountain, Remove hence to yonder place; and it shall remove; and nothing shall be impossible unto you" (Matt. 17:20).

At that time the mustard seed in Israel was the smallest of the seeds. It was as small as a grain of salt, but it grew into the largest tree. So Jesus is saying that if your faith is the kind of faith that grows, if you make it as a seed, it will increase. Once you get the understanding of Seed-Faith into your heart, no one can keep you from receiving your increase.

Miracles are coming toward seed-faithers every day. They're coming toward you or past you. *If you are not expecting them, you won't recognize them. They will pass you right by.*

Many times I've asked, "God, why didn't You do this?" He always reminded me that I wasn't expecting; therefore, I couldn't recognize what I wasn't expecting.

You Can Depend on Jesus...Always!

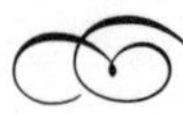

by Evelyn Roberts

There are very few of us who have trouble-free lives. One day I found the most wonderful verse in the Bible that deals with this. Hebrews 2:18 AMP, speaking of Jesus, says, "Because He Himself [in His humanity] has suffered in being tempted (tested and tried), He is able (immediately) to run to the cry of (assist, relieve) those who are being tempted and tested and tried."

That verse says Jesus understands what we're going through, and He's able to run to us immediately whenever we need Him! I like that! He doesn't have to wait a long time. Maybe a doctor or a friend or a family member can't get to us in time. But if we call on Jesus when we're in trouble, He hurries to help us.

We also have God's Word in times of adversity. The Word gives us the power we need to overcome temptations, trials, and tests. Hebrews 4:12 AMP says, "The Word that God speaks is alive and full of power making it active operative, energizing, and effective; it is sharper than any two-edged sword, penetrating to the dividing line of the breath of life (soul) and [the immortal] spirit, and of joints and marrow [that is, of the deepest parts of our nature] exposing and sifting and analyzing and judging the very thoughts and purposes of the heart."

That Scripture continues by saying, "Not a creature exists that is concealed from His sight" (v. 13).

God sees everything we do, and He knows all of our thoughts. He is everywhere we are. We may feel alone, but God is with us! When I'm in trouble, I like knowing that Jesus will run to me and that I can depend on Him...always!

God's Plan for Your Success

by Eastman Curtis
Destiny Church

I can't tell you what a difference it made in my life when I found out that God loved me and wasn't mad at me. I grew up thinking God had a big lightning bolt with my name on it, and He stood in heaven ready to zap me every time I messed up. You know, "Gotcha, boy!"

For some unknown reason, I always thought that God was going to make me do something I didn't want to do. Jeremiah 29:11 NIV is one of my favorite Scriptures because it helped me understand and know God better. It says, "'For I know the plans I have for you,' declares the Lord, 'plans to prosper you and not to harm you, plans to give you hope and a future.'" God is not out to beat your brains out. He wants to bless you.

God's plan for your life is bigger than your own. Many people are fearful about giving God their dreams, their ambitions, and their goals because they think, *God, if I give You my dream, if I give You my plan, You're going to take it away. You're going to reduce it and give it back.*

That's not the way God does things. Whenever you give your life to God, you can expect Him to give it back to you, good measure, pressed down, shaken together, and running over! (Luke 6:38.) God is on your side! He's not against you; He's for you! Romans 8:32 says, "He that spared not his own Son, but delivered him up for us all, how shall he not with him also freely give us all things?"

What does that tell you? God is a giver. He is not a "take-awayer." God wants to give you good things, not take them away. God is into your success even more than you are!

The Real Jubilee

by Billy Joe Daugherty
Victory Christian Center Church and School

If you've had years stolen from you by sickness and disease, by broken family situations, or by financial reversals, take heart! God says in Joel 2:25 that He restores to you the years that have been lost!

This is the message of Jubilee. In biblical times, every 50 years Israel celebrated the Year of Jubilee. Jubilee was a time when God would set right what had gone wrong throughout the previous years. Whatever land had been lost would be returned to its original owners. Those who had become slaves were given their freedom. And all debts were cleared from the books. It was a time like no other.

When Jesus came, He read these words in the synagogue at Nazareth: "The Spirit of the Lord [is] upon Me, because He has anointed Me...to preach the good news (the Gospel) to the poor; He has sent Me to announce release to the captives and recovery of sight to the blind, to send forth as delivered those who are oppressed [who are downtrodden, bruised, crushed, and broken down by calamity], to proclaim the accepted and acceptable year of the Lord [the day when salvation and the free favors of God profusely abound]" (Luke 4:18,19 AMP). Then He said, "Today this Scripture has been fulfilled while you are present and hearing" (v. 21). Jesus was proclaiming that He was the Jubilee!

What that means to you today is that Jesus came to restore your losses. Whatever has been broken, He can mend. Where there is devastation, He can bring healing. God has provided the way. Your part is to believe Him, step out in faith, and claim it!

How Jesus Did Spiritual Warfare

by Joyce Meyer
Joyce Meyer Ministries

I used to think spiritual warfare was screaming at the devil in prayer, "I rebuke you!" One day the Holy Ghost said to me, "Joyce, you ought to be Me and have to listen to you! Why don't you study the Bible and see how Jesus did spiritual warfare?" So I did. And one of the things I found out is that the devil couldn't control Jesus because He walked in love.

In Matthew 22:36 AMP the Pharisees asked Jesus, "Teacher, which kind of commandment is great and important? the principal kind? in the Law? [Some are light; which are heavy?]." They were asking, "What is the deepest thing that You can teach us?" And Jesus replied, "You shall love the Lord your God with all your heart and with all your soul, and with all your mind (intellect). And...You shall love your neighbor as [you do] yourself" (vv. 37,39).

Understand, first of all, that you can't fight a spiritual battle with something you don't have. Many people can never walk in love because they have never received the love of God for themselves. Knowing something in our heads is one thing; knowing by revelation is another. If you really know the love of God, no matter what you go through, nothing will be able to steal that love from you. (Rom. 8:35-39.)

Jesus ministered through love. By following Him, so can we. The Holy Spirit said, "Do you know, Joyce, what most of the people want when they come to you? They want you to love them. They're hurting and they want somebody to put their arms around them and say, 'I understand what you're going through. I love you. God loves you.'" Fight as Jesus did—with divine love.

Don't Draw Back!

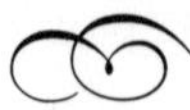

by Jerry Savelle
Jerry Savelle Ministries International

I wouldn't trade places with anyone else on earth. I am a happy man because I am walking with God and fulfilling His destiny for my life. Now I'm not saying I don't have challenges. I face impossible situations every day! But I decided a long time ago that I would never quit or draw back if things got hard in life.

Hebrews 10:38 says, "The just shall live by faith: but if any man draw back, my soul shall have no pleasure in him." That phrase "draw back" means to compromise, give up, or give in. Notice, God didn't say we'd go to hell or He wouldn't love us if we draw back; He said He would have no pleasure in us. We don't bring God pleasure by quitting or giving up under pressure when things get rough. What does give God pleasure is when we stand on His Word, trust Him, and believe that He is fulfilling His promises.

Look what verse 39 says: "We are not of them who draw back unto perdition; but of them that believe to the saving of the soul." That Scripture is referring to us! We are not quitters; we are winners! We don't compromise or give up under pressure. If we don't make that choice in our minds, then the devil can beat up on us for the rest of our lives. We have to make it clear to him that we will live by faith and not draw back, and then we have to remind him because he forgets. Remind him of your choice right now as you say this out loud with me: "I am not one of those who draw back! I'm not a quitter; I'm a winner!"

Sow Into Another's Dreams

by Marilyn Hickey

Marilyn Hickey Ministries

I believe that we must sow into the dreams of others before we can reap our own dreams. How? You encourage someone. You pray for them. Or maybe you sow seed into their dream.

If you're going to see your purpose come to pass, you've got to bless the purposes of other people. This is one of the most powerful truths I've ever known.

Remember Joseph? He sowed his interpretation of the dreams of Pharaoh's butler and baker while in prison, asking them to remember him. They forgot, but two years later the chief butler did remember Joseph's accurate dream interpretations and recommended him to Pharaoh, who ultimately released Joseph from prison and placed him second in command over all of Egypt. This fulfilled Joseph's long-held dream that began when he was only seventeen. (Gen. 40.)

Sometimes when I have wanted to do something for God and then some other ministry started doing it, I became so jealous of them! For example, for years I had wanted to be on television in Australia. I went to the government and couldn't get on. I prayed and prayed, but nothing happened. The next thing I heard Kenneth Copeland was on, then Joyce Meyer was on!

Do you know what God said to me? "If you'll sow into their purposes, I'll bless yours." So I began to sow into the ministries that were on television in Australia. It took only about six months for someone from Australian TV to call and say, "We feel you should be on our network." I said, "I feel I should be too." And I got on, but only after I had sown into someone else's dream first. The same thing will work for you.

God Honors Faith Where He Finds It

by Billy Joe Daugherty
Victory Christian Center Church and School

God is no respecter of persons in the sense that He would ever favor one individual over another. It is faith that God honors wherever He finds it, regardless of a person's background, nationality, social status, or which church they attend.

Hebrews 11 outlines for us many of the men and women of faith in the Bible and what they accomplished by simply believing God's word to them.

These were people from all walks of life, but they acted on their faith. Verse 1 NIV defines faith as "being sure of what we hope for and certain of what we do not see." In other words, we can believe God to move in a situation even before we see the evidence of His moving. That is faith in action—believing for what has not yet happened.

No matter what test or need has come into your life, believe that God is going to move on your behalf. Stand on God's Word and be assured that the situation is going to turn around. It may take time, and there is no guarantee the situation will turn out exactly like you want it to, but God is faithful to honor faith where He finds it.

Blazing Glory

But for you who revere my name, the sun of righteousness will rise with healing in its wings. And you will go out and leap like calves released from the stall. Then you will trample down the wicked; they will be ashes under the soles of your feet on the day when I do these things," says the Lord Almighty.

Malachi 4:2,3 NIV

by Kenneth Copeland
Kenneth Copeland Ministries

I imagine you are probably just as tired of having Satan get in the middle of your affairs as the next guy. You're tired of him causing trouble in your family and messing with your friendships. It doesn't have to be that way, you know. Read today's verse again.

Notice that this Scripture says "S-U-N of righteousness," and not "S-O-N of righteousness"? That's not a mistake. Malachi was talking about a bright, blazing glory. The wings he refers to aren't bird's wings; they're flames of fire that are shaped like wings.

Most exciting of all is the fact Malachi didn't say, "He will go out." He said, "You will go out."

You and I are the ones who will ensure Satan's defeat in our lives. We have all the power we need to destroy Satan's works and to kick him out of our affairs.

The words you say coupled with your faith are going to pull the glory out of you, and you'll walk in that glory right in the face of all the trouble hell can give you.

You are the one who will go out into the world with this blazing glory—the same glory that raised Jesus from the dead. It's that same glory that you'll use to trample down Satan like ashes under your feet![1]

Step Out of Your Comfort Zone

by Richard Roberts

Do you remember the story in Mark 3:1-5 NKJV of the man with the withered hand? Jesus met him in the synagogue and said to him, "Stand forth!" Perhaps this man had never stood up in front of a lot of people before. Or maybe he was embarrassed or ashamed to do so because of his withered hand. Jesus was telling him, in spite of how he felt, "It's time to step out of your comfort zone."

Then Jesus made what I believe to be one of the most amazing statements in the Bible. He said to the man, "Stretch out your hand." And he stretched it out, and his hand was restored as whole as the other (v. 5). Jesus told the man to do something he couldn't do, and if he did it, his hand would not be withered. Figure that out! I believe Jesus wanted him to get into faith action and obedience.

This story reminds me of when I was ministering in Calgary, Alberta, Canada. A man who had back trouble and hadn't been able to bend over for twenty-five years came forward for prayer. After I laid hands on the man, I told him to bend over three times.

"You don't understand, Richard," he said. "That's why I came for prayer. I can't bend over." Then I said, "The Lord is telling me to tell you to do what you cannot do." Upon hearing that, the man started to bend. The first time he went down only slightly. But he started in faith. The second time, he got down a bit farther. The third time, something happened in his spirit. He went down all the way and touched his toes! And his back was perfectly healed!

The key to this man's healing was obedience. When Jesus gives a word, act on it, even if it means stepping out of your comfort zone. That's what happened in this situation. The man acted on the Word of the Lord, and he got his miracle!

Grace in Abundance

by Evelyn Roberts

Years ago, as each of our crusade services ended, my husband would go to the car. He would be tired, and he usually went straight to the car the moment a meeting was over because he had prayed for a lot of people. I had started out the front door when a lady rushed up and asked, "Oh, my goodness, have I missed the meeting?" She said, "I came here in a boat. The boat was late, and I've got such a headache I can hardly stand here! Brother Roberts was supposed to pray for this headache, and he isn't here."

I said, "Well, let's pray." I put my hand on her head, and I tell you, the power of God jolted her. Not that I had any power, but God wanted that woman healed right then. In the end it didn't make any difference to her who prayed for her. At first it made a difference to her because she had heard Oral Roberts was preaching healing, and naturally she wanted him to pray for her.

The woman received her healing and was so pleased! She said, "Now I can go home without a headache." That made me feel so good, not because I did anything, but because I happened to be there when she had a need. I didn't have much to give, but what I had, I gave to her cheerfully.

That's what Peter and John did in Acts 3:1-10. They said they didn't have any money, but that wasn't what the lame man at the Beautiful Gate needed anyway. He needed what they had. And they happened to have Jesus. You don't have to have a lot of healing power; you just have to have Jesus. Jesus has the healing power.

After you have accepted Jesus Christ, He makes you worthy to pray for somebody. And after you pray for someone, you'll feel like saying, "Lord, thank You because I was here and I could help this person."

Of course the Lord wants us to put our hearts into whatever we do. And as we do, He is able to make all grace come to us in abundance. (2 Cor. 9:8.)

Please Pass the Miracles!

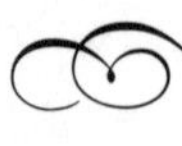

by Oral Roberts

There was a family who sat down to dinner, and they decided to record their conversation and listen to it later. During the dinner, one of their small sons said, "Please pass the butter."

No one heard him. They kept on talking. The second time he said, "Please pass the butter," the others kept right on talking. The third time he said, "Please pass the butter," they still kept right on talking.

Finally, the little boy stood up in his chair and shouted, *"Please pass the butter!"*

"Son, you get down off that chair and go to your room," the father commanded. "You're not going to have any dinner tonight." Quietly, the little boy obediently left for his room.

After dinner, they began to play the recorder. Throughout the conversation they heard a little wee voice saying, "Please pass the butter." A little later, they again heard, "Please pass the butter!"

Someone is up on a chair right now saying, "God, please pass the miracles. Please pass the miracles. Please pass the miracles!"

Jesus *will* hear that little voice! The devil has told you in different ways that God won't hear you. You know this is the truth. And the worse it gets, the more he insists, "God won't hear you!"

I am sure I am speaking to someone who does not believe that God will hear you.

I was a guest on the *Larry King Live* TV program, and he asked me about the twenty-three times I have heard God's voice. He said, "Does God speak to everybody?"

"Yes," I said, "but everybody does not listen."

I'm no special person. I just happen to be listening.

The Joy of God's Presence

by Lindsay Roberts

I thank God for miracles in answer to prayer. I believe in miracles. And when I have a need, there's nothing better than a miracle from God! But I am also thankful for His living presence in my life. It is such a blessing to be able to talk to Him, walk with Him, listen to Him, and have a oneness and a fellowship with Him every day.

For example, I love it when my husband, Richard, gives me gifts. But even better than receiving an occasional gift from him is having a relationship with him. Getting to talk with him and be with him is really a gift that is more special than any other gift he could give me.

That's how God is with us also. Although He loves to pour out His miracles and blessings upon us, His greatest joy is being our Father—having a relationship with us and being present in our lives. It's such an honor to be called His child and to call Him "Father." That's a special name, signifying a very special relationship like no other relationship in our lives.

Psalm 16:11 says, "In thy presence is fulness of joy; at thy right hand there are pleasures for evermore." When we think of all of God's good gifts to us, spending time in His presence is really one of His best gifts to us.

The Biggest Problem Isn't Big Enough

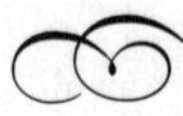

by Kenneth Copeland
Kenneth Copeland Ministries

It doesn't matter what you are facing today...no problem is too big when you factor in God's power! Take hold of His power by expecting something good to happen to you. Grab hold of hope—because you're believing God's promises.

Don't be a stranger to His promises. Dig them out of the Bible. Find out what God has said about your situation. Then start saying, "I expect something good to happen because God promised it!"

Think about those promises. Let them build an image inside you until you can see yourself healed and doing well in every way.

If you'll do that, you'll eventually get bigger on the inside than you are on the outside. Your hope will grow so strong that Satan himself won't be able to beat it out of you.

When we're confronted by impossible situations in this world, we just need to factor in Jesus...His Word...His power!

Some say, "That sounds too easy." Easy?! I don't think so. When Satan throws the noose of hopelessness around your neck with some terrible situation, you have to fight hard. The way you fight hard is by grabbing hold of your hope in God's promises and using it to destroy every thought that contradicts them.

"We demolish arguments and every pretension that sets itself up against the knowledge of God, and we take captive every thought to make it obedient to Christ" (2 Cor. 10:5).

The battleground where hope is won or lost is in your thoughts. So take your stand on that battleground and take control of your thoughts. Begin to expect God's power to destroy the bondage in your life. Begin to expect God to keep His promises to you.[1]

Meditate on the Word

by Pat Harrison
Faith Christian Fellowship International

It's one thing to read Scripture, but it's another thing to meditate on it and make it a part of you. That's what God told Joshua to do when he began to lead the children of Israel. God said, "This Book of the Law shall not depart from your mouth, but you shall meditate in it day and night, that you may observe to do according to all that is written in it" (Josh. 1:8 NKJV).

The question is, how do you meditate on God's Word day and night? Take one verse a day or a week and think about it continually. Memorize it. Say it over and over. Look up the verse in a study Bible and learn what the words actually mean.

Take Timothy 1:7 NKJV, for example. It says, "God has not given us a spirit of fear, but of power and of love and of a sound mind." Who is God? He's my God. He's the God of heaven and earth. That's big. He is El Shaddai. That means He's the God of more than enough in every area of my life. "Has not." That means He never has and never will. "Given us a spirit of fear." What is a spirit of fear? It's a spirit of terror, intimidation, and cowardliness. God has not given us that kind of spirit.

What has He given us? Power. What kind of power? Christ's power. The Holy Spirit's overcoming power. God has given us what? Love. What does God's Word say about love? Perfect love casts out fear. (1 John 4:18.) It can lift us high above every situation or problem. God has also given us a sound mind. What is a sound mind? It's a mind controlled by the Holy Spirit, well-balanced, disciplined, and pure.

You can overcome any situation when God's Word becomes a part of you!

We're All God Has To Work With!

by Jerry Savelle

Jerry Savelle Ministries International

I was inducted into the military in 1967, during the Vietnam War. I'll never forget the day I arrived at Fort Dix for boot camp. A guy who looked like Smokey the Bear ordered us to get off the military transport truck, using words I'd never heard in my life! He told us to fall in. None of us knew what that meant, but it wasn't long before he defined it for us and we stood at attention.

He started chewing on us and screaming at us. Finally, he walked down to the other end of the line, and I thought, *This is my opportunity to see what we've got to work with. I looked around at the recruits.* There was a man in bib overalls; he looked like he'd just come off the farm. Next to him was a man in a three-piece suit; he looked like he'd just come from a bank. Standing next to me was a long-haired hippie who didn't know he was even there—he was stoned out of his mind.

We were a ragtag bunch. As I looked up and down the line I thought, *Dear God, is this all we've got to work with? We're going to war! I'm going to lay my life on the line, and this is all we've got to work with?*

God is fighting a battle against Satan, and we are all He has to work with! Matthew 24:24 warns us that Satan will do his best to deceive God's people and try to get them to depart from the faith. So we have an awesome responsibility. We can't be double-minded. We can't be looking for an excuse to give up or compromise. When we make an unwavering commitment to God and His Word to fight the enemy, He can make us soldiers who are more than conquerors through Him!

A Garden of Vegetables

by Patricia Salem

When I was a young girl, my grandfather taught me about exercising my faith when I pray. He was a wonderful man of God, and he always had a beautiful garden. As we walked through his garden, he would say, "Pat, if you don't do anything with your faith, what good is it? It's like having this garden full of vegetables but never eating them. That won't help you grow strong. The Bible is full of God's promises to us, but if you don't believe them and run with them, then those promises won't do you any good."

First John 5:14-15 NKJV says, "This is the confidence that we have in Him, that if we ask anything according to His will, He hears us. And if we know that He hears us, whatever we ask, we know that we have the petitions that we have asked of Him." We can't ask God for things that are out of line with His Word. For example, we cannot ask for someone else's husband or wife. We're to ask according to God's will; and when we do, the Bible says He hears us.

God wants to answer our prayers, but we have to believe—or have faith—that He hears us and will answer us. Romans 12:3 says that God has given each one of us a measure of faith. But just as it's up to us to pick the vegetables from a garden and eat them if we are to receive nourishment from them, it's up to us to exercise the faith that God has given us in order for it to work in our lives.

Some of us choose to use our faith, and others choose to let it lie dormant. But when we choose to believe what God has said in His Word and run with it, then the Bible says we have the petitions that we have asked of Him.

A New Nature—No Going Back

by Richard Roberts

When the apostle Paul wrote to the Corinthians that they were "new creatures in Christ Jesus," he was reminding them of something they already knew.

Corinth was a busy seaport in Greece—a city of great influence and wealth. It was also a city filled with wickedness, sin, idolatry, and violence. Paul had spent about eighteen months in Corinth building a great church there. Many of the Christians had been deeply involved in the wickedness of the city before they came to know Jesus Christ. They knew how much their lives had changed when they accepted Jesus and were filled with the Holy Spirit.

After Paul left Corinth, he began to hear about problems that were arising in the Corinthian church, and he wrote to them, "Remember—remember—remember." You can almost hear the plea in his voice. "Remember that you are a new creature. The old things are behind you. All things are made new." Paul was also saying to them, "Don't go back!" (2 Cor. 5:17.)

Shortly after I accepted the Lord Jesus Christ as my Savior, during my sophomore year at Oral Roberts University, a friend came up to me and said, "Remember, Richard, when we...." I stopped him short. "No," I said, "I don't remember. That was the old me. I'm a new creature now."

When you become a new creature in Christ Jesus, you must continue to live as a new creature. Don't turn back to your old ways. Start to feed on new information—especially the information about who the Bible says you are! Feed on new inspiration. Begin to serve God with a new dedication. Get a new outlook on life. And stay with it!

Consider your past to be dead. The present and future are alive. Live looking forward in Christ Jesus, not backward—live as a new creature!

You Can Be a Champion for God

by Billy Joe Daugherty
Victory Christian Center Church and School

No matter what your background is, what has happened in your past, or what talents you have or don't have, God has called you to be a champion for Him. God called Gideon to be a champion.

Gideon lived in a time when Israel had sinned and, as a result, the Midianites came in and oppressed the land of Israel. The people were living in abject poverty when the Lord appeared to Gideon and said, "The Lord is with thee, thou mighty man of valour. And Gideon said unto him, Oh my Lord, if the Lord be with us, why then is all this befallen us? and where be all his miracles?" (Judges 6:12,13).

Gideon had a serious attitude problem. He wasn't deeply involved in spiritual affairs; he actually criticized God. Yet the Lord told Gideon that He had chosen him to save Israel from the hand of the Midianites. He said, "Go in this thy might, and thou shalt save Israel from the hand of the Midianites" (v. 14).

Gideon said, "Lord, how can I do that? My family is the poorest of the poor, and I'm the least of the least." Gideon not only had a negative attitude toward God and anger about his situation, but he also had low self-esteem. Despite all that, the Lord chose to make him a champion. He said, "Surely I will be with thee, and thou shalt smite the Midianites as one man" (v. 16).

God speaks to many people who don't have anything, who don't think they are anything, who see themselves as having no ability, and He says, "You can be a champion." He says the same thing to each of us today. "You mighty woman of valor, you mighty man of valor, you can be a champion because I am with you!"

Four Dimensions of Life

by Jesse Duplantis
Jesse Duplantis Ministries

Part One of Two Parts

Because I don't dye my hair, people are always asking me, "Brother Jesse, how old are you?" However, the question shouldn't be, "How long have you lived?" but, "How much have you lived?" How much have you breathed, loved, hurt, and felt? Life has four dimensions: length, breadth, depth, and height. Have you lived enough to understand what people are going through?

Some people live in only one dimension. Methuselah was a one-dimensional man. The Bible says he lived 969 years, begat sons and daughters, and died. That's it! (Gen. 5:27.) His was a one-dimensional life. But Jesus lived only thirty-three years and changed the world forever.

When I became born again, God said, "If you want length, breadth, depth, and height to your life, you're going to have to learn to love some people you don't like. That means praying for those who despitefully use you." (Matt. 5:44.) That was one of those Scriptures I never liked, but I prayed anyway.

I didn't have any breadth in those days. *Breadth* means how wide your life is lived. Never narrow your life to a single interest. Ask yourself, *How far advanced am I in the knowledge of truth?*

My mother had breadth to her life, even though she died at forty-nine. She used to say, "I'll see you saved." I said, "It ain't going to happen." She said, "It is going to happen." And sure enough, before she went to be with the Lord, she saw me saved and preaching the Gospel. Live your life wide enough to change the destiny of another individual.

Your Life Needs Depth and Height

by Jesse Duplantis
Jesse Duplantis Ministries

Part Two of Two Parts

Your life needs depth. Depth—deep underlying purposes and principles of faith—is produced in you through the Bible. Depth produces mission, purpose, and power. After a while you're saying, "Lord, not my will, but Thine be done."

We need depth in the Word so that when the devil attacks us with illness, we say, "I'll stand on the Word of God. By His stripes I'm healed." (Isa. 53:5.)

Finally comes height. *Height* means life is measured by the upward, outward reach of your own aspiration and resolve. Don't rush through your life. Fulfill each part. Moses had all four dimensions. His life had length, breadth, depth, and height. He was a veteran. The title of veteran is attained not by years but by campaigns and battles in which you were found faithful.

God does not stop with one generation. After Moses died, God said to Joshua, "Moses my servant is dead. Now get up and cross the Jordan. Let's go! Move!"

Do you see my point? Teach your children to perpetuate the visions and dreams that God has spoken to you. What God speaks doesn't last only one generation. It lasts forever. God calls your children to be a blessing, and that call will go on and on until Jesus comes. That's length, breadth, depth, and height of life.

A Reason but Not a Right

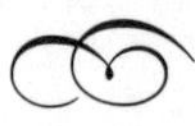

by Lindsay Roberts

I remember a time a when a woman was being really abusive to me, not in a physical sense, but emotionally. I tolerated it year after year until one day it involved my children, and that was it for me. I drew the line!

At that point I became frustrated, and bitterness set in. My mother came to me, and she said, "Lindsay, you have every reason to be bitter." And I thought, *Wow! That justifies how I am feeling.* Then she said, "But you have no right to be bitter, because Jesus Christ took that right away from you at Calvary. You may have a great reason, but according to the shed blood of Jesus Christ, you have no right to remain bitter." Then she said, "It's not up to that person to change; it's up to you to release that person."

That hit me like a ton of bricks, and I suddenly realized it didn't matter if it was a small offense, a medium-sized one, an insult of words, a heinous crime, or whatever, it was just as wrong for me to carry it. I realized at that moment that I was the one who was guilty, and I asked God to forgive me.

Maybe you're struggling with feelings of bitterness and unforgiveness toward someone who has offended you. Jesus said in Mark 11:25-26 that we must forgive to be forgiven. So I ask you from the bottom of my heart to release all bitterness right now. Whatever offense it is that you are carrying, the greatest way to set yourself free is to set somebody else free. Just say, "Father God, I refuse to carry bitterness toward that person. I refuse to harbor unforgiveness. Lord, I release them to You. In Jesus' name. Amen."

Does God Hear You?

This is the confidence that we have in Him, that if we ask anything according to His will, He hears us. And if we know that He hears us, whatever we ask, we know that we have the petitions that we have asked of Him.

1 John 5:14,15 NKJV

by Suzette Caldwell

Windsor Village United Methodist Church

There is a way you can *know* that God hears you when you pray: by praying according to His will. God's Word is His will, so you could say that if we pray according to God's Word, He is listening.

We do this by searching the Scriptures for what God has to say about our situation, then we pray His Word back to Him. For example, I like to pray Psalm 112:1–3 back to God concerning my children: "Father, I praise You. I am blessed because I reverence You. I delight greatly in Your commandments. And because of this, my descendants (here I name my children) are mighty on the earth. They are my generation. I am the upright, and they will be blessed, in Jesus' name. Wealth and riches will always be in their house, and their righteousness will endure forever."

I believe that the Word I have spoken will surround my children as they grow up, and as adults, they will begin to bear fruit from that Word.

Get into God's Word to find out what He has already said about your situation, and then pray that Word back to Him. I believe you can become confident that He hears and answers your prayers![1]

Above All Things

by Evelyn Roberts

Ever since my husband and I started in the healing ministry, I've just been his sidekick. I've walked alongside him and encouraged and helped him along the way. So if I tell stories about what happened to us, they really happened to him. But since I was right beside him, it has to be my story too.

Many things happened in those days. But we both wondered how we would help the people to know and understand that God wanted to meet their needs, because in those days, people didn't know that God really wanted to meet their needs.

When I grew up, we had the idea that if you didn't pay your tithe, there would be a curse put on you. We were not taught that if you do pay your tithe, you will be blessed. Believe me, I took my tithe to church every Sunday. I wasn't about to have a curse on my life!

We didn't have much worldly goods. A neighbor of ours helped us get a brand-new car. When he helped us get that car, it became a symbol to us. To tell the truth, the neighbor was sick of seeing our old rattletrap car on the street. He wanted to help us get something that would make him feel a little bit better about living next door to us. He helped us get a Buick, the most beautiful thing I'd ever seen in my life. It became a symbol to us that if God cared enough about us to give us a new car, He would certainly meet people's needs to whom we ministered.

Then one morning Oral was leaving to go to school, and he realized he had not read the Scripture as he always did every morning. He came back into the house, opened his Bible to 3 John 2, which reads, "Beloved, I wish above all things that thou mayest prosper and be in health, even as thy soul prospereth."

God Wants You To Triumph

by Jerry Savelle
Jerry Savelle Ministries International

Failures are not God-made. God wants you to be a success in every endeavor of your life. I can't find anywhere in God's Word where He says, "Win a few, lose a few." He wants you to win all of your battles. The apostle Paul tells us in 2 Corinthians 2:14 NKJV, "Thanks be to God who always leads us in triumph in Christ."

I like to tell people it's never over until you triumph, just as Paul said. No matter what you're going through, no matter what kind of adversity you may be experiencing, no matter what kind of opposition may come, God always leads you to triumph. Satan is going to do everything he possibly can to keep you from succeeding, but remember the promise found in 1 John 4:4 NKJV: "You are of God...He who is in you is greater than he who is in the world."

If you are facing adversity but striving for triumph, you can pattern yourself after the many people found throughout the Bible who faced incredible odds—brutal enemies, tough adversity, and fierce opposition—but who were unwilling to give up. Hebrews 11:33-34 NKJV describes them as people who through faith subdued kingdoms, worked righteousness, obtained promises, stopped the mouths of lions, quenched the violence of fire, escaped the edge of the sword, out of weakness were made strong, became valiant in battle, turned to fight the armies of the aliens.

These were common people much like you and me who alone weren't strong, but their faith in God's almighty power gave them strength to fight their battles and triumph. If you need strength today to face situations life has given you, use Micah 7:8 NKJV to uphold you: "Do not rejoice over me, my enemy; when I fall, I will arise; when I sit in darkness, the Lord will be a light to me."

Fired Up

by Eastman Curtis
Destiny Church

Just before the Israelites were about to claim the Promised Land, the tribes of Reuben and Gad approached Moses. After wandering in the desert for forty years, they had decided that they were content to keep their flocks and herds in the land they presently occupied. They told Moses, "Don't make us cross over the Jordan River into the Promised Land. We're happy where we are." (Num. 32:1-5.)

Moses was a little miffed because he knew that God wanted the best for His children. But the Reubenites and Gadites were, in essence, saying they didn't want God's best. They were happy to stay where they were. Moses said to them, "Shall your countrymen go to war while you sit here? Why do you discourage the Israelites from going over into the land the Lord has given them?" (vv. 6,7 NIV). He was really saying, "Are you just gonna sit there?"

The Reubenites and Gadites were just sitting there. They were not moving ahead. They were not advancing. They were stagnant, and because of that, they were discouraging their fellow Israelites from receiving all God had for them.

When you are stagnant in your walk with God, you not only can limit yourself to receiving less than God's best, but you can also discourage others and keep them from pressing into the blessing God has in store for them.

Apathy and indifference are contagious. But the reverse is also true. When you are fired up about what God is doing in your life and you're pursuing the destiny that He has given you, you can spread that enthusiasm to others, and their lives can be changed through God's power!

The Holy Spirit Searches Your Heart

by Marilyn Hickey

Marilyn Hickey Ministries

First of Two Parts

The heart is the place of enlightenment and the seat of your affections. Many people listen to their hearts when making decisions. Others' hearts skip a beat when they see a loved one from a distance. The Christian, however, makes a decision for Christ with his heart, and then Christ comes to live in him, thereby guiding his behavior and effecting a change within him.

Two of Jesus' disciples realized this, probably for the first time, when Jesus appeared to them following the Resurrection as they walked the road to Emmaus. After spending time talking with them and explaining the fulfillment of the Scriptures to them, Jesus disappeared from their midst. When they realized it was Jesus, "They said one to another, Did not our heart burn within us, while he talked with us by the way, and while he opened to us the Scriptures?" (Luke 24:32).

Keep A Winning Heart

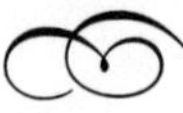

by Marilyn Hickey
Marilyn Hickey Ministries

Second of Two Parts

All of us want a winning heart; yet a winning heart comes only if you have a wise heart. If you seek after God with all of your heart, then you are going to win. A winning heart has no desire to do evil. Second Chronicles 12:14 says that King Rehoboam "did evil because he prepared not his heart to seek the Lord." The main idea in this verse is that you have to prepare your heart to seek the Lord, just as a marathon runner runs daily in preparation for the race.

'Depend on Me'

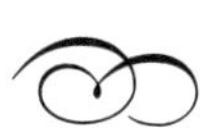

by Lindsay Roberts

Has God ever asked you to do something that you felt you couldn't do? He has me! But if God calls you, He plans to help you, even if you're in uncharted territory.

There was a time in my life when I was so quiet and timid that in public I was happy to sit still and not say two words. Then I married Richard Roberts...and he had a television ministry! At first, I wasn't on television with him. I sat in the audience. But I had to have a bucket next to me, because every time I even thought a camera was coming near me, I lost my lunch. And when I finally did go on television, I shook so badly that I could hardly speak.

I felt that God had made a wrong choice. I didn't think I could live the life He had called me to. But one day as I cried out to God for help, He said, "Lindsay, you didn't call yourself to this life. I called you to it. Depend on Me."

God never makes mistakes. He doesn't call the equipped; He equips the called. Even now, public speaking and being in front of the camera isn't my favorite thing, but I know what God has called me to do, and I depend on Him.

In Isaiah 41:10 God says, "Fear thou not; for I am with thee: be not dismayed; for I am thy God: I will strengthen thee; yea, I will help thee." If God has called you to do something for Him, be obedient and give Him the glory. He will help you!

There Is Only One Way!

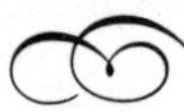

by Terry Law
World Compassion/Terry Law Ministries

First of Two Parts

One night the Lord Jesus walked into a room where I was praying. He said, "I'm going to send you behind the Iron Curtain." Those were the most shocking words of my life.

A few years later, a letter came in the mail inviting us to sing on a university campus in southern Poland. It was from one of the more prestigious institutions of higher learning in eastern Europe. The famous Italian astronomer and physicist Galileo taught at that university!

It's really a scary thing when you move across a border and see border guards with machine guns and guard dogs. They begin going over your bus with a fine-tooth comb, trying to find anything.

When we arrived in Krakow, the city where we were invited to sing, I found we had not been invited by a university group but by the leaders of the Communist Youth Party of southern Poland.

Now if you don't think God has a sense of humor, you ought to minister for Him on occasion. They thought we were a rock-and-roll group. They had no idea our repertoire was Christian music.

Both concerts were sold out. But by the end of the third song, they knew what was happening. I got up to try to break the ice, and as I did, the anointing of the evangelist came on me. You wouldn't want to travel with me when the anointing comes on me because I don't care who you are or what you think, I'll tell you what the Word of God says. There is only one way, and His name is Jesus Christ!

I talked for about twelve minutes, and when I was finished, I walked offstage and left. I was grabbed and hauled downstairs, and the group continued singing.

My "hosts" could not believe we had come to present Jesus. They couldn't believe we would risk our lives for that! Later one of them who became a Christian said, "The reason I became a Christian is because you believed in your Jesus more than I believed in my communism."

A Powerful Testimony!

by Terry Law

World Compassion/Terry Law Ministries

Second of Two Parts

After the men were through talking with me, I began to realize that they had sold out the second concert, and they didn't want to give back the money. They had made a great deal of money, and they said to me, "You can't talk anymore, but the group's got to sing."

I said, "Fine."

The group had already started singing in the second concert before they allowed me to go up on the stage, and our young people were terrified. They thought we were all going to prison. They were standing on the platform, their knees having a "fellowship meeting," and they were praying for the Rapture all at the same time.

Halfway through the concert the anointing fell on the singers, and they forgot their fear. They forgot everything else, and they began to sing to the Lord. I'll never forget that moment as long as I live. There were eight singers and twelve musicians in the band. The singers started to raise their hands. They forgot the audience and sang to Jesus! If you're a young American in the middle of a Communist audience, tears rolling down your cheeks, praying to Somebody they don't even believe exists, it's the most powerful testimony you can give them. Nobody told us this. We didn't understand it. It was what the Spirit of the Lord was doing. I saw one of the guys blowing a slide trombone with one hand in the air! I had never seen that before that night. I saw it! I saw it!

The audience sensed the anointing. They knew something palpable was in the air. Then we sang the last song, "God is moving by His Spirit, moving through all the earth. Signs and wonders, when God moveth. Move, O Lord, in me."

When the song died away, there were about fifteen seconds of dead silence, and then everyone leaped to their feet in one group. It was as if someone had pressed an electric button. Everybody stood and began to put their hands together and applaud!

They demanded one, two, three encores. We were there until 3:30 in the morning leading people to Jesus Christ in the headquarters of the Communist party!

SEPTEMBER 26

God's Word + Hope + Faith = Appearance

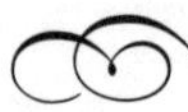

by Kenneth Copeland

Kenneth Copeland Ministries

Therefore, since we have been justified through faith, we have peace with God through our Lord Jesus Christ, through whom we have gained access by faith into this grace in which we now stand. And we rejoice in the hope of the glory of God.

Romans 5:1,2 NIV

God's Word + Hope + Faith = Appearance. This spiritual process always works the same way. Hope forms the image, then faith rises up and gives substance to that image, making it a reality in the natural, physical realm.

Now, I have a question I'd like you to seriously consider: In the light of all God has promised us in His Word, what are you and I to expect? What should we be hoping for?

Certainly, healing is great. Financial supply is wonderful. But could it be that God has something even better for us to hope for?

Yes, He does. He tells us what it is in today's verse.

This Scripture, in the last phrase, says we're to rejoice in the hope of the glory of God! We're to expect the glory, not just the healing or the finances!

As long as you're just expecting healing, you'll always be battling it out with your old sinful nature, but if you're expecting the glory, you'll be raising your spiritual sights to something bigger than healing. You'll be expecting the very presence of God to rise up in you so powerfully that, instead of believing for healing every six weeks, you'll walk in divine health every day!

I've experienced touches of glory, and believe me, I'm eager for more! So start expecting the glory. Raise your expectations to a new level. The results will be glorious![1]

True Therapy

by Vicki Jamison-Peterson

Vicki Jamison-Peterson Ministries

First of Two Parts

Laughter is an important part of a healthy life. Like a nutritious diet and exercise, positive emotions are necessary to keep us on an even keel physically and psychologically. Laughter helps reduce anxiety and tension in school, at work or at play, with relationships, and just everyday living.

The ability to laugh is one of the most important characteristics we can give children. It profoundly affects their coping abilities and relationships with the world around them. Parents can start to teach their children about the healthy benefits of laughter with a few of these facts. When people laugh very hard, their heart pace quickens, and their lungs expand and fill to capacity. Their throat goes into uncoordinated spasms. All capillaries open, and the pituitary gland is stimulated to produce natural painkillers a hundred times more powerful than morphine.

The effect is like taking the body on an internal jog. Other health-care professionals extol the curative powers of laughter. Dr. Annette Goodheart recommends faking it in order to feel better. "Go someplace private," she advises, "and start pumping out those familiar sounds, ha, ha, ha."

Oxygen floods the blood and the cardiovascular system dilates, which is why the face gets flushed. The muscles relax, which is why you fall out of your chair if you laugh hard enough. The diaphragm convulses, which is why you get a pain in your side.

According to Dr. Goodheart, the internal organs get massaged. This is true therapy. If you start every morning with fifteen minutes of laughter, it will take care of the rest. Start with fifteen seconds and work up to what you can tolerate. Try it! It works!

Rejoice and Be Glad in It

by Vicki Jamison-Peterson
Vicki Jamison-Peterson Ministries

Second of Two Parts

People say, "What is the fruit of this?" And pardon the pun, but we are the fruit of this. To the physical body, to the emotions, the fruit of joy is a strengthener.

The word *strengthener* reminds me of the verse in Nehemiah 8:10 that we always quote: "The joy of the Lord is your strength." The joy of the Lord comes into our natural bodies, into our spirits, and becomes a physical, spiritual, and emotional strength. The Holy Spirit's office is that of strengthener, so why would He not know how to bring us into joy to strengthen us?

In the morning, begin to laugh just however long you can—fifteen seconds, if that is as far as you can go—and go ha, ha, ha. Would it not make sense that in the spirit world, God, being all-knowing, who created our bodies to be self-healing, also created us as emotional beings, that the body, the emotions—all of that—would work together so that our spirit man can be more profoundly dominant?

It is noted that a good laugh changes blood pressure. So if you have high blood pressure, it will raise it and then lower it to a healthy area, reduce muscle tension, and improve digestion. If you laugh hard enough to cry, tears will be released that contain bacteria-killing agents.

Joy is an aspect of God's nature, but it's the curative, restorative aspect of God doing psychotherapy, physical therapy, spiritual therapy, to help us get above our circumstances that we might be energized and empowered with His presence to do what we are called to do.

"You have made known to me the ways of life: you will make me full of joy in Your presence." —Acts 2:28 NKJV

Know God Is a Good God

by Evelyn Roberts

One of the first things I heard my husband preach when he began the healing ministry was "God is a good God." I'd never heard anybody say that before, and I asked him, "Where did you get that? How do you know God is a good God?"

Oral said, "Evelyn, you know that the Lord saved you, and He has saved me." Yes, I knew that to be true. God didn't have to save us; we didn't do anything to deserve it or earn it. The Bible says, "But God commendeth his love toward us, in that, while we were yet sinners, Christ died for us" (Rom. 5:8). It is a good God who saves us!

There are more reasons why I believe God is a good God, and they come straight from the Bible. You can't get a better source than the Bible for what you believe. God said that He confirms His Word to us out of the mouths of several witnesses.

John 10:10 says, "The thief cometh not, but for to steal, and to kill, and to destroy: I am come that they might have life, and that they might have it more abundantly." Everything we count as good in our lives comes from our good God! It is a good God who comes to give us life, and not just ordinary life but abundant life!

In James 1:17 we read, "Every good gift and every perfect gift is from above, and cometh down from the Father of lights, with whom is no variableness, neither shadow of turning." Everything we count as good in our lives comes from our good God! He's the Creator of every blessing, the Author of every good word, the Giver of every miracle.

Matthew 7:11 gives us these words of Jesus: "If ye then, being evil, know how to give good gifts unto your children, how much more shall your Father which is in heaven give good things to them that ask him?" God is a good God, and it is His nature to give good gifts.

Let's praise God for His goodness. Let's praise Him for the good gifts He has given us and the good things He has done for us. Let's believe God for something *good* to come into our lives today!

You Have To Know What You Have

by Lindsay Roberts

John 8:32 says, "Ye shall know the truth, and the truth shall make you free." John 17:17 says that God's Word is truth. But it's only when you know the truth of God's Word that it can make you free. The promises in the Word of God are available to you all the time, but you need to know what you have in order for them to work in your life. Let me give you an example of what I mean.

One Sunday morning Richard and I were hurrying to get ready to go to church—it was one of those mornings. You know how they go. Just as we were about ready to leave, Richard came running down the stairs in a panic, holding his hairbrush in his left hand. He said, "Lindsay! I'm running late, and I can't find my hairbrush anywhere!"

I looked at him and asked, with a completely straight face, "Where have you looked?" He told me he had looked upstairs and downstairs, but couldn't find his brush.

Then I asked the crucial question: "Have you looked in your left hand?" He looked and said, "I can't believe it! How did it get there?"

The hairbrush was there all the time! But Richard didn't know he had it, so he couldn't use it. That's just like the Word of God. God's promises have been there for us all along, but if we don't know they're there, they are of no value to us.

When you need help, don't be tempted to go running here and there, to this place and that place, or turning to the world for answers. Look in God's Word. You can find help there for whatever you're facing.

Living Without Fear!

by Richard Roberts

Young people these days have a slogan that can be seen on everything from backpacks to T-shirts to bumper stickers: "No Fear!" They usually intend it to mean that they have no fear of scaling mountains, surfing waves, skateboarding, or other such activities. But it is a good slogan for all of us to adopt. However, this is easier said than done.

After the events of September 11, 2001, many people are living in fear as any number of disasters threaten from every side. People ask me, "Richard, aren't you afraid of what might happen?"

My answer to them is, "I do not live in fear."

How are we able to stand with confidence in these uncertain and perilous times? The Bible tells us that "God has not given us a spirit of fear, but of power and of love and of a sound mind" (2 Tim. 1:7 NKJV). We do not have to be tormented or controlled by a spirit of fear.

Nothing can happen in this world that will knock God off His throne. He provides comfort for His children, and we can say, like the psalmist, that even if we walk through the valley of the shadow of death, He is with us. (Ps. 23:4.)

When you know who is in charge of your life and that He is trustworthy, you can rest in Him and live in His peace.

Your Loving Father

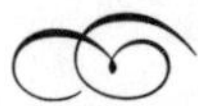

by Jerry Savelle

Jerry Savelle Ministries International

Don't ever forget that God is on your side. Romans 8:31-32 says, "If God be for us, who can be against us? He that spared not his own Son, but delivered him up for us all, how shall he not with him also freely give us all things?" God is always working on your behalf. He's not going to stand by and let the devil beat up on you without doing something about it. He's your loving Father!

I know this because I am a father too. I have two daughters. They're both grown, with families of their own now, and they've blessed me with five grandchildren. But I don't care how old they get or how many children they have, they're still my little girls. I still like for them to come sit beside me and tell me what a great daddy I am.

I'm doing my best to live a godly life, but if you were to start bothering my girls, you would find out that even though I'm godly, I'm not totally sanctified. I would hurt you and repent later, because those are my girls! You see, I'm a loving and caring father. I'm not going to stand by and let someone abuse my children. I'm not going to tell my daughters, "I love you, and I'm allowing this to teach you something." God doesn't do that either! He's not a child abuser, and He won't let anybody abuse His children, particularly the devil.

When God is for you, no one can successfully be against you. God loves you, and He cares about every detail of your life, both large and small. He wants you to have all the blessings that He has promised in His Word. You can count on it!

Led By the Holy Spirit

by Evelyn Roberts

Learning to be led by the Holy Spirit is important because it helps you make decisions based on God's Word and His will for your life.

When you seek the Holy Spirit's guidance...

- You learn to listen for God's voice to direct you,
- You allow Him to fill you with His Spirit, and
- He confirms by His Word what He has said to you.

But we must be careful when we feel that God is telling us to do something. We need to question God to make sure it is His voice. He will confirm it in His own way.

For example, Acts 10 tells how the apostle Peter was praying when he had a vision in which a sheet came down from heaven with all kinds of animals inside. He heard a voice telling him to kill and eat whatever he wished. But being a Jew who observed strict dietary laws, Peter questioned God, saying, "I have never eaten anything unholy and unclean." God replied, "What God has cleansed, no longer consider unholy" (vv. 14,15 NASB).

At the same time, God spoke to Cornelius—a devout Gentile—telling him to send for Peter to come and share God's Word with his household. Because of his vision, Peter realized he wasn't to consider Cornelius unworthy because he was a Gentile. God confirmed His Word. Peter obeyed the Lord and the Gospel was opened up to all people!

First John 4:1 NKJV says, "Do not believe every spirit, but test the spirits, whether they are of God." God promises to lead us, and when He tells us something, He will work it out His way and in His time. Our part is to pray and trust Him to lead us by His Spirit.

What Is a Shallow Christian?

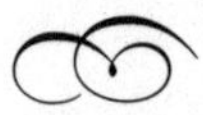

by Joyce Meyer
Joyce Meyer Ministries

Do you know what a shallow Christian is? A shallow Christian is someone who walks in the flesh, not the Spirit. They live out of what they want, what they think, and what *they* feel, instead of what God wants, thinks, and feels. They are people who walk in the soulish, carnal realm. They're not walking in the Spirit according to Galatians 5:16. And Romans 8:6 says "to be carnally minded is death; but to be spiritually minded is life and peace."

A shallow Christian isn't spiritually dumb. Their spirit has been born again, they are alive to Christ, and they have some understanding of what the Holy Spirit is leading them to do. It's just that they let their flesh be stronger than the Spirit.

My mind does not tell me what God thinks. It tells me what I think. My feelings don't tell me how God feels. They tell me how I feel. I know this because sometimes I may feel like giving up on somebody, but God doesn't feel like giving up on them. Sometimes I may feel like slapping somebody, and God will tell me to send them a present. That's a real flesh-burner spiritually!

Jesus said, "Love your enemies, bless them that curse you, do good to them that hate you, and pray for them which despitefully use you, and persecute you" (Matt. 5:44). God wants us to do good to those who despise us and hatefully misuse and abuse us.

The point is, God wants us to grow up and not be shallow Christians so that the inheritance Jesus died to give us and that is already ours in heaven will be released!

Power in Your Words

by Billy Joe Daugherty
Victory Christian Center Church and School

There is power in your words. Hebrews 11:3 says, "Through faith we understand that the worlds were framed by the word of God." In Genesis 1, the phrase "God said" is found nine times. God spoke everything into existence.

Now you may ask, "What relevance does that have to do with me?" We all face desperate situations, and when we do, we need to know how to overcome. We were made in the image of God, and He has placed the power of the Word in us for our concerns.

I was introduced to that truth by a hometown friend who was an Oral Roberts University student. His family didn't have any more money than mine, and I asked, "How can you afford that school?" He told me that Philippians 4:19 says, "My God shall supply all your need according to his riches in glory by Christ Jesus." He said, "I've been speaking those words, and God has paid for my schooling."

I didn't understand what he was saying, but it sounded good. A few weeks later, I drove to ORU with him. About 100 miles from Tulsa we ran into freezing rain, sleet, and snow. Driving was treacherous and there were accidents all over the place. As we drove, my friend put his hand on the dashboard and prayed, "Father, I thank You that the angels are surrounding us and that You're going ahead of us to make our way safe." I had never heard a prayer like that, but I agreed with him! And we made it to ORU without any trouble. That's when I came to realize that there is power in the words we speak.

'Only Believe'

by Lindsay Roberts

And, behold, there came a man named Jairus, and he was a ruler of the synagogue: and he fell down at Jesus' feet, and besought Him that He would come into his house. For he had one only daughter, about twelve years of age, and she lay a dying.

Mark 5:22,23

Look at the story of Jairus's daughter. When she was dying, Jairus left her. She was at the point of death. Do you know the miracle of faith that it had to take for a father to leave his daughter at the point of death and go to find Jesus? As he was going on the road, he found Jesus, and as they walked the road together, Jairus told Him, "My daughter is dying. She's sick. She is at the point of death."

And Jesus said, "Okay, I will come and heal her."

As they were on their journey, along came a woman who had an issue of blood. Thank God, she went to Jesus and found her miracle! Praise God! After twelve years, the issue of blood immediately dried up. She was no longer at the point of death. When Jesus stopped and healed this woman, she told Him about her life.

Meanwhile, Jairus got word from his messenger. Jairus was the man of faith who left his house in faith, spoke the word of faith, talked faith, and acted his faith. But the messenger came to say, "Don't bother the teacher anymore. Your daughter is now dead."

But Jesus said to Jairus, "Only believe," and his daughter was healed.

'Am I Still in God's Will?'

by Richard Roberts

First of Four Parts

Psalm 37:23 says, "The steps of a good man are ordered by the Lord: and he delighteth in his way." Jeremiah 29:11 in the *Amplified Bible* reads: "I know the thoughts and plans that I have for you, says the Lord, thoughts and plans for welfare and peace, and not for evil, to give you hope in your final outcome."

Everybody wants to be in God's will. When the storms of life rush in and the world hits us up beside the head with a lead pipe, when the battle comes, we inevitably begin to ask questions: "Am I still in the will of God? Is He still directing my steps?"

Surely those are the same questions the disciples asked that night when they were on the storm-tossed waters of the Sea of Galilee. Each of them must have asked, "Am I still in God's will? Is He still directing my steps?"

No matter what storm you are in, God is still directing your steps. Romans 8:23 says that if you love God, you are called according to His purpose, and He will cause all things to work together for your good. Your life will fit into His plan.

After Jesus was baptized, the Bible says in Matthew 4:1 that the Spirit led Him into the wilderness. When He reached the wilderness, the devil was there. Wherever you go, you're going to find the devil. The devil will be there because he is your adversary, who, as a roaring lion, walks to and fro seeking whom he can devour. (1 Peter 5:8.) Wherever you go in life, the devil will be there. Why? Because you are dangerous to the devil, and he knows that if you obey God, you will make a difference in the kingdom of God!

The Lord is my light and my salvation; whom shall I fear? —Psalm 27:1

Listen to God's Voice

by Richard Roberts

Second of Four Parts

Genesis, chapter 37, tells the story of a young man named Joseph. He was his father's favorite son, and his father had given him a coat of many colors. Joseph was a dreamer. He dreamed many dreams and shared them with his brothers, which made them angry.

One day when they were out in the field, the brothers took Joseph's coat of many colors and doused it in animal blood. They then threw him into a pit and later sold him into slavery.

Many years passed, and certainly Joseph must have been wondering if he was in God's will. But all along, God, in His time, was ordering Joseph's steps and directing his path, causing all things to work together for his good.

God will do the same for you if you will be obedient, if you will listen to His voice.

I want to share something with you concerning the will of God for your life. It is this: You cannot share your dream with just anybody. Joseph shared his dream with his brothers, and they hated him for it. So they said, "Let's kill him: then let's see what becomes of his dream."

When you share indiscriminately with everybody, somebody will misunderstand. Someone will not understand your dream. Proverbs 19:2 says, "Also, that the soul be without knowledge, it is not good; and he that hasteth with his feet sinneth." It is not good to be hasty and miss the mark! You must not share your dream with just anybody. Listen to God's voice, and hold it close!

The Lord knoweth the days of the upright: and their inheritance shall be for ever. —Psalm 37:18

OCTOBER 9

Learn To Resist Temptation!

by Richard Roberts

Third of Four Parts

God will show you whom to share your dream with. Sometimes that means rising above the past in your family. Joseph's family were liars. They were cheaters and tricksters. His own father stole the birthright of his brother, Esau. His mother was a manipulator. The Bible says that Joseph's brothers went to Shechem one day and killed all the men of that city.

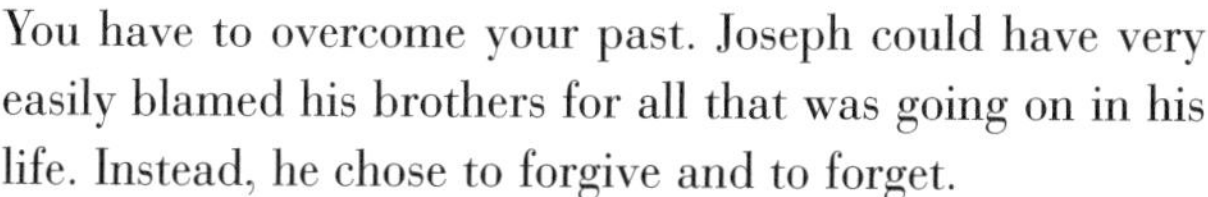

You have to overcome your past. Joseph could have very easily blamed his brothers for all that was going on in his life. Instead, he chose to forgive and to forget.

Isaiah 43:18-19 says, "Remember ye not the former things, neither consider the things of old. Behold, I will do a new thing; now it shall spring forth; shall ye not know it? I will even make a way in the wilderness, and rivers in the desert." Man may forget you, but God never will. Genesis 39:2 says, "And the Lord was with Joseph, and he was a prosperous man; and he was in the house of his master the Egyptian."

It is inevitable that you're going to face temptation. Learn to resist it! Joseph was doing wonderfully in the house of Potiphar. But he had one big problem—Potiphar's wife.

Joseph was not immune to temptation. Verses 12-20 tell us, "And she caught him by his garment, saying, Lie with me: and he left his garment in her hand, and fled, and got him out. And it came to pass, when she saw that he had left his garment in her hand, and was fled forth, that she called unto the men of her house, and spake unto them, saying, See, he hath brought in an Hebrew unto us to mock us; he came in unto me to lie with me, and I cried with a loud voice: And it came to pass, when he heard that I lifted up my voice and cried, that he left his garment with me, and fled, and got him out. And she laid up his garment by her, until his lord came home...."

And Joseph's master took him, and put him into the prison, a place where the king's prisoners were bound: and he was there in the prison.

The Steps of a Good Man

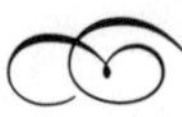

by Richard Roberts

Fourth of Four Parts

Once again, Joseph found himself in prison. While he was there, two of his cellmates had dreams. One of them was Pharaoh's baker and one of them was his chief butler. Joseph interpreted their dreams. When the butler and baker were released from jail, Joseph asked them to remember him, and the chief butler did. He said to Pharaoh, "There's a man in jail who can interpret dreams. His name is Joseph." And Pharaoh called him forth. Joseph interpreted Pharaoh's dream, and it pleased him so much that he not only released Joseph from prison, but he also made him the number two man in government.

It's no big deal when you suffer because of something you've done wrong and you take it patiently as 1 Peter 3:20 tells us. The big deal is when you do right and you suffer for it. This is what God finds acceptable. For the steps of a good man are directed by God to work out His will and His plan for that man's life.

Make That Decision

by Kenneth Copeland
Kenneth Copeland Ministries

If God has called you to do something, something that you think is impossible, chances are Satan has been bombarding you with thoughts of doubt, fear, and discouragement.

Don't let him lead you down that road. Don't let him keep you from remembering that God has the ability and faithfulness to get the job done. Resist the temptation to think about your problems and inabilities—resist the temptation to worry.

Stop struggling and start resting. Relax. God knows that what He has called you to do is impossible. He knows you are having a problem with that fact. He doesn't mind waiting while you draw on His promises and develop the courage you need for the task.

You don't have to panic. Just keep reminding yourself that as long as you have your Bible and your faith, you can do anything God tells you to do.

Put thoughts about your own weaknesses behind you, and focus instead on God's awesome ability. Start saying to yourself, "God is with me! He will not, He will not, HE WILL NOT leave me helpless, forget me, nor let me down!"

Then open your Bible and choose to believe what it says about you. Treat it as God's blood-sworn oath to you. Keep it in front of your eyes. Keep it in your ears. Keep it coming out of your mouth. Make a rock-solid decision to stick with it until the strength of God Himself rises up within you and overwhelms the fear.

Once you make that decision, there's no turning back. It's on to bigger and better things![1]

Confessing the Word

by Lindsay Roberts

Proverbs 4:24-27 says to put away from you false and dishonest speech, and willful and contrary talk. Put it far from you. Let your eyes look right with a fixed purpose, and let your eyes gaze straight before you. Consider well the path of your feet. Let all your ways be established and ordered right. Turn not to the side, to the right hand or to the left, and remove your foot from evil.

Proverbs 4:20-21,25 says, "My son, attend to my words; incline thine ear unto my sayings. Let them not depart from thine eyes; keep them in the midst of thine heart.... Let thine eyes look right on, and let thine eyelids look straight before thee."

Three things are covered—your eyes, your ears, and your heart. What you say and what you see will determine what you believe. What we have been saying and seeing is sometimes in contrast to the Word of God.

What do you watch on television? What do you listen to all day long? I can tell an awful lot about your personality if you will give me your checkbook and your calendar, because where you spend your time and your money determines what you are. How much of your time are you giving to the Word of God? How much of your finances are you giving to the Word of God?

Jeremiah 15:19-21 tells us, "Therefore thus saith the Lord, If thou return, then will I bring thee again, and thou shalt stand before me: and if thou take forth the precious from the vile, thou shalt be as my mouth: let them return unto thee; but return not thou unto them. If you will return and give up this mistaken tone of distrust and despair, I will give you again a settled place of quiet and safety." If you have any doubt about God's loving you or caring for you, His faithfulness, His goodness, or His healing, there are seven thousand promises in the Bible. Isn't that like God to go exceedingly abundantly above whatever we face?

God's Secret Place

by Keith Butler
Word of Faith International Christian Center

Psalm 91:1 NKJV says, "He who dwells in the secret place of the Most High shall abide under the shadow of the Almighty."

What is the secret place of the Most High? A secret place is one that other people don't know about. It's a place others cannot access. The secret place of the Almighty is a place where no weapon the enemy brings against you can get to you unless it goes through God.

How do you dwell in God's secret place? By having full and complete confidence in God's love for you against all evil *and* in your love for Him. It's a two-sided deal. It involves God's love for you and your love for Him.

Most of us have grown up hearing that God is love, and we know it's true from a mental standpoint. But we often struggle to get that knowing down into our hearts. Galatians 5:6 says that faith works by love. And the more you believe in your heart that God loves you, that He wants you to be healed, wants you to be delivered, wants you to be provided for, and wants you to overcome, the easier it is for you to dwell in the secret place of the Most High.

First John 4:16 NKJV says, "We have known and believed the love that God has for us. God is love, and he who abides in love abides in God, and God in him." When the devil comes against you with all kinds of pressure and trials, you need not fear because you are protected from his evil plots as you abide under the covering of God's love.

Get Up!

by Jerry Savelle

Jerry Savelle Ministries International

There's not one of us who has never made a mistake or sinned. But when we fail, it doesn't mean that God doesn't love us or that He will never forgive us. After we've fallen, the most natural thing to do is get up.

If I were to fall off a platform while I was preaching, someone would undoubtedly come to my aid and ask if I was hurt. If I said no, that person would ask if he could help me up. What if I were to say, "You don't understand. I've fallen. It may be God's will that I'm down here. He may be teaching me a lesson." If that sounds crazy, it's because it is.

If I were to accidentally fall off a platform, I would get up quickly and hope no one saw me fall. It would be embarrassing. I know, because I did fall off a platform once when I was preaching at a farm in Arkansas. It was a makeshift platform about four feet wide and twelve feet long, much like a runway.

As I was preaching, I got excited and moved too close to the edge. I fell off the back of the platform and landed in a base drum. My arms and legs were sticking out everywhere. I prayed, "Lord, what do I do?" The Lord said, "Micah 7:8, 'When I fall, I shall arise.'" Then He added, "And do it quick, son!" So I climbed out of the bass drum, got back on the platform, took up where I had left off, and never even mentioned falling.

Some people live a limited lifestyle because they major on their mistakes. But God says, "Get up and brush yourself off. I will forgive you. It's not over yet. Come on, get a new start." That's the kind of God we serve.

Make the First Move

by Lindsay Roberts

Have you ever been under such stress that you caught yourself whining, griping, and complaining to God, thinking He had forgotten you? Or asked, "Why doesn't God come and help me?" God has already done His part. He is waiting for us to do ours. Scripture is clear that you and I must initiate the action.

In Matthew 11:28 Jesus said, "Come unto me, all ye that labour and are heavy laden, and I will give you rest." A sentence like this in English grammar is a command that carries an understood "you" at the beginning. "You come unto Me." The process begins with us. Let's learn to make that first move.

Be Strong in Grace

by Gloria Copeland
Kenneth Copeland Ministries

Paul instructs us to be strong in grace. But what is grace? And what does it do? Titus 2 tells us, *"For the grace of God that bringeth salvation hath appeared to all men, Teaching us that, denying ungodliness and wordly lusts, we should live soberly, righteously, and godly, in this present world"* (vv. 11,12).

Grace teaches us. It teaches us how to live in freedom in this world.

Whenever the Spirit of God corrects you, whenever He points out a mistake you're making or speaks to you about something you're doing that is grieving Him, don't be mad. Be glad! It's the grace of God teaching you something to make your life better.

Grow strong in that grace by spending time every day in prayer. Live each day expecting the Spirit of God to counsel and instruct you about the things in your life—big and small.

Expect to hear from Him. If you don't, you won't listen for Him, and you're not likely to hear Him because He speaks in a still, small voice. As a rule, His words are quiet words. They're not overwhelming words. If you don't have a spiritual ear tuned to heaven, you'll miss them.

So, every morning of your life spend time praying in the spirit, talking to the Father, and reminding yourself that the Holy Ghost is inside you, constantly teaching and guiding you. Become strong in the grace of God.[1]

God's Loving Correction

by Patricia Salem

When I was a child my father had an explosive temper, and his correction was harsh. As a result, it was difficult for me to learn to trust my heavenly Father. I was fearful. I thought if I did the slightest thing wrong, God would come after me.

It was many years before I realized that God wasn't out to get me or hurt me. He loved me. Not until I had a personal relationship with Jesus Christ did I learn just how much God loves me. I learned that when He corrects me, it is to keep me on the right path and to spare me from harm. The Scripture says, "My child, don't ignore it when the Lord disciplines you, and don't be discouraged when he corrects you. For the Lord disciplines those He loves" (Heb. 12:5,6 NLT).

I have learned to trust God more over the years and respond to His correction. Sometimes when I pray at night, the Lord will speak to my heart and let me know that He wasn't pleased with how I handled a particular situation. He doesn't holler at me or say He will not give me another chance. He gently corrects and redirects me. And I say, "Lord, I'm sorry. I repent, and I'll listen more carefully next time. Where You direct me, I will follow."

God doesn't abuse or malign. He corrects and redirects. He puts our feet upon the right path if we just ask. Psalm 32:8 NKJV says, "I will instruct you and teach you in the way you should go; I will guide you with My eye." That's the correction and redirection of a loving heavenly Father!

'Peace, Be Still'

by Evelyn Roberts

I love the story of Jesus calming the storm found in Matthew 8:23-27 NKJV. Jesus and the disciples were in a boat going across the Sea of Galilee. The Lord had had a busy day ministering to the multitudes, and He was asleep in the back of the boat. "Suddenly a great tempest arose on the sea, so that the boat was covered with the waves.... Then His disciples...awoke Him, saying, 'Lord, save us! We are perishing!'...Then He arose and rebuked the winds and the sea, and there was a great calm."

We've all had tempests, or problems, come upon us. And many times, like the storm on the Sea of Galilee, they come suddenly out of nowhere. Tempests are very real, and it is easy to become very afraid.

A tempest can take many forms. It might come in the form of sickness, the loss of a job, or trouble with your children. A tempest can be a marriage grown cold, a misunderstanding, or a heartache. And it can wash over your life and make you feel as if you are going under. Even when you know God is your Source of help, it is easy to become filled with fear and find yourself asking, "What will I do? How am I going to get out of this?"

It's important to remember—especially when the tempest seems at its worst—that God cares and He is with you. He is there any time you call on Him, day or night, to speak the wonderful words, "Peace, be still!" (Mark 4:39 NKJV). When the disciples called on Jesus, He calmed the storm and let them know that He was in control. He can do the same for you.

A Listening Heart

by Taffi L. Dollar
World Changers Church International

Most of us want to know God's purpose for our lives and how to have success. But how can we know these things? I believe we do it by spending time in God's presence and getting to know His voice through His Word—by seeking to hear His voice every day as if our very survival depended on it.

John 5:25 NLT says, "The time is coming, in fact it is here, when the dead will hear my voice—the voice of the Son of God. And those who listen will live." When Jesus says, "Those who listen will live," He is not talking about a mere existence or barely making it from one day to the next. He's talking about developing intimate communication with God in order to live a life of purpose and fulfillment. God wants to speak to you so you can succeed.

You were made to hear God's voice. He told Moses in Deuteronomy 4:36, "Out of heaven I made you to hear My voice, that I might instruct you."

God is speaking all the time. But to hear Him, we must have a listening heart. It's up to us to tune our spiritual ears to hear God's voice through His Word, and as He speaks, to obey. He wants us to hear Him so that He can divinely direct us in every area of life. Psalm 85:8 says, "I will hear what God the Lord will speak." It takes determination on our part. But as we tune in to God's voice and obey Him, we can find His direction and fulfillment for our lives.

Standing on the Word

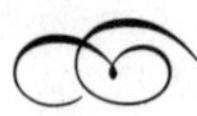

by Lindsay Roberts

I drove past a billboard once that said, "Isn't it funny that people believe television but question the Bible?" I thought, *That sign is pretty catchy. But it's more than that.*

The Word of God is true: "The entirety of Your word is truth" (Ps. 119:160 NKJV). It is powerful: "The word of God is living and powerful, and sharper than any two-edged sword" (Heb. 4:12 NKJV). Jesus was the Word clothed in flesh: "The Word [Christ] became flesh and dwelt among us" (John 1:14 NKJV). God spoke the world into existence with His Word: "Then God said...." (Gen. 1:3-31 NKJV).

At the time I saw the billboard, I was frustrated by a situation I was facing. I couldn't seem to see the light at the end of the tunnel. A friend kept saying, "Lindsay, you've got to stand on the Word of God." So one day, in total frustration, I put the Bible on the floor and literally stood on it. I cried out, "God, I am standing on Your Word, and I am not going to be moved until I hear from You!"

As I stood there, I realized I was standing on the most powerful force on the face of the earth—the Word of God. Jesus said, "Heaven and earth will pass away, but My words will by no means pass away" (Matt. 24:35 NKJV). My faith began to rise up, and I knew that if I believed God's Word, something was going to happen. And He brought healing to my situation.

Literally standing on the Word of God may seem extreme to some, but it helped me realize that, according to the Word of God, there is no area of our lives that is beyond hope.

Have Confidence

by Eastman Curtis
Destiny Church

When I was a little kid, my dad would come home from work and occasionally bring me my favorite peanut butter candy bar. I used to stick my face up against the window and watch for my dad to pull up and get out of his car. I'd see the candy bar sticking out of my dad's shirt pocket and get so excited! When he opened the door, I'd grab him around the legs and hang on as he dragged me across the floor to his big recliner. Then I'd climb up in his lap, lean up against his chest, and ask, "Is that a candy bar in your pocket?"

"Oh!" my dad always said in surprise. "How did that get there?" Then he'd take the candy bar out of his pocket, unwrap it slowly, and hand it to me. I'd shove it into my mouth and let the crumbs fall on him and me.

How do you think my father would have felt if I had crawled across the floor to him and said, "I'm so unworthy! I don't even deserve to look at that candy bar. But could I just look at it for a minute and eat the crumbs that fall on the floor"? My dad would have said, "Hey! You're the reason I got this candy bar! I don't want it. It's for you!"

How often we go to God in prayer feeling unworthy to receive His blessings! Yet Ephesians 1:6 says that if we have received Jesus Christ as our Savior, we are accepted as God's beloved. Hebrews 4:16 NKJV tells us to *"come boldly to the throne of grace, that we may obtain mercy and find grace to help in time of need."* What a wonderful invitation from our Lord!

Many times we think we've got to try to earn God's favor, but He has qualified us because of what Jesus did on the cross. We don't have to earn it. We can approach Him with confidence, knowing that all He has is ours because we are His children! (Luke 15:31.)

Surrender Your Life

by Sharon Daugherty
Victory Christian Center Church and School

We often think of surrender as losing something. But when Jesus willingly went to the cross so that we could have abundant life, we didn't lose anything. We gained everything! It was the ultimate act of surrender.

Webster's Dictionary defines *surrender* as the act of yielding oneself to the power, control, authority, or influence of another. Jesus showed us what surrender is. He was totally surrendered to God.

First, He surrendered His position in heaven to come to a world that didn't even know who He was. Isaiah 53:3 says that He was despised and rejected of men. He surrendered His will to His heavenly Father every day when He walked on the earth, and He surrendered in the Garden of Gethsemane when He prayed, "Father, if thou be willing, remove this cup from me: nevertheless not my will, but thine, be done" (Luke 22:42). Then He surrendered when He went to the cross, knowing that all the sins of the world would be laid on Him and He would suffer like no one had ever suffered. His surrender led to ultimate victory.

We are all surrendered to something in our personal lives. Some people surrender themselves to busyness, to money, to drugs, or to sexual sins—whatever is more powerful and more important to them than God. But Jesus said, "No one can serve two masters; for either he will hate the one and love the other, or else he will be loyal to the one and despise the other" (Matt. 6:24 NKJV).

When you switch your allegiance over to Jesus and surrender your life to the heavenly Father as He did, the power of ungodly influences and their dominion over your life can be broken.

God's Glory

by Joyce Meyer

Joyce Meyer Ministries

We hear a lot about the glory of God but not about what the term really means. Over the years I have studied the glory of God and have come to what for me is a good understanding of it.

There are several ways you can approach the glory of God. You can talk about the miracles, signs, and wonders that follow when the power of God comes into a service. Or you can talk about the honor that is due to God. Both of those definitions are accurate.

But I like to be practical. I want to know how I can benefit from the glory of God in my everyday life. I have found that glory is not only the honor due to God, but it's also the manifestation—the bringing out in the open where it can be seen—of God's excellence.

Second Corinthians 5:20 AMP says, "We are Christ's ambassadors, God making His appeal as it were through us." If Jesus is making His appeal to the world through us, people need to see something that will impress them. God wants us to get His glory out in the open where it can be seen.

Bringing out God's glory means walking in excellence. It means making the right choices in the hundreds of decisions we face every day—how we talk to people, how we talk about people, how we spend our money, what kind of entertainment we choose, and so on.

On the night before He was crucified, Jesus prayed, "Father, glorify Me so I can glorify You" (John 17:1). We can all pray a similar prayer: "God, help me be more excellent so I can show people how excellent You are."

Go to War With Praise

by Kenneth Copeland
Kenneth Copeland Ministries

Praising God and giving Him thanks are integral parts of prayer. After you made the decision to believe for something, then you need to praise God for the answer. Thank God that what you prayed for will happen.

Offering praise and thanks involve more than just speaking nice words to God. There is power in praise. Praise was set apart by God for a definite reason.

Psalms 8 and 9 point out some things about praise that every Christian should know. Psalm 8:1-2 says, "O Lord, our Lord, how majestic is your name in all the earth! You have set your glory above the heavens. From the lips of children and infants you have ordained praise because of your enemies, to silence the foe and the avenger."

From these Scriptures, we see that God ordained praise—He brought it into existence. Why? "To silence the foe and the avenger." Praise stops Satan cold. It is strength. It's a weapon we can use to stop whatever Satan's throwing at us.

Psalm 9:1-4 says, "I will praise you, O Lord, with all my heart; I will tell of all your wonders. I will be glad and rejoice in you; I will sing praise to your name, O Most High. My enemies turn back; they stumble and perish before you. For you have upheld my right and my cause; you have sat on your throne, judging righteously."

When you praise, your enemies will turn back! Remember: Our struggle is not against flesh and blood, but against Satan's forces. (Eph. 6.)

Whatever trouble is challenging you today, begin to praise God. Exercise this vital weapon against Satan and his forces. Your enemies will have to turn back. They will fall and die before you, and the peace and victory that Jesus bought for you will be yours.[1]

Breaking Destructive Soul Ties

by Lindsay Roberts

God has given each of us a spirit and a soul. Your spirit is the part of you that will live forever, even after it leaves your body. Your soul includes your mind, will, emotions, and decision-making processes. God designed the spirit to rule over the soul.

When it comes to the close relationships in your life, you knit your soul to another person's as a relationship grows. You develop a *soul tie* to that person. The danger comes when you knit yourself to someone who is not allowing the Spirit of God to lead them, someone who can pull down your soul so much that they eventually pull down your spirit. *That's a destructive soul tie.*

Perhaps you have left a bad or even abusive relationship, thinking that would end your connection with that person. But until you ask God to help you break that destructive soul tie, that relationship may still be influencing your other relationships and decisions.

God can create a "clean slate" in your soul, freeing you to begin again. Ask God to break any destructive soul ties you have. Then begin renewing your mind with the Word of God. Let the washing of God's Word begin to transform your life as you allow God to speak to your spirit and lead you into new and healthy relationships in Him.

Big Problem, Huge God

by Keith Moore
Faith Life Church

When I first went into the ministry and began counseling people from all walks of life, many times they'd get angry with me if I did not agree with them about the severity of their problem. I've had people tell me, "You're not taking my problem seriously enough. You don't understand. This is not your common, run-of-the-mill problem."

We've probably all felt that way at times, but the Bible says our problem is common. First Corinthians 10:13 NIV says, "No temptation [trial or problem] has seized you except what is common to man. And God is faithful; he will not let you be tempted beyond what you can bear. But when you are tempted, he will also provide a way out so that you can stand up under it." In other words, your problem is common. God has seen it before, and He has promised to provide a way for you to stand up under it!

So instead of magnifying your problem, tell your big problem about your huge God! Psalm 34:3 says, "O magnify the Lord with me." Make God bigger, and according to God's Word, you can begin to see a change in your life!

A Merry Heart

by Richard Roberts

Many in the medical profession are beginning to realize that laughter is an important part of a healthy life. The ability to laugh helps reduce anxiety and tension. And like a nutritious diet and exercise, positive emotions are necessary to keep us on an even keel physically and emotionally.

Actually, medical science is confirming what the Bible says: "A merry heart doeth good like a medicine: but a broken spirit drieth the bones" (Prov. 17:22).

Laughter is not only a healing medicine for our souls, but it also affects our bodies. When people laugh hard, their pulse rate quickens, their lungs expand and fill with oxygen, their capillaries open, and the pituitary gland is stimulated to produce natural pain killers. The overall effect is like taking the body on an internal jog.

God knows that we can't do what we are called to do without His joy, which is our strength. No doubt that is one of the reasons Jesus' departing message to His disciples concerned joy. He said, "I have told you these things that My joy and delight may be in you, and that your joy and gladness may be full measure and complete and overflowing" (John 15:11 AMP). When Jesus fills our hearts with His joy, He can lead us through the most difficult circumstances with a deep gladness that permeates our very being. Such joy comes from knowing God personally and walking in daily fellowship with Him.

The Gift of Faith

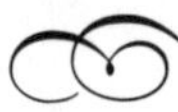

by Richard Roberts

First of Two Parts

The gift of faith is supernatural. The gift of faith comes into operation when our own faith stops or reaches its limit. God will drop a gift of faith into a believer's heart.

The first time this happened to me, I was a boy and I wasn't aware of how the gift of faith works. I was ten years old and I had twenty-two warts on my left hand. We had prayed and believed, but nothing was happening.

My mother said, "We're going to the doctor." As I had grown older, the warts had spread and became more numerous, and she said, "We're going to get them burned off!"

Then my father said, "We're going to get down to business with God. We're going to pray. Now when I pray, Richard, I want you to release your faith."

"How do you release your faith?" I asked.

"You let it go," he answered.

"Well, how do you let it go?" I questioned.

"You release it," my father said. "You need a point of contact."

"What's a point of contact?" I asked.

"A point of contact is something you do," my father answered. "When you do it, you release your faith." He pointed at the light switch and said, "That light switch has no power, but it's hooked up to the power company. When you flip the switch, you touch the power company, and the lights come on.

"You have faith in your heart. God is manifesting faith in your heart, but you have exhausted your faith. As a little boy, you've prayed and believed and expected, but so far nothing has happened. Now we're going to call on God."

My father didn't use those exact words, but as I've thought about it over the years, he was saying, "I believe that God is going to manifest something in you to help you go beyond your human faith limit to believe."

'That Is When the Miracles Come!'

by Richard Roberts

Second of Two Parts

My father continued, "Now your faith in your heart is like that light switch. When you release your faith, you touch God's power company. That is when the miracles come!"

He prayed. I looked at my hand. Nothing had changed. He said, "Now this time we're going to expect!"

Within two weeks every wart disappeared, and I learned how to get a point of contact for the releasing of my faith. I learned something, even though I didn't understand what I was learning. I learned something as a boy; and as I've grown older, I've begun to understand even more of what happened that day. The gift of faith was operating in my life to heal my warts.

The gift of faith is what came into Daniel when they cast him into the lions' den. (Dan. 6:16-23.) God manifested a gift of faith. If Daniel could sit there with those hungry lions and not fear, not worry, not be terrorized, he had faith!

It was the custom of the kings in those days not to feed the lions for a few days so that when they threw someone into the pit, they could watch the lions literally tear the humans limb from limb. They made sport of it.

Apparently it didn't bother Daniel, because God manifested a gift of faith in him to believe that those lions would do him no harm. Daniel believed!

Daniel 6:20 says, "When he [the king] came to the den...the king spake and said to Daniel...servant of the living God, is thy God, whom thou servest continually, able to deliver thee from the lions?"

Verse 22 explains, "My God hath sent his angel, and hath shut the lions' mouths, that they have not hurt me: forasmuch as before him innocency was found in me; and also before thee, O king, have I done no hurt."

Daniel had faith, and the miracle came!

The Table Is Set

by Marilyn Hickey
Marilyn Hickey Ministries

In Psalm 23:5 we read, "Thou preparest a table before me in the presence of mine enemies: thou anointest my head with oil; my cup runneth over." What does God do? He prepares a table for us. Where does He prepare it? In the presence of our enemies. How does He help us in that time? He anoints us. And why does He do it? So our cup will overflow!

When my husband and I started Happy Church in Denver, Colorado, now called Orchard Road Christian Center, I began to host home Bible study groups. I found that many people who would never have come to a church service would come to a home Bible study. Over a cup of coffee and a cookie, they would get saved.

About that same time, a prominent minister visited our church, and he said to me, "Marilyn, of all the pastors' wives I know, you are the biggest example of a failure." He went on, "A pastor's wife ought to be leading the music or playing the piano or organ. Or you should be in charge of the women's missionary council."

Well, I knew if I led the music, nobody would come to church. Furthermore, I couldn't play the piano or the organ, and I couldn't crochet or knit. Rather than be discouraged at what he said, however, I was encouraged! I knew that I was in the presence of an "enemy" of God's plan and purpose for my life, and therefore, I was in for an anointing that would cause my cup to overflow!

What happened? Those home Bible study groups began to grow and multiply until we eventually had twenty-two of them each month. Out of those Bible studies a five-minute-a-day radio program was started. And shortly thereafter, God gave me a word that He had called me to cover the earth with the Word, which we are now doing through print and television.

Has someone given you a negative word today? Don't be discouraged! Look for God's table to be prepared for you there. Expect to be anointed, and expect your cup to overflow!

The Tiniest Stake

by Oral Roberts

When an elephant is young and being trained for a particular purpose, it is often chained to a stake buried in a concrete slab. Again and again the young elephant will strain to pull the stake loose so it can be free. Finally, it stops struggling because it learns that struggling is in vain.

Once the elephant believes it cannot get loose, the keeper can tie it to the tiniest stake driven only a few inches into the ground, and the animal will not escape. Of course, it is not the tiny stake that holds the elephant but the memory of its former failures. It does not try anymore.

One of the most pathetic sights in the world is the person who has quit trying, who believes he is a failure. This is the way wrong believing can control our lives. We start to think we are too weak to live a victorious life in Christ. Then we look at our past failures and we think it must be true. Finally, we start living down to that level of believing, and we stop trying anymore.

Jesus came to free us from wrong believing. John the apostle wrote, "Whatsoever is born of God overcometh the world: and this is the victory that overcometh the world, even our faith" (1 John 5:4).

When you accept the Lord into your life, you become a new person in Him, and you are no longer chained to your past failures. Victory is yours through your faith. Romans 8:37 says that Jesus makes you more than a conqueror. He gives you the power to start living up to your potential in Him.

Take It Back!

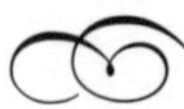

by Billy Joe Daugherty
Victory Christian Center Church and School

When the devil came to Adam and Eve in the Garden, he came to steal the righteousness, dominion, wholeness, freedom, peace, and joy that God had placed in their hands. When they sinned, they lost their relationship with God.

At that moment God put into action a plan to restore what the devil had stolen. That plan was for His Son, Jesus Christ, to come and get back what had been taken from Adam and Eve and also from us. That included a renewed relationship with God, but it also takes into account everything that has been stolen from us.

In Joel, chapter 2 NKJV, we find a situation where Israel had sinned against God. And sin opens the door for the enemy to come in and steal, kill, and destroy. God told Israel through His prophet, "Rend your heart, and not your garments; return to the Lord your God, for He is gracious and merciful, slow to anger, and of great kindness; and he relents from doing harm" (v. 13). Then in verse 25 He promised, "I will restore to you the years that the swarming locust has eaten."

God says, "Even when everything is gone, I will restore!" Maybe you have lost years in a wrong relationship or the bondage of an addiction. The devil may have stolen the peace and joy from your family. If so, this is the time to open your heart to God and get in a position to rise up and say, "I'm taking it back!" Go after it with your faith. Nothing is too hard for the Lord!

You're on God's Mind

by Jerry Savelle

Jerry Savelle Ministries International

Years ago my friend John Osteen, who's in heaven now, would call me up on the telephone every once in a while and say something like this: "Hello, Brother Jerry. I just wanted you to know that Dodie and I had you on our minds today, and we're praying for you. Bye." I wouldn't even get to talk. He would hang up before I could say anything! But it would just make my day to know that John Osteen and his wife had me on their minds and were praying for me.

One time I was in Australia, and I was awakened with a phone call at 3 A.M. It was Kenneth Copeland. He said, "Jerry, where are you? You're the hardest guy in the world to find. I've called every office you have in the world, and I finally found you. I just wanted you to know that Gloria and I had you on our minds during our prayer time today, and whatever you're going through, you're going to make it. Praise God!" And he hung up. I had a hard time going back to sleep that night, just knowing that I was on Kenneth Copeland's mind and he was praying for me.

Now, I don't get those kinds of phone calls every day. But I know that I am on God's mind twenty-four hours a day, and the thoughts He thinks toward me are good. (Jer. 29:11.) Psalm 8:4-5 NIV says, "What is man that you [God] are mindful of him, the son of man that you care for him? You made him a little lower than the heavenly beings and crowned him with glory and honor."

You are constantly on God's mind, and He loves you more than you can imagine. That thought ought to make your day!

Mixing Praise and Worship

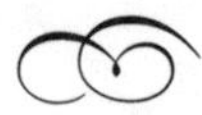

by Richard Roberts

Did you know that praise and worship play an important role in developing your faith? It's true. When God promised Abraham that he and Sarah would have a son in their old age, Abraham never wavered in believing God's promise. Romans 4:20 says he was strong in faith, giving glory to God. Now that's praise and worship!

Why is it so important to mix praise and worship with your faith? So that when the tests of your faith come, you'll be ready. Abraham experienced the miracle of having a son in his old age, but a few years later he experienced the ultimate test. (Genesis 22:1-13.)

One day God spoke to him and said, "Take your only son, Isaac, whom you love so much, and go to Moriah and sacrifice him." But Abraham was prepared for the test. He had experienced God's faithfulness, and he knew he could trust Him. Abraham told his servants, "The lad and I will go yonder and worship, and we will come right back." Abraham believed that even if he had to sacrifice his son, God would raise him up. After placing Isaac on the altar, Abraham raised the knife above his beloved son. But God said, "Don't do it! I know that you trust Me." At that precise moment, Abraham saw a ram caught by his horns in a bush. God miraculously provided the sacrifice.

Abraham was in tune with God. He had developed an intimate relationship with God, and when the time came for him to prove his trust in God, he was up to the challenge. God didn't disappoint him. He honored his faith and obedience. We, too, can develop a faith relationship with God so that we can praise and worship Him in every situation and pass our "trust tests" with flying colors!

Cultivating a Relationship With the Holy Spirit

by Pat Harrison
Faith Christian Fellowship International

First of Three Parts

I love the Holy Spirit because He's everything to me that Jesus said He would be. If He's not everything to you that Jesus said He would be, it could be that you're not giving Him that opportunity.

Who is the Holy Spirit? The Holy Spirit is not an "it." He's the third person of the Trinity. God left Him here on earth for us when Jesus was resurrected and went to sit at the right hand of God the Father. It is important that we know who the Holy Spirit is so that we can hear Him and learn to be led by Him.

A relationship with the Holy Spirit is something you cultivate. When we come into the family of God, the Holy Spirit comes to live within us. Ephesians 2:18 AMP says, "For it is through Him that we both [whether far off or near] now have an introduction (access) by one (Holy) Spirit to the Father—so that we are able to approach Him."

When you receive Jesus as Lord, you come into the family of God. You become a new creature in Christ. But the process continues. You don't just say, "Praise God, I'm born again" and that's it. You have to grow and allow the power of the Holy Spirit to work in you, through you, and out of you. And you can do that through fellowship with Him, by studying the Word of God and making it part of your daily life. You begin developing an intimate relationship with Him so that you know Him, not just about Him.

The Holy Spirit is present to do a work in you. What is that work? To lead you in the manner in which God would have you live out your destiny here on earth.

Giving God Top Priority

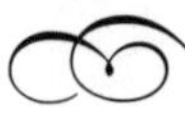

by Pat Harrison
Faith Christian Fellowship International

Second of Three Parts

To have a meaningful relationship with the Holy Spirit, you put God first in your life. He has priority.

In the natural, most likely your mother or father taught you how to feed and clothe yourself and keep yourself clean. You learned to accept the daily responsibilities of caring for yourself. In the same way, you grow and mature spiritually by being responsible to diligently seek God through His Word and prayer each day and asking for His guidance as to how He would have you live. (Heb. 11:6.)

Meditating on the Word of God develops a relationship with the Holy Spirit. Why do you need to meditate on the Word? So the Word becomes part of you, living on the inside of you, so that it creates your world and all that pertains to you. James 1:22 AMP tells us, "Obey the message; be doers of the Word, and not merely listeners to it." Meditation without practice is not enough to allow us to walk in the fullness of the Spirit.

To be successful, business owners go over their past experiences, look at their goals, and make sure they are in line with their priorities. It is the same with Christians in the Spirit realm. We have to continually go back to the Word so that we know we are setting our goals according to God's will.

If you have a personal relationship with the Holy Spirit, He will give you wisdom and understanding on how to accomplish God's purpose for your life. We're human, so we may not always hit the mark, but the Holy Spirit is there to guide us. We learn to listen for the voice of the Holy Spirit, through prayer and by studying the Word of God.

Who the Holy Spirit Is

by Pat Harrison
Faith Christian Fellowship International

Third of Three Parts

In John 14:16-17 AMP, Jesus tells us who the Holy Spirit is: "I will ask the Father, and He will give you another Comforter (Counselor, Helper, Intercessor, Advocate, Strengthener and Standby) that He may remain with you forever...for He lives with you [constantly] and will be in you."

So who is the Holy Spirit, the third person of the Trinity?

He is the action behind the Father's will. (John 6:63.)

He is a Comforter. He is there to comfort you and keep you in a state of well-being at all times. (Gal.5:22,23.)

He is your Advocate, the One who supports and defends you. (John 16:8.)

He is your Strengthener. He is strong and powerful, and because He resides in you, He gives you that power to resist any force that comes against you. (Rom. 8:31.)

He is your Standby. He is dependable and is always ready to serve as a substitute for you. (Eph. 1:13,14.)

He is your Helper, ready to assist you, to give you aid and relief. He has the power to change your life. (Luke 11:9,10.)

He is your Counselor, your Advisor. He can give you guidance if you ask for it. (John 14:26.)

He is your Intercessor. He prays for you, stands in favor for you, and pleads for you. (Rom. 8:26,27.)

It's important that we learn to walk in, and be led by, the Holy Spirit so we can fully walk out God's will for our lives—His destiny for us!

God's Benefits!

by Lindsay Roberts

You have wonderful benefits as a Christian. Psalm 103:3-5 NKJV says that God forgives all your iniquities…heals all your diseases…redeems your life from destruction… crowns you with lovingkindness and tender mercies… [and] satisfies your mouth with good things, so that your youth is renewed like the eagle's.

Although those benefits are yours, if you don't know they exist, you can't obtain them. It's as if your spouse went to the mall at Christmastime and purchased gift certificates for you from all of your favorite stores. Once you received the certificates, you'd probably get to the mall as quickly as possible to pick up what was rightfully yours. After all, they'd already been paid for!

However, if you didn't know that your spouse had purchased those gift certificates, they would still exist and they would still be yours, but you wouldn't receive anything from them because you failed to use them.

In a similar way, everything that God promises in His Word is rightfully yours because Jesus purchased them for you with His own blood, which was shed on the cross at Calvary. Your part now is to claim your benefits and use them to live the joyous, abundant life He came to bring you. (John 10:10.)

Faith Comes by Hearing the Word

by Oral Roberts

I grew up in Oklahoma, and as a young boy, they struck oil in Pontotoc County. My father had been called to preach, and he sold our farm one year before oil was struck right where we had lived, and also across the road on his brother's land. His brother, who had been poor, got rich!

I learned then how they got oil out of the ground. The driller drilled down into the earth, through the rock, until they hit oil. The oil had been there for thousands of years, but nobody knew it. And when they struck the oil, up it came, flowing high above the oil derrick, which in those days was made out of wood, going hundreds of feet in the air. And if they didn't have a container for it, the oil would be lost. They didn't have big tanks in those days, so they dug out ponds, and the oil would fill up those ponds. Now that is how you got oil.

Romans 10:17 says, "So then faith cometh by hearing... the Word of God." How does faith come? It comes when the preacher preaches the Word; he is the driller. The Word is the drill bit, and it drills down inside you where your faith is. When it hits your faith, it explodes! It comes up out of you and touches God and brings the miracle right toward you. It comes toward you or goes past you, depending on *you,* because God is sending it. If you're expecting your miracle, you'll reach out and get it. If you're not, it will pass you by, and you'll say, "Oh, where is my miracle?" because you weren't looking for it.

So, remember where your faith comes from. As the Word is preached, it drills down and touches faith, and up it comes. So faith comes by hearing the Word of God!

For the Wind Was Contrary

by Keith Butler
Word of Faith International Christian Center

First of Three Parts

Matthew 14:22-28 says, "And straightway Jesus constrained his disciples to get into a ship, and to go before him unto the other side, while he sent the multitudes away. And when he had sent the multitudes away, he went up into a mountain apart to pray: and when the evening was come, he was there alone.

"But the ship was now in the midst of the sea, tossed with waves: for the wind was contrary. And in the fourth watch of the night Jesus went unto them, walking on the sea. And when the disciples saw him walking on the sea, they were troubled, saying, It is a spirit; and they cried out for fear. But straightway Jesus spake unto them, saying, Be of good cheer; it is I; be not afraid. And Peter answered him and said, Lord, if it be thou, bid me come unto thee on the water."

Jesus had just finished ministering to thousands of people. He'd had a supernatural manifestation of the power of God when five thousand men, besides women and children, were fed supernaturally from a little boy's lunch. And then He tells His disciples, "I want you to go to the other side; I'm coming after a while." They obeyed, got in the boat, and began to head across the sea.

I know this is a literal event that took place, but there are also certain things that we can learn from the incident. The sea is the life which you and I live. We live on an earth where things change daily. Satan will use the wind to create waves in your life. The boat is the place of home, a place of safety.

As soon as you begin to do what the Lord tells you to do, waves will come along right away. Satan is the one who sends the wind in life, and it is Satan who uses people to come against you.

Get Out of the Boat!

by Keith Butler

Word of Faith International Christian Center

Second of Three Parts

The ship was in the midst of the sea, tossed with waves, for the wind was contrary. The disciples were in a wooden boat that didn't have any real covering. They were out on the sea in the middle of the night. It was the fourth watch, early in the morning, and the wind was blowing. The waves were smashing up against the boat, and the rain was coming in their faces. They could hardly see, and they were beginning to be a bit concerned about whether or not they were going to make it to the other side.

Then they saw something very strange. It was a figure coming in their direction, seemingly walking over the whitecaps on top of the water! Matthew 14, verses 26 and 27, tell us, "And when the disciples saw him [Jesus] walking on the sea, they were troubled, saying, It is a spirit; and they cried out for fear. But straightway Jesus spake unto them, saying, Be of good cheer; it is I; be not afraid."

Since they were out on the water in the middle of a storm with the waves lapping up against their boat, "Peter answered him and said, Lord, if it be thou, bid me come unto thee on the water" (v. 28). Peter saw the Lord doing something supernatural—walking on the water—and he knew whatever the Lord was doing, he could do too. "And [Jesus] said, Come. And when Peter was come down out of the ship, he walked on the water, to go to Jesus" (v. 29).

Now walking on the water of life is going beyond what you can do in your own strength, doing what you can do beyond your own ability, and doing what you can do beyond your own education. God wants to do more in your life than what you can think of doing. He wants to do more in your life than anyone has ever thought could happen in your life because the Lord, of course, is supernatural. But you have to be willing to get out of the boat! You have to take the first step.

'Where's the Kitchen?'

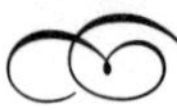

by Keith Butler
Word of Faith International Christian Center

Third of Three Parts

I was a Bible student graduating from Bible school when the Lord spoke to me and said, "I want you to open up a church. I want you to go into the ministry full time."

At that time, my wife and I had a little boy. We'd had a little daughter, who was born while we were students in Tulsa. We didn't see how we were going to make it as we believed God for food every day. We used our faith and believed God would provide our needs daily.

Any time you're going to walk on water, you won't be able to see how you're going to do it. Peter couldn't see how he was going to be able to do it, and neither could we!

One evening we were sitting in the living room praying for food, as the only thing we had in the house was a jar of water.

A knock came on the door. As I opened it, there stood a brother I knew with a bag of groceries in his arm. "Where's the kitchen?" he asked as he brushed on past me and headed toward the kitchen. Then there was another knock on the door. I turned around, and there was his wife with another big bag in her arms, asking, "Where's the kitchen?"

About that time I figured out what was going on. I still had a little bit of pride. I didn't want to receive that charity. But my friend said, "The Lord told me to bring you this food." And they kept bringing in bag after bag after bag. On the way out, he gave me one of those holy handshakes that was filled with money. Then he ran down the sidewalk, jumped in the car, and sped off.

The Father provided for us supernaturally, but it happened only when we got out of the boat!

A Secret About Giving

by Joyce Meyer

Joyce Meyer Ministries

Let me share with you a secret that I've learned about giving. If you keep anything that God tells you to give, the devil will either take it away from you or you will never enjoy it.

Here is how God taught me this secret about giving. I have a bracelet that is an antique. It has a bow on the front, with rhinestones around it. The second time I wore the bracelet, God told me to give it to a particular girl. And I made so many excuses! Maybe she doesn't like silver. It's probably too fancy for her. I really just wanted to keep it, but I finally ended up giving it to her.

I would moan over the loss of that bracelet every time I saw the girl wearing it. I would think, *Oh, I just love that bracelet! I wish I had my bracelet back.*

Then one day the girl gave it back to me. She said God had told her to return the bracelet. I believe God told her to give it back to me to teach me a lesson! I used to love that bracelet, but since she gave it back to me, it lies in my drawer, and I don't ever wear it. I don't even like it now!

Because God asked me to give something away and I still held on to it in my heart and eventually got it back, that thing does not give me joy at all. God's blessing for me was off that bracelet from the moment He asked me to give it away. This is what God taught me: When He tells you to give something away, His blessing is off it for you. And if you keep it, either the devil will steal it or you'll never enjoy it. So if God is telling you to give something away, don't keep it, for "God loves a cheerful giver" (2 Cor. 9:7 NKJV).

A Man After God's Heart

by Patricia Salem

We are prone to think that God only calls those who are perfect to do His work. David was one of God's chosen, but being called by God didn't make him perfect. He spent his life making mistakes. He committed adultery and murder and strayed from God's teachings. But God still called him "a man after His own heart" (Acts 13:22).

How could David be favored by God when he sinned in so many ways? Because when David realized he had made a mistake, he would repent. And God would forgive him and continue to love him. God knows that we're going to make mistakes. But, like David, if we will go to Him when we do something wrong and say, "God, I'm sorry. I goofed up. Please help me do right," He can help us get back on track.

Nothing we do can be too terrible for God to forgive if we are willing to genuinely repent. We are reassured of God's forgiveness in Romans 3:22-24 NLT, which says, "We are made right in God's sight when we trust in Jesus Christ to take away our sins. And we can all be saved in this same way, no matter who we are or what we have done. For all have sinned; all fall short of God's glorious standard. Yet now God in his gracious kindness declares us not guilty. He has done this through Christ Jesus, who has freed us by taking away our sins."

God loves each of us, just as He loved David, who was imperfect. "The unfailing love of the Lord never ends!... Great is his faithfulness; his mercies begin afresh each day" (Lam. 3:22,23 NLT). If you need forgiveness, all you have to do is repent and ask God for it.

The Joyful Jesus

by Eastman Curtis
Destiny Church

I think many of us miss out on the joy that Jesus walked in because the picture of Him in our minds is one of a weeping Jesus carrying the weight of the world on His shoulders. And He looks sad—like somebody has just beaten Him with a depression stick.

That's the way the devil would love for you to see Jesus. Why? As a disciple of Christ, you are being conformed into His image, and if your picture of Jesus is one of His being depressed, sad, and discouraged, you're going to become like that. Jesus said, "A disciple is not above his teacher, nor a servant above his master. It is enough for a disciple that he be like his teacher, and a servant like his master" (Matt. 10:24,25 NKJV).

I believe Jesus was full of joy. How do I know that? Just read the four Gospels and Acts. Jesus not only attracted men and women to hear Him preach, teach, and heal, He also attracted children. At one point the disciples told the little kids to stay away, but Jesus turned around and rebuked the disciples, saying, "Forbid them not: for of such is the kingdom of God" (Luke 18:16).

Children are attracted by joy. Imagine a Jesus who looks like the sad, depressed pictures many of us have of Him in our minds. If Jesus had really been like that, when children were around Him they would have jumped behind their mothers, crying, "No, Mama, no!"

Joy attracts people. Why is the devil out to steal your joy? Because he knows it is a powerful force. Nehemiah 8:10 says, "The joy of the Lord is your strength." If the devil can steal your joy, he can steal your strength. That's why it's important to hold on to your joy—no matter what comes your way!

God of the Hills

by Marilyn Hickey
Marilyn Hickey Ministries

Part One of Two Parts

God is the God of the hills and the valleys. Ahab, the king of Israel, learned this when he faced the Syrian army. Even though the enemy army looked to be more powerful, the Lord told Ahab through a prophet that if he would be obedient, he would win the battle on the hill. Ahab did as he was directed, and the opposing army was defeated. (1 Kings 20:13-21 NKJV.)

The prophet came to Ahab again, warning him that the Syrian army would be back in the spring. Because the Israelites lived in the valleys, the enemy's plan this time was to attack in the valley because their king had been told, "Their gods are gods of the hills. Therefore they were stronger than we; but if we fight against them in the plain [valley], surely we will be stronger than they" (v. 23).

That attitude must have challenged God, for He told Ahab, "Because the Syrians have said, 'The Lord is God of the hills, but He is not God of the valleys,' therefore I will deliver all this great multitude into your hand, and you shall know that I am the Lord" (v. 28). And God gave the Israelites their second victory over the Syrians.

There are times in our lives when we find ourselves facing the enemy on high hills, and we are wondrously victorious. But there are also times when we encounter the enemy in the darkest valleys, and we're tempted to be fearful. But God's Word assures us that we need not be afraid because our God is the God of the hills and the valleys. He is with us at all times and in all places to fight for us.

God of the Valleys

by Marilyn Hickey
Marilyn Hickey Ministries

Part Two of Two Parts

Joseph of the Old Testament was someone who experienced many valleys in his life. He was thrown into a pit by his brothers and sold into slavery. Later Potiphar's wife tried to seduce him, and then he was thrown into prison. (Gen. 37:24; 39:7-23 NKJV.) But God was faithful to Joseph in his hard times. When Joseph interpreted Pharaoh's dreams, he released him and made him administrator over all of Egypt!

Joseph could have gotten egotistical in his high government position, but he didn't. He knew the Lord of the valleys had turned his suffering into fruitfulness. Joseph named one of his sons Ephraim, meaning fruitful in suffering, in recognition of what God had done in his life.

Later, Joseph's father, Jacob, prophesied over him, saying, "Joseph is a fruitful bough...by a well; his branches run over the wall" (Gen. 49:22). Because he let God be real in his valleys, Joseph was blessed, and his branches ran over the wall to bless others as well. God saved his family and generations later through them brought forth the Messiah, Jesus Christ.

The story of Joseph can help us learn an important lesson: Life is full of ups and downs, but God can make us fruitful in our valley times. When we let God be God of the hills—the good times—and God of the valleys—the low times—not only are we blessed, but we become a fruitful bough that grows and blesses others as well.

'My Day of Reckoning'

by Patricia Salem

I never lived on my own. I went directly from my father's house to my husband's after we married. I never had to be the one to pay the bills or be responsible for financial matters...until my husband died. I was a 38-year-old widow with three children between the ages of 10 and 15.

After my husband's death, so many circumstances came against me! One day I realized that I couldn't cope by myself any longer. I went into my bedroom, closed the door, and began to talk honestly to God. "I can't do this," I told Him. "I can't handle these problems. I don't know what to do. My three children need a father, but I can't be the mother and the father. I don't know how."

Quoting Psalm 68:5, I said, "God, Your Word says that You are a father to the fatherless and a defender and protector of the widows. Okay, I'm going to take You at Your Word because You look after Your Word to perform it. (Jer. 1:12 NASB.) You are going to be my Husband and a Father to my children. Now it's up to You to take care of us."

That was my day of reckoning. I could have been drawn into a negative frame of mind by Satan, and there is no telling how our lives would have turned out. Instead, I turned to the Father to get my strength to carry on, and by doing that, He was able to bring His perfect peace to me and my household. By relying on Him, I knew He would be beside me when I faced the trials ahead.

The bottom line is this: You can take God at His Word. Just learn to rely on Him 100 percent!

God Watches Over His Word

by Lindsay Roberts

Jeremiah 1:12 says that God watches over His Word to perform it. When we go along with exactly what the Word of God says, He is obligated to watch over His Word to perform it.

When I tell my children, "I give you my word. Mama promises this is what she is going to do," my children can turn around to me and say, "Mama, you promised!" I'm obligated to honor what I said. You see, they are not making a demand on what *they* said; they are making a demand on what *I* said. I put myself in the position to watch over my word to perform it. I obligated myself. God did the same thing. When holy men moved by God's Spirit wrote the Word and God said it would work, and He told us to use His Word in Jesus' name, then He said He would watch over His Word to perform it. We are not forcing Him to perform it, because we can't force God to do anything. He is simply doing what He said He would do.

Protection by Listening to Your Spirit

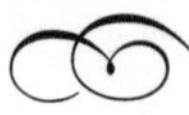

by Kellie Copeland Kutz
Kenneth Copeland Ministries

When it comes to protecting your children and those you love, it is so important to learn to listen to your spirit. God is always speaking to us. I don't believe one calamity ever happens to us that the Holy Spirit doesn't speak to our spirits beforehand to warn us. John 16:13 says that the Spirit of truth will show us things to come. He knows what the enemy is trying to do. If we are in tune with His voice, He can protect us from the devil's attacks.

I strongly encourage you to pray what I prayed: "Lord, I want to be able to hear You when You speak to me. I want to know what You sound like." God took me to school after I prayed that prayer! He put me through one little exercise after another, and His training caused me to grow light-years in my spiritual walk!

First Peter 5:8 tells us to be sober and vigilant because the enemy walks about as a roaring lion, seeking whom he may devour. Be ever watchful. Keep your spiritual antenna up, always listening on the inside for the Holy Spirit's leading. As you listen to your spirit and heed the Holy Spirit's voice, you can make sure the enemy never has the opportunity to devour you or your family![1]

One of the Best Ways

by Terry Law
World Compassion/Terry Law Ministries

Part One of Two Parts

I have traveled all over the world preaching healing, and I've seen God perform healing miracles. But in 1988 I noticed something was wrong in my body. I was getting cramps in my legs and had to change the prescription of my glasses three times in a two-month period. I could feel my strength beginning to wind down.

One morning I woke up on the verge of a coma. I went immediately to see my doctor. After some tests, he said, "Terry, you have the highest blood sugar count I've ever seen." He put me into the hospital immediately.

I knew I needed faith for healing, and Romans 10:17 says that faith comes by hearing the Word of God. So I asked a friend to bring me every teaching tape on healing he could find. As I listened to the Word, my faith began to grow.

One tape was nothing but healing Scriptures. I remember that I began to focus on Mark 11:23-24:

"Whosoever shall say unto this mountain, Be thou removed, and be thou cast into the sea; and shall not doubt in his heart, but shall believe that those things which he saith shall come to pass; he shall have whatsoever he saith.... What things soever ye desire, when ye pray, believe that ye receive them, and ye shall have them."

As I heard those words, God spoke to me, saying, "Your healing is in those verses." I began to meditate on those Scriptures. As God led me toward my healing, I learned that one of the best ways to be healed is through meditating on the Word of God.

Chew On the Word

by Terry Law
World Compassion/Terry Law Ministries

Part Two of Two Parts

Joshua 1:8 says we should meditate on God's Word day and night so we'll obey it. Then we'll prosper and have good success. The word *meditate* comes from the same Hebrew word that means "to chew," like a cow chews its cud. I learned in a biology class in high school that a cow has the ability to take food into its mouth, swallow it, then bring it back up and chew on it again. It's called "chewing the cud."

And that's similar to what God tells us to do with His Word—chew on it for a time, then let our spirits rest. After a while, we're to bring it back up to our mind and meditate on it some more. Gradually the life that's in God's Word will begin to permeate our spirits, and it can bring total healing to our flesh.

That is essentially what happened to me in the hospital. After chewing and meditating on Mark 11:23-24 over and over, the power of God came upon me, and I said, "That's it! I'm healed!"

I rang the bell for the nurse. She came running, and I told her, "I'm healed!" She said, "I'd better call your doctor." The doctor ordered more tests, and the results showed my blood sugar level was back to normal. I was healed! And I'm still walking in that healing today!

Confess the Good

by Eastman Curtis
Destiny Church

Once I was preaching in Florida, and I met a couple and their teenage son. "Eastman," the father said, "our son watches your television program and wanted to meet you." I thanked him and introduced myself to their son.

Then, with his son right there beside him, the father said, "You know, my boy used to be great. I don't know what's happened. He's sleeping all the time. He's not doing well in school. He's not involved in the youth group like he used to be. He's a loser."

As the father spoke, I watched the son. He was looking down, and you could see him shrinking inside. I grabbed his hand and said, "You're a winner! You've got the potential of God flowing through you. He's got big plans for you." As I began to confess the good over him, you could see the air come back into his lungs.

I spoke to the boy's parents privately and explained to them the power of speaking positive words over their son, not just in his presence but also in his absence. The young man's life turned around. After graduation he attended a Bible college, and today he is serving God with all of his heart.

It's amazing what effect words can have in a person's life. If we speak degrading, negative words over our children, it's likely they will start to believe them and act out exactly what we're confessing over them. Hebrews 10:24 NLT says, "Think of ways to encourage one another to outbursts of love and good deeds." Confess the good over your family and see what changes God can bring!

Your True Destiny

by Kenneth Copeland
Kenneth Copeland Ministries

Did you know that right here, in the midst of the same environment that's dragging the world into defeat...right here in the midst of the same storms that are tearing the world apart...you and I and every other born-again child of God can live in victory?

We can put on the whole armor of God, walk right into the midst of the worst circumstances the world has to offer us, and none of them will be able to bring us down.

That's why God told us to put on His armor in the first place! He knew it would protect us. The Word of the living God and the full armor of God is bulletproof. It's sickness-proof, debt-proof, recession-proof. It will cause you to stand when everything around you is falling apart!

But you have to get dressed. You have to walk in it!

You can't just give it a passing nod and then go on watching what the world watches and saying what the world says. If you keep copying the world's ways, you're going to share in the world's destiny. But if you'll copy Jesus—if you'll say what He says and nothing else—you'll share His destiny. It's your choice.

Romans 12:2 says, "Be not conformed to this world: but be ye transformed by the renewing of your mind, that ye may prove what is that good, and acceptable, and perfect, will of God." You won't find the will of God by copying the world. You'll find it by copying Jesus. "If ye continue in my word, then are ye my disciples indeed; And ye shall know the truth, and the truth shall make you free" (John 8:31).

So put on the whole armor, that you will be able to stand. For victory, my friend, is your true destiny.[1]

Giving Thanks in Tough Times

by Lindsay Roberts

The best time to give thanks to God may be in the tough times. Did you know that Thanksgiving Day was founded in the midst of war? In 1863, at the height of the Civil War, President Abraham Lincoln made a decree that America would celebrate "a day of Thanksgiving and Praise to our beneficent Father."

Sadly, many people come into Thanksgiving with mixed emotions. In our family, some of the saddest things happened right at Thanksgiving time. This may be your first Thanksgiving without a certain loved one. Or the holiday may serve as a reminder of some other hurt in your life. Your circumstances may tell you that you don't have anything to be thankful for. But while God doesn't tell us to be thankful *for* all situations, He does tell us to be thankful *in* all situations: "In everything give thanks" (1 Thess. 5:18).

Psalm 34:1 says, "I will bless the Lord at all times; his praise shall continually be in my mouth." The pressures of life can be overwhelming sometimes, but we have a choice to be thankful or not. Richard and I have made a pact that when things start to overwhelm us, we will start giving thanks to the Lord...not for all situations, but in all situations. That gets us focused more on the solution than on the problem. That one decision has changed our lives, and I believe it can change yours too. When you give thanks to God in the midst of your trials, you can expect to see things start to change for the better!

Made in His Image

by Jesse Duplantis
Jesse Duplantis Ministries

First of Four Parts

I was praying as I was being taken to a church service in Johannesburg, South Africa. I said within myself, *Lord, I just can't live without You.* And I thought the Lord was saying, "That's nice, Jesse. Thank you. Jesse, I can't exist without you. I tried to exist without man. I created wonderful cherubims, archangels, and angels, and I created the universe and planets and moons and stars. And I called it good, but it wasn't My best. But when I created you, you looked just like Me!"

Made in His image! I was so excited that I sat down and rested myself, and I've been looking at the body of Christ ever since.

We preachers have a responsibility because we represent Jesus. The Bible says that in prison Paul's and Silas's backs were bleeding. Paul was doing a phenomenal work for God, and he said, "Sing Silas." And the Bible tells us that the prisoners heard them singing and praising God. (Acts 16:25.)

There's an unseen audience listening and watching each of us. So we have a responsibility to Jesus every day to live clean in a dirty world.

Romans 10:13 tells us, "For whosoever shall call upon the name of the Lord shall be saved." That's whosoever, which means "anybody." Then in verse 14, Paul says to the church at Rome, "How then shall they call on him in whom they have not believed? and how shall they believe in him of whom they have not heard? and how shall they hear without a preacher?"

God answered those questions: *How shall they call on Him in whom they have not believed?* First, you've got to believe in something. "How shall they believe in him of whom they have not heard? Faith cometh by hearing" (Rom. 10:17).

'I'll Take Him! I'll Take Him!'

by Jesse Duplantis

Jesse Duplantis Ministries

Second of Four Parts

Without divine knowledge, men cannot believe. Without faith, men cannot call upon God. Without calling upon God, men cannot be saved. And how shall they hear without a preacher? The Gospel lives and conquers by means of human contact.

Lightning is not supposed to affect an airplane, but it blew a hole in the top of one I was in, and I could see daylight right over my seat. The stewardess freaked out, "We're going to die!" I grabbed her and said, "No, we're not! Remember your training. You're freaking out everybody on this plane. Sit down!" I figured if I was going to die, I was going to get somebody saved before I went down. I leaned over to one man and asked, "Listen, do you know Jesus? If you don't, you'd better get to know Him now. You haven't time to tarry. Meet Jesus now!"

He said, "I'll take Him! I'll take Him!"

It was pretty rough, but we landed safely. The captain came back and said, "Reverend, I want to thank you for putting my stewardess back in line. I wish you could have come up in the cockpit. We were shaking too."

How shall they believe in him of whom they have not heard? The church is God's agent in this world. It is a common meeting place for saints and sinners. Jesus was a churchgoer. The Bible says that as was His custom, He went to the synagogue on the sabbath day. (Luke 4:16.) It was His custom. Jesus went to church for thirty years and sat down and listened to people talk about what He wrote.

Ephesians 5:1 says, "Be ye therefore followers of God as dear children."

The Lord Is in This Place

by Jesse Duplantis
Jesse Duplantis Ministries

Third of Four Parts

"For God so loved the world [because of salvation] that he gave his only begotten Son [the cost of salvation. Salvation is free to you today, but it definitely isn't cheap.], that whosoever believeth in Him [the condition of salvation] should not perish, but have everlasting life [the consequence of salvation]" (John 3:16). If you understand the cost, the condition, and the consequence, then you understand salvation.

How shall they believe in Him of whom they have not heard? Faith comes by hearing the Word of God. If you are to influence men, you must be influenced by God. If you are going to influence your community, you've got to be influenced by God. If you want to touch your world, you've got to take care of the biggest problem where you are.

Who made David king? We know Samuel anointed him, but who made David king? Goliath! No one paid attention to David before Goliath. He had a dysfunctional family, and his father didn't even pay attention to him. He told David, "Just stay on the back hill. Watch the sheep." When Samuel asked, "Don't you have any more sons?" David's father replied, "Yes, but you don't want to see him."

David didn't have the love of his father. That is why he and Jonathan, King Saul's son, knit together. Jesse didn't bother with David, but when those two boys got together, their hearts bonded. They had the same background. Jonathan loved David so much that he said, "My kingdom is yours." That's truly a minister of the Gospel, a servant, a son who serves.

Goliath made the boy David a king. Your adversity will make you king. David became king that day because God was a blessing to him.

The Gospel Lives by Human Contact

by Jesse Duplantis
Jesse Duplantis Ministries

Fourth of Four Parts

How shall they believe him of whom they have not heard? The Gospel lives and conquers by means of human contact.

People read books. I like what President Reagan said during his presidency. If he were stranded on an island, and he had the libraries of the world and could choose only one book, he said he would choose unequivocally the Bible. When he was asked why, he answered, "You can read it a million times and get something new out of it every time you read it."

How shall they hear without a preacher? Personality is a powerful expression used by God. The Gospel is the revelation of the personality of God in the personality of Jesus. Jesus said, "When you see Me, you've seen the Father" (John 14:9). Does God laugh? Does He cry? Jesus did, so evidently the Father does. God's personality was transmitted into Jesus.

Paul directed Timothy to commit the teachings of Christ to faithful men. I thank God for Billy Graham who preached the Gospel to me.

There's no one better than you are. God created you, and He created you in His image and likeness. He loves you. You're only one word from His ear. All you have to say is "Jesus," and He is there. If you make a mistake, say, "Forgive me," and He will. He'll love you, and He'll help you. And if you don't know what to do, ask God. He said, "If any of you lack wisdom, let him ask of God...and it shall be given him" (James 1:5).

For the Lord giveth wisdom: out of his mouth cometh knowledge and understanding. He layeth up sound wisdom for the righteous: he is a buckler to them that walk uprightly. —Proverbs 2:6,7

Expectant Faith

by Lindsay Roberts

When a woman becomes pregnant, she says, "I am expecting." Each time I was pregnant, I couldn't see inside my body, but I knew that I was expecting a baby. I knew by my faith that God was creating something miraculous inside me, and soon I would have a baby. That's expectant faith.

Faith for your needs works the same way. When you have a need, take it to God and say, "Father, this is what is broken in my life, and I believe You can fix it. I need Your healing touch on this situation, and I'm expecting a miracle."

You may not see God's answer to your prayer right away, just as I couldn't see the baby growing inside me for nine months; but 2 Corinthians 5:7 tells us that we walk by faith, not by sight. Begin to say, "In Jesus' name, no matter what I see, no matter what I feel, no matter what's staring me in the face, my God said, 'The just shall live by faith,' and by faith I'm receiving my miracle according to God's Word!" That is having expectant faith!

During the nine months I was pregnant with each of my children, I didn't have a break. I was expecting the entire time. On good days, bad days, happy days, sad days. It didn't matter; I was still expecting. Treat your faith like that. Stay in an attitude of expectancy. No matter what is happening around you, hold on to the Word of God and expect a miracle.

An Open Door for Miracles

by Gloria Copeland
Kenneth Copeland Ministries

When people came to Jesus and asked, "What must we do to do the works God requires?" Jesus answered, "The work of God is this: to believe in the one he has sent" (John 6:28,29). All through the Bible, every time something awesome happened, somebody had to trust God enough to act on what He said and open the door.

That's what happened to me the day I made Jesus my Lord. I read Matthew 6:26 and found out that God cares even for birds—and faith burst into my heart. I didn't know the first thing about becoming a Christian. Yet when I spoke that faith out—that I believed in Him—I opened the door just a crack and God's mercy and love flooded my heart and changed me forever.

It's still true today. However wide you open that door of faith is how much of God's mercy and goodness will flow into your life. He wants to do great things in your life and give you all the benefits of salvation. When I say salvation, I'm not just talking about a ticket to heaven. Salvation means freedom—from depression, poverty, sickness, danger, fear—anything you need freedom from!

Psalm 68:19 says God loads us with the benefits of salvation daily. Start each day by opening the door of faith. Don't just open it a crack—rip it off the hinges![1]

We Need Each Other

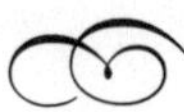

by Keith Butler
Word of Faith International Christian Center

If you have accepted Jesus as your Lord and Savior, you are a part of the body of Christ. First Corinthians 12:22,27 NLT says, "The human body has many parts, but the many parts make up only one body. So it is with the body of Christ.... Now all of you together are Christ's body, and each one of you is a separate and necessary part of it."

Your body parts don't operate independently of each other. Your hand doesn't say, "I'm tired of operating with this wrist. I get my instructions from the head, and I don't need this wrist anymore." No, even though the instructions come from the head, they have to go through the neck and shoulder, down through the arm to the wrist, and all the way to the hand in order for the hand to do its job.

That's the way God has created the body of Christ. No one person has all the gifts and talents. No one person has all the revelation. God has built a certain interdependency into His body of believers.

Jesus said, "By this all will know that you are My disciples, if you have love for one another" (John 13:35 NKJV). God expects us to love and receive our brothers and sisters in Christ because we are all part of the same body. We can all learn something from each other, and we need each other!

If You Don't Know How To Pray...

by Patricia Salem

Many people feel as if they don't know how to pray. But I believe that if you know how to talk to someone, you can pray, because when you pray, you are talking to God.

I was widowed at a young age, and I quickly learned that if I was going to make it as a single parent with three children, I was going to have to rely solely on God. I learned to think of Him as my best friend, my confidant, and my helper. But to develop that kind of relationship with Him, I had to pray—talk to Him—about whatever I was facing. I had to become close to Him and trust Him with my whole heart.

Many times during those years I would ask Him, "Father, what should I do about this situation?" Usually by the next morning, He had given me the answer. The children and I would be at the breakfast table, and I'd say, "I've been praying, and this is God's answer to what we're facing." I still do that today.

Think of God as your best friend. He loves you more than anyone else. And you can talk to Him just as you would to your best friend. Tell Him your problems, your needs, your hurts. Tell Him where you need His healing touch in your life. But most of all, tell Him how much you love Him and trust Him.

That's how the psalmist prayed. He said, "I will give thanks to your name for your unfailing love and faithfulness, because your promises are backed by all the honor of your name. When I pray, you answer me; you encourage me by giving me the strength I need" (Ps. 138:2,3 NLT). I believe such heart-to-heart prayers go straight to God's listening ear.

In Your Weakness God Is Strong

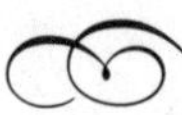

by Jerry Savelle

Jerry Savelle Ministries International

When I read about the apostle Paul, it seems to me that he was a man who enjoyed a good fight. I've often said I wish they would make a movie about his life, and I think Clint Eastwood should play the part. I can just see Paul saying to the devil, "Okay, punk, make my day!"

It's not that Paul was a tough guy in his own ability. He was human, just like you and I, with human weaknesses. But in 2 Corinthians 12:10 he said, "I take pleasure in infirmities, in reproaches, in necessities, in persecutions, in distresses for Christ's sake: for when I am weak, then am I strong." Paul had discovered that when he was at his weakest, that was when the power of God came on him the strongest. When he was beyond his own strength and ability, that's when he sensed the greater anointing, the greater presence of God, on his life. He knew, and we can too, that when we are at our weakest point, God can show up strongest for us!

'This Is My Harvest!'

by Lindsay Roberts

One Christmas a couple of years ago my mother and I went shopping together. My mother had all the stuff she wanted in her cart and had just pulled into the area by the cashier's line when we noticed some people counting heads. What we didn't know at the time was that every one-hundredth customer that went through one certain line got their whole cartful of items free. Others apparently had figured it out, and they were trying to work the system.

Then I told my mother, "You go right there," pointing to a certain line, "and I'll go here." I wanted to count my money and get my purse organized before I reached the cashier.

All of a sudden, someone shouted at my mother, "You're it!" Totally ignorant of what was going on, my mother answered, "What?"

"You're the one-hundredth customer! Everything in your cart is free!" they said. Just then a woman said to my mother, "This must be your lucky day."

My mother answered her, saying, "No, no. I have sowed my seed to God. This is my harvest!" And right there she began to preach Seed-Faith.

Not only did my mother recognize that this was *not* just her lucky day, but God was multiplying her seed and she was given an opportunity to give a testimony because of what had happened.

Unashamed Witnesses

by Billy Joe Daugherty
Victory Christian Center Church and School

Wimps don't witness. It takes a real Christian to stand up and boldly witness for Christ. As never before, I believe this is an hour when God wants the unashamed witness of His Son, Jesus Christ, proclaimed in every arena of life. Romans 10:13-14 says, "Whosoever shall call upon the name of the Lord shall be saved. How then shall they call on him in whom they have not believed? and how shall they believe in him of whom they have not heard? and how shall they hear without a preacher?"

That's a powerful word exhorting us to proclaim the Gospel. You may say, "I don't need to talk about Jesus—my life is a witness." While a good example is necessary, if all that was needed was for you to live a good life, Jesus should have never died on the cross. He would have only needed to show us how to live a good life. The problem is that every person has sin in his or her heart, and our good life cannot take sin out of our heart. It was the death, burial, and resurrection of Jesus that paid the price for sin.

If we don't speak up and sound the voice of God's Word, we are like a lifeguard who is sitting on his tall chair at the beach, looking out over the water. He looks good, he's in shape, and he has the best equipment at his disposal. Suddenly some people out in the water get caught in a riptide, and they scream for help. But the lifeguard just sits there, looking at them through his binoculars. The lifeguard is prepared and equipped, but if he doesn't do something, those people will drown!

God hasn't called us simply to look good as Christians. He has called us to be bold, ready witnesses to win the lost to Jesus.

'Are You Buying?'

by Jesse Duplantis
Jesse Duplantis Ministries

Growing up, our daughter, Jody, was always polite when we went out to eat. We would often have adult guests with us, so Jody usually brought along a friend or two to keep her company during the meal. When she was about fourteen, I began to notice that as we were sitting at the table, I'd get an elbow in my side. "Dad, are you buying?" she'd ask.

I'd answer, "Yes, I'm buying."

Then she'd turn to her friends and say, "Order whatever you want. Dad's buying."

How many times have we sat down at a spiritual table with God and asked, "Excuse me, God. Are You buying?"

Of course God is buying! We are His beloved children! When we sit at His table, we can have what we want and how much we want because He has the power to give us not only what we need but also things we desire or want.

Philippians 4:19 NKJV says that God shall supply all your need according to His riches in glory by Christ Jesus. God's Word also says that the Lord will guide you continually and satisfy your desire. (Isa. 58:11 ESV.) And we are told in 2 Chronicles 1:7 NIV that God appeared to Solomon and said to him, "Ask for whatever you want me to give you." God wants to be our Source for everything we could possibly yearn for!

God's table is full of abundance, and we are invited to His feast. The meal has already been paid for with the life of His precious Son, Jesus. It gives God great pleasure when we take advantage of His marvelous provision for us.

God's Destiny for You

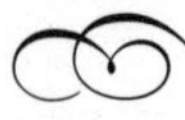

by Marilyn Hickey
Marilyn Hickey Ministries

First of Three Parts

Before you were born, no one had a fingerprint like yours; no one had the same chromosome code or the same genetic code. You are unique. God created you for a purpose for such a time as this.

How can you find your purpose—your destiny? The One who designed you—the Lord—can reveal it to you. You weren't an accident. God has a plan and purpose for each individual. Pray and ask Him to reveal to you His destiny for your life.

There is no happiness, no joy, like being in God's plan and His destiny. You may be going through the toughest of times, facing the greatest of challenges, and experiencing the worst demonic attacks, but you can be happy when you know you're in His plan.

The story of Joseph in Genesis 37 tells of finding one's destiny. Joseph found his at seventeen. It doesn't take forever. You may not know all the details and the process, but God will begin to speak to your heart in a still, small voice and reveal it to you. It may be a little piece here and a little piece there, but you will begin to see that God has His hand on your life.

Joseph had two dreams. In one, he dreamed that the sun, moon, and stars bowed down to him. (vv. 6-11.) That sounds egotistical, doesn't it? Often, when you begin to hear from God, you may think, *God, I can never do that. That's too big, too far-out.* But remember what God said to Abraham and Sarah in Genesis 17:6? "Kings shall come out of thee." And if you're born again, you are the seed of Abraham.

You may affect a nation, a leader, or a corporation. Inside you is a potential beyond what you can imagine, because it is the plan and purpose of God.

Practice Wherever You Are

by Marilyn Hickey
Marilyn Hickey Ministries

Second of Three Parts

Practice your calling wherever you are. Joseph's purpose involved his administrative ability, which he practiced when he was only seventeen on his father's estate. Later, he worked hard for Potiphar, who said, "This man has wonderful administrative ability, so I'll put him over my estate." (Gen. 39:1-6.)

It's important to keep doing the things you know God wants you to do no matter what discouragement you meet. Joseph was practicing his calling when Potiphar's wife tried to seduce him and he was put into prison. Joseph knew his purpose, and he fled the temptation. When circumstances are against you, God can make a way—if you stay in your purpose and practice. Joseph continued to practice his purpose in prison, and the prison officials noticed him. "We need an administrator," they said, "and he has an administrative gift."

Joseph was called upon to interpret the dreams of two men in the prison, which he did successfully. One of the men was put in the high position of Pharaoh's cupbearer. Joseph said to him, "Don't forget me," but the man forgot him. Then Pharaoh had a dream, and suddenly the cupbearer remembered Joseph. Joseph interpreted Pharaoh's dream, and at nearly forty, Joseph was placed in a position of authority over the entire land, second only to Pharaoh! (Gen. 41:39-43.)

Joseph could never have become the administrator of a nation if he had not been practicing at home with his father, practicing at Potiphar's house, and practicing in prison. God knew the potential in Joseph because He put it there. He knows your potential also. So stay in your purpose and keep practicing. It will pay in the end!

He Talked About God

by Marilyn Hickey
Marilyn Hickey Ministries

Third of Three Parts

Forgiveness is the key to having the power and anointing to perform God's full purpose for your life. Some people will say, "You can't do it," but you have to stay with your purpose. Once the people at a TV station said to me, "Lady, we can tell you're not television material." But now they aren't around.

You have to forgive. Joseph's brothers threw him into a pit, Potiphar's wife falsely accused him of trying to seduce her, and the cupbearer totally forgot him. Joseph had many opportunities to get bitter, but if he had gotten bitter, if he had not forgiven, he would have missed his purpose.

I believe Joseph was just as human as anyone. How could he forgive? How could he stay with his purpose? To teach me, the Holy Spirit led me to read everything Joseph ever said, because out of the abundance of the heart the mouth speaks.

When Joseph was approached by Potiphar's wife, he said, "I can't go to bed with you. Your husband is my master, and God would be displeased with me." He talked about God. Imprisoned, he said to the two men who came to him with their dreams, "God interprets dreams." What did he talk about in prison? God.

Then when his brothers came to ask him, "Are you going to kill us?" Joseph replied, "No. What you did you meant for evil, but God meant it for good" (Gen. 50:20). He talked about God.

What will uphold you during trying times? Forgiving those who have hurt you and focusing on God. Pray this prayer: *Father, help me forgive, and show me how to walk in the power and the anointing of Your purpose planted in me. In Jesus' name. Amen.*

Doctors Treat, but God Heals

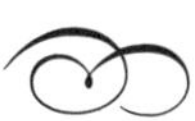

by Richard Roberts

There are several time-honored Bible ways of receiving your healing. One method is by the laying on of hands. Jesus said all believers "will lay hands on the sick, and they will recover" (Mark 16:18 NKJV). That verse doesn't say anything about your needing a special calling. Every born-again believer is to have a ministry of healing.

Healing can also come through medical treatment. Jesus put His stamp of approval on medical science when He said, "Those who are well have no need of a physician, but those who are sick" (Matt. 9:12 NKJV). God approved of prayer for healing in James 5:15 NKJV which says, "The prayer of faith will save the sick, and the Lord will raise him up."

The concept that the streams of medical science and prayer work together to bring healing came through my father's ministry many years ago. In the Bible the apostle Paul laid hands on the sick and they were healed; Luke, the physician, treated them medically and they were cured.

I don't limit God in the way He heals. When I get a headache, all I want to do is get well. So I pray and take a couple of pain relievers. I don't really care which one works. I don't put my faith in the prayer, nor do I put my faith in the medicine. I put my faith in God, who is the Source of both. No matter which one works, I give the glory for the healing to Him.

As you seek the healing you need, focus on and give the glory to God, the Source of each and every healing miracle!

Worry in Reverse

by Pat Harrison
Faith Christian Fellowship International

You probably know people who brag that they've read fifty or more pages of the Bible in one sitting, or they've read Isaiah thirty-three times, or they can quote the Bible "six ways backwards." But in many instances, the Word didn't get in them—they were just reading print on pages.

The Bible tells us that we are to meditate on the Word day and night. (Ps. 1:2.) That's totally different from just reading the Word.

How do you meditate on the Bible? You take a verse, then look at each word and think about the words. The verse might say, "But he"—who is he? He is Jesus. Who is Jesus? Jesus is our Savior, our Deliverer, our Healer. That's how you meditate on the Word. You take each word and meditate on it and think about it.

I like to think of meditation as the opposite of worry, or "worry in reverse." Instead of meditating on the wicked and the evil, or dwelling on a bad report you may have received, you meditate on the Word of God. You absorb the Word. That's how you retain the Word. Then when you retain it, the Word becomes part of you and your world. And when it gets inside you, it's got to come out, because out of the abundance of the heart your mouth speaks. (Matt. 12:34.)

You sow the Word into the garden of your heart. Then when trouble comes—when Satan tries to attack you—the Word will come up out of your mouth, and he will be defeated in the authority of Jesus' name!

Take It Back!

by Sharon Daugherty
Victory Christian Center Church and School

First Samuel 30 tells the moving story of David and his mighty men who returned to their city of Ziklag after a great battle. When they arrived home, they found their city had been burned by the Amalekites, their families kidnapped, and all of their belongings stolen. It was a devastating homecoming. Verse 4 says, "Then David and the people that were with him lifted up their voice and wept, until they had no more power to weep."

In their distress, David's men turned on him and planned to stone him, blaming him for their plight. But verse 6 says that David encouraged himself in the Lord his God. He sought God, and the Lord told him to pursue the enemy army, for he would overtake them and recover everything that had been lost. God said to David, "Go, take it back!"

So David and his men obeyed the Lord. They rose up from the place of weeping and pursued the enemy army until they found them eating, drinking, and dancing in a field. David and his men fought them from the twilight to the evening and defeated them soundly. Verse 18 says, "David recovered all that the Amalekites had carried away: and David rescued his two wives." He took back everything the enemy had stolen from him!

I want to encourage you today. You may have been through some things that have devastated you, and you may feel that all hope is gone. But it's never too late with God. He wants you to rise up and believe that He can help you take back what the devil has taken from you!

The Result of God's Blessing

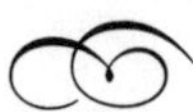

by Dr. Creflo A. Dollar

World Changers Church International

In Genesis 12:1-2, the Lord told Abram, "Get thee out of thy country, and from thy kindred, and from thy father's house, unto a land that I will shew thee: And I will make of thee a great nation, and I will bless thee . . . and thou shalt be a blessing."

Once when I read that Scripture, I thought, *Lord, I always thought blessings were a car or house—tangible stuff that I could touch.* And the Lord answered, "Son, blessings are spiritual."

I asked God for a Scripture, and He referred me to Ephesians 1:3, which says He has blessed us with all spiritual blessings in heavenly places in Christ. I said, "Well, what about the blessings of a house or car? What about healing and the good life?"

"Those are the result of the blessing," God said. "They're not the blessing. They are the result of the invisible, the intangible."

Blessed means to empower to prosper. What does it mean when somebody is empowered? It means you give legal power or authority to that person. God is saying, "I have authorized you as an authorized dealer of My anointing in this world to have success."

Blessed is a word that talks about enablement from God more than a material manifestation from that enablement. God is saying, "I promise to bless you, to empower you, and to anoint you to have success. I didn't say I'd give you a house or a car, but that I would give you an enablement, an ability from Me; and with that ability you can get the results of that anointing."

The Lord's anointing empowers you with ability and wisdom, with ideas and concepts to make you rich. Proverbs 10:22 says, "The blessing of the Lord, it maketh rich, and he addeth no sorrow."

God's Unexpected Ways

by Lindsay Roberts

Most of my life I wanted to be a kindergarten teacher. One of my favorite things to do is sit in a chair and teach—whether it be the Word of God or the ABC's! But God had other plans. When He told me to begin the television program, *Make Your Day Count,* I was excited. This was my big chance! I couldn't wait to sit in a chair before the TV cameras and teach the Bible. Of course, there were to be other parts to the show, such as cooking segments, guests, and music, but I wanted to instruct people in the Word of God!

The responses we began to get from viewers surprised me. "You make me laugh," read one letter. One man told my husband, "I like to watch your wife cook!" No one seemed to realize the importance of my teaching! Frustrated, I tried all the harder to portray myself as a serious Bible teacher, but all I could seem to do was make others laugh. I said, "Lord, this is not working."

Then one day I received a letter from a woman who wrote, "If I didn't have your show to make me laugh, I don't know what I'd do." She had breast cancer and was going through chemotherapy. Our show was the bright spot in her day. I suddenly realized that God was using the program to reach people in His way. God says, "My ways [are] higher than your ways" (Isa. 55:9 NKJV). I believe if we are open to how God wants to use us—even if it's not how we expect—we can be a blessing to others and be blessed in return.

Facing the Lions' Den

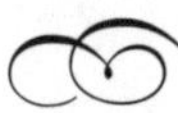

by Richard Roberts

We all go through times of trouble when we feel as though we've been thrown into a den of hungry lions. That literally happened to the prophet Daniel.

The Bible says Daniel had distinguished himself above the king's governors. He had an excellent spirit, and the king considered placing him over the empire as his administrative officer. Because of this, the governors hated Daniel. So they devised a plan to trick the king into decreeing that no one could pray for thirty days. Anyone who disobeyed would be thrown into a den of lions.

Daniel paid no attention to that decree, and he continued to pray to his God as usual. The prophet's actions were reported to the king, who soon realized he had been tricked, but he had to keep his word. Much to his chagrin, he had Daniel thrown into the lions' den. But God delivered Daniel! He sent His angel and shut the lions' mouths! (Dan. 6:22 NKJV.) Verse 23 says that Daniel came up out of the den without any harm or injury because he believed in his God!

You may be facing a lions' den right now. It may be a lions' den of fear, discouragement, or depression. Perhaps it's a den of sickness or debt. But when you stand strong in your faith and obey God's Word, you have a Bible right to expect God to fulfill His Word. He has the power to deliver you just like He delivered Daniel!

The Safest Place To Be

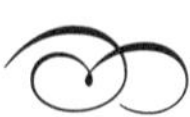

by Lindsay Roberts

My husband Richard's ministry takes him all over the United States and around the world. Whenever he boards an airplane to go to faraway places, there are always possible dangers. There could be mechanical difficulties with the plane, or the country to which he's traveling could be experiencing unrest. And now our oldest daughter, Jordan, is beginning to travel and minister with him. Even though it means she, too, may face dangerous situations, she tells me, "Mama, I have to go because God has called me."

Knowing my concern for my loved ones, the Lord spoke to me about the situation, saying, "Lindsay, the safest place they can ever be is in the center of My will." That made sense. The safest place any of us can be is in the center of obedience to God's will.

Sometimes when we ask for God's guidance, He tells us, "Not yet." Other times He may tell us, "Now." Ecclesiastes 3:1-5 NKJV says, "To everything there is a season, a time for every purpose under heaven: a time to be born, and a time to die; a time to plant, and a time to pluck what is planted...a time to break down, and a time to build up; a time to weep, and a time to laugh...a time to embrace, and a time to refrain from embracing."

We may not feel comfortable with what God is calling us or our loved ones to do, but God has a time and a season for everything. God wants us to listen to His voice and go His route. Then we will be in the safest place possible—the center of His will.

Overloaded With Joy

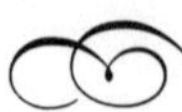

by Kenneth Copeland
Kenneth Copeland Ministries

Joy...it's a traditional part of the Christmas season. In December, people who hardly crack a smile all year send out cards with messages about joy. Carolers chirp out "Joy to the World!" as grumpy shoppers push their way through crowded malls. Glittering banners wave the word *joy* over city streets jammed with irritated drivers who just want to get home.

The truth is, with all the pressures people face this time of year, it's easy to let joy slip through your fingers, but don't do it. Instead, get a true understanding of joy that you can hang on to all year 'round.

Joy used to be my weakest area. I spent so much time focusing on faith that I didn't pay much attention to it; however, the Lord taught me that you can't live by faith without joy. That's because it takes strength to live by faith. The natural pull of the world is always negative. When you leave things alone and don't work against that negative flow, they always get worse.

To move toward life, you must constantly swim upstream. If you ever get too weak spiritually to do that, you'll find yourself being swept back toward defeat. So you can never afford to run out of strength.

No wonder the apostle Paul wrote to rejoice in the Lord always! To rejoice means to re-joy, to back up and get another load!

Paul understood the link between joy and strength. That's why he prayed for the Colossians to be "strengthened with all might, according to His [God's] glorious power, for all patience and longsuffering with joy" (Col. 1:11 NKJV). The heart of that sentence says we are strengthened with might and joy!

Paul reaffirmed this basic truth: The joy of the Lord is our strength! (Neh. 8:10.) So back your truck up...and get another load![1]

How To Get the Fear Out

by Lindsay Roberts

First of Two Parts

The Bible says in 2 Corinthians 5:7 that we walk by faith and not by sight. If you walk by sight, the sight of things today will kill you. Second Timothy 1:7 tells us, "For God hath not given us the spirit of fear; but of power, and of love, and of a sound mind." Power, love, and a sound mind can come only when you get out of the spirit of fear. God has not given you the spirit of fear. If God has not given it to you, but you are possessing it, then God can't give you what He wants to give you because you won't let go of the things you have that He did not give you!

In order for you to get power, love, and a sound mind, it is essential to get fear out. How do you do that? "Faith comes by hearing, and hearing by the word of God" (Rom. 10:17 NKJV).

If fear and faith are total opposites, like darkness and light, and they can't dwell together in the same place, then in order to get faith in, fear has to be driven out.

Faith comes by hearing the Word of God. Psalm 1:1 says, "Blessed is the man that walketh not in the counsel of the ungodly, nor standeth in the way of sinners, nor sitteth in the seat of the scornful." God said in James 1:17 that every good and perfect gift comes from Him. He is not going to tell you something bizarre. It may be different from the way the world thinks and talks, but it is not going to be bizarre. God talks like He writes, and He writes like He talks. He will never say something to you that doesn't line up with the Word of God.

God has power, but that power comes from the Holy Spirit entering into you, coming upon you, and being stirred up within you.

Bless the Lord With Your Mind, Will, and Emotions

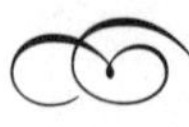

by Lindsay Roberts

Second of Two Parts

Isaiah 41:10 tells us, "Fear thou not; for I am with thee: be not dismayed; for I am thy God: I will strengthen thee; yea, I will help thee; yea, I will uphold thee with the right hand of my righteousness."

For months I had been praying for the healing of a little child. I became so frustrated one day that I called Oral Roberts. I said, "I can't do this anymore. I can't pray anymore. I feel like I am just going crazy."

God spoke to me through Oral, who said, "Let me say one thing first. You have a will, and you're using it wrong. Read Psalm 103:1, which says, 'Bless the Lord, O my soul.'" Then he asked, "What does *soul* mean? Mind, will, and emotions. Bless the Lord with your mind, your will, and your emotions."

He continued, "Your mind and emotions are headed for a crash. Why? Because you are not using your will in the right direction. You have to exercise it. Use it! Use it in the right direction!"

So I began to say, "Self, line up with the Word of God. I will bless the Lord today with my mind. I will bless the Lord today with my will. I will bless the Lord today with my emotions."

I began to pray with every fiber of my being: "Bless the Lord, O my soul: and all that is within me, bless his holy name. Bless the Lord, O my soul, and forget not all his benefits: who forgiveth all thine iniquities; who healeth all thy diseases; who redeemeth thy life from destruction; who crowneth thee with lovingkindness and tender mercies; who satisfieth thy mouth with good things; so that thy youth is renewed like the eagle's" (Ps. 103:1-5).

God Is on the Job

by Jerry Savelle

Jerry Savelle Ministries International

Part One of Two Parts

I believe that we are in the last of the last days. Sometimes the pressure is intense. From the *Message Bible*, 1 Peter 4:7 says, "Everything in the world is about to be wrapped up, so take nothing for granted. Stay wide-awake in prayer." Then verse 12 goes on to say, "When life gets really difficult, don't jump to the conclusion that God isn't on the job." And verse 19 says, "If you find life difficult because you're doing what God said, take it in stride. Trust Him. He knows what he's doing, and he'll keep on doing it."

I don't know about you, but it energizes my faith to know that no matter what's going on around me, God is still on the job, working behind the scenes. Right now He's rearranging things. If necessary, He's causing His angels to maneuver situations to help us.

Many of us are under some of the greatest pressure we've ever experienced. There is a lot of potential for stress today because of unrest, not only around the world but also in our personal lives. It seems that Satan is intensifying his efforts against Christians. And attacks don't just come one at a time anymore; they come in bunches.

But never forget that no matter how impossible your situation might look, God is at work, and He knows what He's doing. Keep on trusting Him! Don't ever think that nothing good is happening just because you can't see it with your natural eyes. Something good is happening, because God is on the job!

'I'm Taking Care of That'

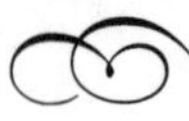

by Jerry Savelle

Jerry Savelle Ministries International

Part Two of Two Parts

One time I needed $50,000 for a ministry project in Kenya. On my way to preach a meeting in Toronto, Canada, I prayed, "Lord, I would appreciate it if You would arrange for the $50,000 I need for this project in Kenya." And He said, "I'm already taking care of that."

As I arrived at the church where I was to preach, I met a couple who said, "Brother Jerry, we were believing God that we would get to talk to you during this meeting." They said my ministry had made a tremendous impact on their lives. As we said good-bye, they put an envelope into my suit pocket, but I didn't have time to look at it then.

After the service, I said, "Lord, I want to thank You for that $50,000 You said You were arranging for." And He said, "Didn't I tell you I was taking care of that?" I answered, "Yes, You did, and I want to thank You for it."

This went on for five days. Every day I would remind the Lord of my request. Finally, on the last day of the meeting, the Lord said, "Son, would it surprise you to know that I've already taken care of that? Go look in the suit you wore the first day of the meeting." When I did, I found the envelope, and it held a check for $50,000!

First Thessalonians 5:24 says, "Faithful is he that calleth you, who also will do it." We don't always know how God is going to work on our behalf. But I do know that if we are trusting Him, He is behind the scenes taking care of whatever we're believing for, even when we can't see anything happening!

Hearing God's Voice

by Taffi L. Dollar
World Changers Church International

I believe the only way we will be able to stand against the onslaughts of the devil that are coming against us today is by being able to hear and obey God's voice. We were made to hear our heavenly Father's voice. Deuteronomy 4:36 says, "Out of heaven he made you to hear his voice, that he might instruct thee." In the same way that children recognize the voice of their mother so she can instruct, correct, and encourage them, we were made to hear our Father's voice.

We recognize the voices of our parents and children. If they call on the phone, we don't have to ask them to identify themselves. We know the sound of their voices. It's familiar to us. This is the same familiarity our heavenly Father wants us to experience when He speaks to us.

God is not silent. He is speaking all the time in many ways—in a song, in a word from someone, in that still, small voice inside of us. But we must have a listening heart. We have to tune our ears and our spirits to hear from Him through His Word. God speaks clearly, not in vague impressions, but in specific details. In Genesis 6 when He spoke to Noah about building the ark, He gave him specific instructions about every aspect needed to successfully complete the job.

God desires to speak to us just as clearly today and to give us specific direction for our lives. He wants us to make a quality decision to learn to recognize His voice and listen to His instruction so we can have peace and be free from confusion and frustration.

The Christmas Story

by Oral Roberts

First of Three Parts

As I read Luke's account of the first Christmas, these thoughts came to me. I hope you follow me in these reflections so you may also better understand the real meaning of Christmas.

Mary was a young girl engaged to be married when the angel, Gabriel, visited her with a message from God. Mary and her fiance´, Joseph, were looking forward to their marriage. Engagement vows in those days were almost like marriage vows are today, and the entire community considered Mary and Joseph's betrothal binding.

One day while Mary was alone, an angel appeared. This must have been a startling experience for she drew back in fear. But he spoke gently and said, "Fear not, Mary" (Luke 1:30).

Then the angel explained that she had been chosen to give birth to God's Son, Jesus. She would be with child before her marriage to Joseph, but the child would be begotten of God.

This message from the angel was full of implications for a young woman already engaged. Her marriage hopes would be jeopardized; no one would understand. Mary had to have incredible trust in God, for only the vaguest details of the birth were revealed to her. We have but an inkling of the terrible problems such a situation would have brought to Mary and to Joseph. The natural reaction would have been for Joseph to have broken his vows with Mary. But God sent an angel to Joseph in a dream, quieting his fears and telling him that he should go ahead with his plans to accept Mary as his wife.

Mary's cousin, Elisabeth, was visited by the same angel, Gabriel, and told that she would give birth to a child in her old age. This child would become John the Baptist. Several days later, Mary went into the hill country of Judea to see her cousin, who was in her sixth month. As she entered the house, the baby in Elisabeth's womb leaped for joy, and the spirit of prophecy fell upon Elisabeth! She told Mary that because she had believed the angel, God would perform all the things He had said would come to pass.

Just a Hand Away

by Oral Roberts

Second of Three Parts

The ordeal of childbearing must have been difficult. There were no hospitals or soft beds. There was only a stable for Mary's baby, a manger for His bed. Mary considered it a great honor and sang from the depth of her spirit, "My soul doth magnify the Lord, and my spirit hath rejoiced in God my Saviour" (Luke 1:46,47).

The night Jesus was born, God sent a heavenly choir of angels to fill the heavens with joyous song. One said to the startled shepherds, "Fear not: for, behold, I bring you good tidings of great joy, which shall be to all people. For unto you is born this day in the city of David a Saviour, which is Christ the Lord. And this shall be a sign unto you; Ye shall find the babe wrapped in swaddling clothes, lying in a manger" (Luke 2:10-12).

I believe every angel in heaven wanted to be the first with the glad tidings that Christ the Lord was born. What a glorious privilege!

The shepherds left their flocks to see the new baby. Men of the fields, sons of toil, went to the manger to pay homage to Mary's infant child.

Wise men from various parts of the world discovered a new star and set off on a journey that took many months to take gifts of royalty to the newborn King.

Such was God's performance because of Mary's believing!

When the baby Jesus was eight days old, Mary and Joseph took Him to Jerusalem to present Him to God. Simeon, a just and devout man, who had waited for the consolation of Israel and who was filled with the Holy Spirit, had received a message from God that he would not see death before he had seen the Lord's Christ. "And he came by the Spirit into the temple: and when the parents brought in the child Jesus, to do for him after the custom of the law, then took he him up in his arms, and blessed God, and said, Lord, now lettest thou thy servant depart in peace, accorSding to thy word: for mine eyes have seen thy salvation" (Luke 2:27-30).

To Change the World

by Oral Roberts

Third of Three Parts

Has there ever before been a baby like this? As the baby lay in Mary's arms, the world knew His power. Because of Him, hosts of angels visited the earth, heaven bent low, and the glory of God descended upon mankind in a way never known before, with the comforting message of joy and peace.

It has been said that when God gets ready to lift an empire, to change the course of human history, or to save the world, He has a baby born somewhere. For the greatest task of all, the salvation of mankind and the fulfillment of all God's precious promises, God had the baby Jesus born of the virgin Mary. "For," said the angel, "he shall save his people from their sins" (Matt. 1:21).

Mary gave the fruit of her womb, asking nothing in return. But she recorded all these things in her heart, for she had faith in God.

I have often imagined that Luke visited with Mary and asked her to tell him all about the angel's visit, the birth of the Child, and all she had to go through. No one else told it as he did. Its beauty and truth have blessed men through the centuries.

Such is my version of the Christmas story in the Gospel of Luke, as I visualized it that Christmas Eve. Through this intimate picture of Mary's believing, I gained a new understanding of Christmas. Suddenly I knew that the next day would be the happiest Christmas in my life. I knelt and thanked God for His answers to the questions that had perplexed my heart.

I wish that all people everywhere might know the true meaning of Christmas and that little children, as well as their parents, might grasp the significance of God's gift to humanity.

Christmas is a time of spiritual rebirth, of searching our hearts, and of asking the heavenly Father to make us more like His holy Son, Jesus.

Christmas is a time to praise God for His goodness. Glory to God in the highest!

No Fear

by Keith Moore
Faith Life Church

My grandmother was a Partner with Oral Roberts, and she hung his letters on the walls of her home for encouragement. Through Oral's letters, as a teenager I became a believer in God's power to heal.

In the ministry, I've seen that one of the biggest challenges to receiving healing is not only dealing with the physical part of the problem but also with the spiritual part. I thank God for the medical profession and how God works through them, but doctors themselves will tell you that they can't make the body heal itself. That takes the healing power of God, and it involves the spirit of man.

How can you tap into that spiritual dimension of healing? Your faith can be the catalyst that lays hold of God's healing power. But how do you know if you are in faith? Hebrews 4:3 says, "We which have believed do enter into rest." When you believe God's promises and you put your trust in God, you can rest in Him. The devil wants you to give him a legal right to enforce whatever sickness or disease has tried to find a place in you. Fear can give him that right. Often when you hear a frightening diagnosis, panic tries to paralyze you, and thoughts that you're going to die can try to grip your mind. If you embrace that bad report rather than resting in your trust in God, you can hinder His healing power.

But, thank God, He has done something about fear. We don't have to have it. Psalm 27:1 says, "The Lord is my light and my salvation; whom [or what] shall I fear?" Hear God speaking those words into your spirit, and it can take away fear and heaviness. God's healing power is greater than disease. Use your faith and believe God's Word for your healing to begin now!

Take Your Dream Off the Shelf

by Richard Roberts

Do you have a dream that needs to be resurrected? Years ago when my father was preaching a crusade in Seattle, Washington, a man by the name of William Skrinde was in the audience. He had failed in business and was working for only 75 cents an hour in a nursing home. He was 66 years old and his future looked bleak. But during the crusade he received Christ.

One night my father explained the concept of Seed-Faith, and it opened up Mr. Skrinde's eyes to giving out of a heart of love and with expectancy. But he had little to give. My father said, "There are those of you listening to my voice who have invented or created something, and you've laid it on the shelf. Perhaps it's even in your attic. Look around. See what God has given you."

The Holy Spirit inspired Mr. Skrinde to go up into his attic, where he found the plans he had drawn up years before for a part for four-wheel-drive vehicles. He felt led to try one more time to sell the product. This time the company bought it, and Mr. Skrinde became a wealthy man. He was a great supporter of our ministry until the day he died at age 92. He described the change in his life this way: "Right at the time I should have retired, I got 'refired.'"

Does your dream need to be revived? Ecclesiastes 3:1 says, "To everything thing there is a season, and a time to every purpose under the heaven." Maybe it's time for you to go to your "attic," take your dream off the shelf, and see what God can do through you.

The Word Is Truth

by Kenneth Copeland
Kenneth Copeland Ministries

Notice that this verse doesn't say, "Thy Word is fact." Truth goes beyond facts. The fact may be that you don't have any money. The fact may be that the doctor said you have an incurable disease. But what does the truth have to say about it?

You see, the truth is absolute. Truth doesn't yield. Truth doesn't change. Thus, facts are subject to truth.

It can be a fact that you are sick as can be, but God says you were healed by the stripes of Jesus when He died on the cross. That's the truth. Now you have a choice. You can apply the truth of God's Word to the fact that you're sick and the fact will change—or you can agree with the facts and things will stay like they are.

I'll tell you right now, it will be much easier just to agree with the facts, because facts scream a lot louder than the Word of God does. God's Word will be quiet—until it starts coming out of your mouth.

But once that Word begins to come out of your mouth in faith, it will be the final word. If it's God's Word about healing, you'll be healed. If it's His Word about prosperity, you'll be prosperous. If it's His Word about deliverance, you'll be delivered.

God has given you His contract. When you do your part by believing, speaking, and acting on a heart full of faith, God's Word will come to pass. No circumstance on earth and no demon in hell can stop it.

So forget all those stories you have heard about so-and-so who believed the Word and it didn't work for him. Quit asking questions and settle it once and for all. God's Word is truth.[1]

Barrier Breakers

by Marilyn Hickey
Marilyn Hickey Ministries

The Bible says, "As [a man] thinketh in his heart, so is he" (Prov. 23:7). So if I think a certain level is as high as I can go and God thinks I can go higher, I'll never go as high as God wants me to because I have created a barrier. I'm only going to go as high as I think I can. I believe God breaks the barriers of what the enemy would like to limit us with. God is an unlimited God. And in Psalm 78:41 it says, "Yea, they turned back and tempted God, and limited the Holy One of Israel."

Don't tell God He can't use you because you have a past, because God doesn't know that. Turn to Judges 11 and read the story of Jephthah, who is one of my favorite people in the Bible. He was illegitimate. His father had him by a prostitute and took him home for his legal wife to raise. You can imagine how that woman felt about that little boy when she saw him.

Jephthah's father died, and his half-brothers kicked him out because they said, "You can't have any of our father's inheritance." But the Bible says something about this man that is very powerful, something that will break barriers as much as anything I know. Jephthah was Spirit-filled. "Then the Spirit of the Lord came upon Jephthah" (Judg. 11:29). Praying the Word of God is what begins to break barriers.

An enemy called the Ammonites came against the Israelites. There were no armies but Jephthah's, and it was a little army. His half-brothers came to him and said, "Would you take your army and protect us from the Ammonites?" And Jephthah said, "I will do it, if you will let me be the judge if I win and if you will accept me in leadership." They said, "If you win, you can be the judge." He won! And Jephthah judged Israel six years.

Jephthah could have said, "Oh, I can never do anything because of my past." I'm tired of hearing about people's pasts and how it affects their present. God doesn't know that your past will hinder you. He has redeemed your past. God can use you because He has redeemed you.

First Thessalonians 5:16-18 NIV tells us, "Be joyful always; pray continually; give thanks in all circumstances." Be joyful. Pray. Be thankful. If you will do these three things, you'll always come out smelling like a rose.

God Will Make a Way

by Richard Roberts

Everyone has something in his past that he doesn't want to remember—a struggle, a heartache, a problem. I know I do. I know you do too. You'd like to forget the past, but the devil doesn't.

It's interesting to me that when something has gone wrong the devil will continue to bring it across your mind again and again. Just about the time you feel like you're about to break loose and be free of it, the devil will bring up your past again. You begin to wonder, *Am I ever going to be free of this thing?*

Is the devil throwing something from the past up to you right now? Then Isaiah 43:18 is for you: "Remember ye not the former things, neither consider the things of old." That means don't remember those things that are in the past. Don't think about them. And don't consider doing things the same old way either.

I saw a sign the other day in a store window. It showed a picture of an employee talking to an employer, saying, "But we've always done things this way!" You may be caught up in doing things the same old way, but God has a new way for you to do things in your life. He has new thoughts for you to think, new actions for you to take. He says, "Behold, I will do a new thing." And He goes on to say, "Now it shall spring forth; shall ye not know it?" (v. 19). That means this new thing is on the way into your life *now*, so get ready for it.

God further says, "I will even make a way in the wilderness, and rivers in the desert." Do you have a wilderness or dry desert in your life?

God did a new thing in my life, and He wants to do a new thing in your life. He has a way of having you prepared for something new after the devil throws something at you. Will you forget the past and receive it? If you will, a fresh, new miracle from God will come your way.

Immanuel

by Richard Roberts

Two missionaries imprisoned by the Chinese Communists were placed in a small, guarded room and forbidden to communicate with each other.

As the Christmas season approached, they longed to talk about the birth of their Savior. On Christmas morning one of the men started to call a special greeting to his friend across the room, but dared not. Then he had an idea. Casually, he pulled some straw from under his mattress and used it to spell the word *Immanuel*, meaning God with us.

The other missionary understood his message. They both rejoiced that God was with them even in this dismal circumstance of life.

Christ came to show us what God is like, to make God real to us, not only on Christmas but also on every other day of the year. God is with us when all is well. But what comfort it brings to know that He is also with us when everything is going wrong!

When you are discouraged, remember that God is with you. Act upon this belief, and your sagging spirits will rise. Your circumstances may be disheartening, but an awareness of God's constant presence will bring you strength and grace for the situation until the victory comes.

Endnotes

Building God's Dreams

Kenneth and Gloria Copeland, *Pursuit of His Presence*, (Tulsa, OK: Harrison House Publishers) February 20.

God's Not Mad at You

Lindsay Roberts, *Make Your Day Count Devotional for Teens* (Tulsa, OK: Harrison House Publishers) pp. 176-177.

God Has a Place for You

Lindsay Roberts, *Make Your Day Count Devotional for Women* (Tulsa, OK: Harrison House Publishers) pp. 98-99.

Don't Buy the Lie!

Kenneth and Gloria Copeland, *Pursuit of His Presence*, (Tulsa, OK: Harrison House Publishers) December 1.

Knowing God

Lindsay Roberts, *Make Your Day Count Devotional for Women* (Tulsa, OK: Harrison House Publishers) pp. 150-151.

Extreme Lengths

Lindsay Roberts, *Make Your Day Count Devotions for Women* (Tulsa, OK: Harrison House Publishers) pp. 14-15.

A Life of Abundance

Lindsay Roberts, *Make Your Day Count Devotional for Women* (Tulsa, OK: Harrison House Publishers) pp. 32-33.

An Ambassador of Love

Lindsay Roberts, *Make Your Day Count Devotions for Women* (Tulsa, OK: Harrison House Publishers) pp.104-105.

Good Luck? Bad Luck? Yeah, Right.

Kenneth and Gloria Copeland, *Load Up Devotional* (Tulsa, OK: Harrison House Publishers, 2002) p. 20.

We're Not Civilians!

Kenneth and Gloria Copeland, *Pursuit of His Presence*, (Tulsa, OK: Harrison House Publishers) October 28.

Protected by the Blood of Jesus

Lindsay Roberts, *Make Your Day Count Devotional for Women*, (Tulsa, OK: Harrison House Publishers, 2004) pp. 80-81.

Sitting on the Edge of His Seat
Kenneth and Gloria Copeland, *Load Up Devotional* (Tulsa, OK: Harrison House Publishers) p. 65.

How We Learned To Live by Faith
Lindsay Roberts, *Make Your Day Count Devotional for Women* (Tulsa, OK: Harrison House Publishers) pp. 56-57.

Dare To Step Out
Kenneth and Gloria Copeland, *Pursuit of His Presence*, (Tulsa, OK: Harrison House Publishers) September 11.

Not Guilty
Kenneth and Gloria Copeland, *Load Up Devotional* (Tulsa, OK: Harrison House Publishers) p. 79.

Healing Power
Kenneth and Gloria Copeland, *Load Up Devotional* (Tulsa, OK: Harrison House Publishers) p. 85.

None of These Things Move Me
Kenneth and Gloria Copeland, *Pursuit of His Presence*, (Tulsa, OK: Harrison House Publishers) August 27.

God Really Does Love You!
Lindsay Roberts, *Make Your Day Count Devotions for Teens* (Tulsa, OK: Harrison House Publishers) pp. 34-35.

He's Given You Peace
Kenneth and Gloria Copeland, *Load Up Devotional* (Tulsa, OK: Harrison House Publishers) p.101.

Blazing Glory
Kenneth and Gloria Copeland, *Load Up Devotional* (Tulsa, OK: Harrison House Publishers) p. 120.

The Biggest Problem Isn't Big Enough
Kenneth and Gloria Copeland, *Load Up Devotional* (Tulsa, OK: Harrison House Publishers) p. 160.

Does God Hear You?
Suzette Caldwell, *Make Your Day Count Devotional for Women*, (Harrison House Publishers: Tulsa, OK; Copyright © 2004).

God's Word + Hope + Faith = Appearance
Kenneth and Gloria Copeland, *Load Up Devotional* (Tulsa, OK: Harrison House Publishers) p. 304.

Make That Decision
Kenneth and Gloria Copeland, *Load Up Devotional* (Tulsa, OK: Harrison House Publishers) p. 335.

Be Strong in Grace
Kenneth and Gloria Copeland, *Pursuit of His Presence,* (Tulsa, OK: Harrison House Publishers) July 21.

Go to War With Praise
Kenneth and Gloria Copeland, *Load Up Devotional* (Tulsa, OK: Harrison House Publishers) p. 339.

Protection by Listening to Your Spirit
Lindsay Roberts, *Make Your Day Count Devotional for Women,* (Tulsa, OK: Harrison House Publishers) pp. 160-161.

Overloaded With Joy
Kenneth and Gloria Copeland, *Load Up Devotional* (Tulsa, OK: Harrison House Publishers) p. 357.

Your True Destiny
Kenneth and Gloria Copeland, *Pursuit of His Presence,* (Tulsa, OK: Harrison House Publishers) June 9.

An Open Door for Miracles
Lindsay Roberts, *Make Your Day Count Devotional for Teens* (Tulsa, OK: Harrison House Publishers) pp. 28-29.

The Word Is Truth
Kenneth and Gloria Copeland, *Pursuit of His Presence,* (Tulsa, OK: Harrison House Publishers) June 24.

Prayer of Salvation

God loves you—no matter who you are, no matter what your past. God loves you so much that He gave His one and only begotten Son for you. The Bible tells us that "...whoever believes in him shall not perish but have eternal life" (John 3:16 NIV). Jesus laid down His life and rose again so that we could spend eternity with Him in heaven and experience His absolute best on earth. If you would like to receive Jesus into your life, say the following prayer out loud and mean it from your heart.

Heavenly Father, I come to You admitting that I am a sinner. Right now, I choose to turn away from sin, and I ask You to cleanse me of all unrighteousness. I believe that Your Son, Jesus, died on the cross to take away my sins. I also believe that He rose again from the dead so that I might be forgiven of my sins and made righteous through faith in Him. I call upon the name of Jesus Christ to be the Savior and Lord of my life. Jesus, I choose to follow You and ask that You fill me with the power of the Holy Spirit. I declare that right now I am a child of God. I am free from sin and full of the righteousness of God. I am saved in Jesus' name. Amen.

If you prayed this prayer to receive Jesus Christ as your Savior for the first time, please contact us on the Web at **www.harrisonhouse.com** to receive a free book.

Or you may write to us at

Harrison House

P.O. Box 35035

Tulsa, Oklahoma 74153

Oral Roberts Evangelistic Association

Oral Roberts Evangelistic Association, located in Tulsa, Oklahoma, was founded in 1947. A non-profit evangelistic ministry now under the leadership of Richard Roberts, OREA has been taking the saving, healing, delivering power of Jesus Christ around the world for more than fifty years. Among its many outreaches, the Oral Roberts Ministries produces a daily interactive healing program, "The Hour Of Healing"—hosted by Richard and Lindsay Roberts—and a daily program for women, "Make Your Day Count"—hosted by Lindsay Roberts.

Oral Roberts University was chartered in 1963 and accepted its first students in 1965. The campus now has 22 major buildings and over 5,500 students enrolled in 64 undergraduate concentrations, 15 graduate level programs, and 2 doctoral level programs. Now under second generation leadership, Richard Roberts serves as President of ORU. Oral Roberts serves as Chancellor.

The Prayer Tower, located at the center of the University's campus, houses the Abundant Life Prayer Group which operates 24 hours a day, 7 days a week, and receives more than 2,000 calls a day for prayer from around the world.

For more information on ORU or Oral Roberts Ministries,
log on to **www.oru.edu** or **www.orm.cc**.

For prayer any time,
call the Abundant Life Prayer Group at 918-495-7777.

Send e-mails to: prayer@orm.cc

Or write:
Richard and Lindsay Roberts
Tulsa, OK 74171

All royalties from the sale of this book will go towards the
Make Your Day Count scholarship fund.

For more information on the contributors in this book, please contact:

Tommy Barnett
Phoenix First Assembly
13613 North Cave Creek Road
Phoenix, Arizona 85022
602-867-7117
www.phoenixfirst.org

Mark & Janet Brazee
Mark Brazee Ministries
8863 E. 91st Street
Tulsa, Oklahoma 74145
918-258-1734
www.brazee.org

Keith Butler
Word of Faith International Christian Center
20000 W. Nine Mile Road
Southfield, Michigan 48075
248-353-3476
www.woficc.com

Jeanne Caldwell
Agape Church
701 Napa Valley Drive
Little Rock, Arkansas 72211
501-225-0612
www.agapechurch.org

Suzette Caldwell
Windsor Village United Methodist Church
6000 Heatherbrook Drive
Houston, Texas 77085
713-723-8187
www.kingdombuliders.com

Kenneth & Gloria Copeland
Kenneth Copeland Ministries
Fort Worth, Texas 76192-0001
800-600-7395
www.kcm.org

Eastman & Angel Curtis
Destiny Church
1700 S. Aspen Ave.
Broken Arrow, Oklahoma 74012
918-259-9080
www.destinychurch.com

Billy Joe & Sharon Daugherty
Victory Christian Center
7700 S. Lewis Ave.
Tulsa, Oklahoma 74136
918-491-7700
www.victorytulsa.org

Dr. Creflo A. & Taffi L. Dollar
Creflo Dollar Ministries
P.O. Box 490124
College Park, Georgia 30349
866-477-7683
www.creflodollarministries.org

Cathie Dorsch
Agape Church
701 Napa Valley Drive
Little Rock, Arkansas 72211
501-225-0612
www.agapechurch.org

Jesse & Cathy Duplantis
Jesse Duplantis Ministries
P.O. Box 20149
New Orleans, Louisana 70141-0149
985-764-2000
www.jdm.org

Pat Harrison
Faith Christian Fellowship International
P.O. Box 35443
Tulsa, Oklahoma 74153-0443
918-492-5800
www.fcf.org

Marilyn Hickey
Marilyn Hickey Ministries
P.O. Box 17340
Denver, Colorado 80217
303-770-0400
www.mhmin.org

Dr. I.V. & Dr. Bridget Hilliard
New Light Christian Center Church
1535 Greensmark Drive
Houston, Texas 77067
281-875-4448
www.newlight.org

Suzanne Hinn
Benny Hinn Ministries
P.O. Box 162000
Irving, Texas 75016-2000
817-722-2000
www.bennyhinn.org

Vicki Jamison-Peterson
Vicki Jamison-Peterson Ministries
P.O. Box 700030
Tulsa, Oklahoma 74170
918-494-7777
www.vjpm.org

Kellie Copeland Kutz
Kenneth Copeland Ministries
Fort Worth, Texas 76192-0001
800-600-7395
www.kcm.org

Terry Law
World Compassion/Terry Law Ministries
P.O. Box 92
Tulsa Oklahoma 74101
918-492-2858
www.terrylawonline.com

Kate McVeigh
Kate McVeigh Ministries
P.O. Box 1688
Warren, Michigan 48090
586-795-8885
www.katemcveigh.org

Joyce Meyer
Joyce Meyer Ministries
P.O. Box 655
Fenton, Missouri 63026
800-727-9673
www.joycemeyer.org

Keith Moore
Moore Life Ministries
P.O. Box 1010
Branson, Missouri 65615-1010
417-334-9233
www.moorelifenow.org

Terri Copeland Pearsons
Kenneth Copeland Ministries
Fort Worth, Texas 76192-0001
800-600-7395
www.kcm.org

Patricia Salem
Oral Roberts Ministries
Tulsa, Oklahoma 74171
918-495-7777
www.orm.cc

Jerry Savelle
Jerry Savelle Ministries International
P.O. Box 748
Crowley, Texas 76036-3155
817-297-3155
www.jsmi.org

Art Sepúlveda
Word of Life Christian Center
550 Queen Street
Honolulu, Hawaii 96813
808-528-4044
www.wordoflifehawaii.com

Brenda Timberlake-White
Timberlake Ministries International
P.O. Box 100
Creedmoor, North Carolina 27522
919-528-1581
www.timberlakeministries.com

Bob Yandian
Bob Yandian Ministries
P.O. Box 55236
Tulsa, Oklahoma 74155
800-284-0595
www.precepts.com

For Women Only!

God wants you to enjoy every day. And when you make your day count for something good, you do. Lindsay Roberts and friends, like Joyce Meyer, Gloria Copeland, Taffi Dollar, and Marilyn Hickey will help you start spiritually every day with the *Make Your Day Count Devotional.* You'll also find practical applications, time-saving tips, and easy recipes!

ISBN: 1-57794-662-2

The Make Your Day Count Devotional Series ministers to the needs of Women, Mothers, Teachers, and Teen girls. You'll find that God wants you to live your days rejoicing and laughing, sharing your faith and loving others, praying and growing—becoming enthused and changing your world! Start today and make it count!

ISBN: 1-57794-365-1

Available at fine bookstores everywhere or at www.harrisonhouse.com.

Teachers ISBN: 1-57794-660-X

Teens ISBN: 1-57794-661-8

www.harrisonhouse.com

Fast. Easy. Convenient!

- New Book Information
- Look Inside the Book
- Press Releases
- Bestsellers
- Free E-News
- Author Biographies
- Upcoming Books
- Share Your Testimony

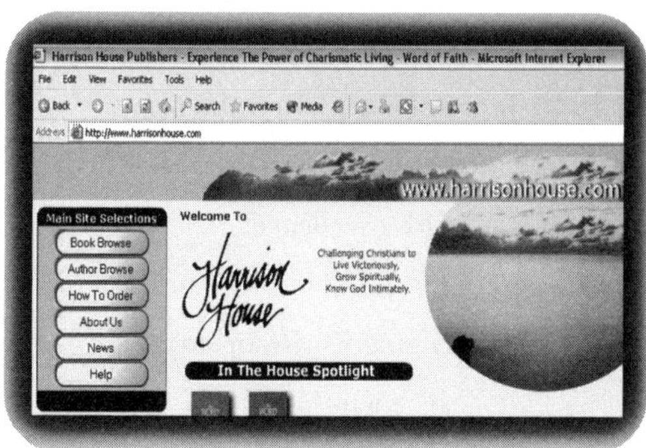

For the latest in book news and author information, please visit us on the Web at www.harrisonhouse.com. Get up-to-date pictures and details on all our powerful and life-changing products. Sign up for our e-mail newsletter, *Friends of the House,* and receive free monthly information on our authors and products including testimonials, author announcements, and more!

Harrison House—
Books That Bring Hope, Books That Bring Change

The Harrison House Vision

Proclaiming the truth and the power
Of the Gospel of Jesus Christ
With excellence;

Challenging Christians to
Live victoriously,
Grow spiritually,
Know God intimately.